THE INSTRUME DIRECTOR'S SOURCE BOOK

A compendium of practical
ideas and helpful
information for today's
school band and orchestra
director

by
John
Kinyon

ALFRED PUBLISHING CO., INC.

Alfred Publishing Co., Inc.
15335 Morrison Street
Sherman Oaks, California 91403

Library of Congress Cataloging in Publication Data
Kinyon, John.
    The instrumental music director's source book.

    Bibliography: p.
    1. Conducting.   I.   Title.
MT85.K54   785   82-4028
ISBN 0-88284-164-5   AACR2

ACKNOWLEDGEMENT

An acknowledgement of indebtedness must be made to the many hundreds of students who, over the years, have each in turn and in their own unique way challenged my mind, charged my spirit and enriched my life. We have been friends and together have made music, and for that I shall be forever grateful. Along the way and through that special relationship which music teachers are privileged to share with their students, each of you has contributed to this book.

John Kinyon

CONTENTS

FOREWORD

O f the many teaching fields in public school education, instrumental music is one of the most challenging as well as one of the most rewarding. It is a profession unique in its demands; its practitioners must not only be knowledgeable and skillful in their chosen field of music, but also in unrelated areas, including pedagogy, psychology and administration. More basic still is a concern of the heart . . . a love of children. Indeed, so vast and varied are the personal prerequisites and professional training requirements for instrumental music teachers that no one text, nor four-year college course of study, could hope to be comprehensive enough to cover completely the groundwork necessary to ensure teaching success. Even in the most advantageous of situations the usual stint of undergraduate internship teaching is sometimes destined to fall somewhat short of the mark. Most would agree that the ripest time for learning occurs *after* college, during the first years of professional teaching, for there is no substitute for actual experience.

Then too of course, in estimating the probability of success in instrumental teaching, student teachers must reckon with their own more personal aspects. Despite similar opportunities of college training and experience, all graduates are *not* created equal. This is to say that although the skills and knowledge which are absolutely essential for success in instrumental teaching may have been mastered, the human factor of *personality* must also be figured in the total equation for success. There are few, if any, college courses designed for the student's improvement of *self*. Maturation is left to natural development with little or no guidance offered in matters of alteration and improvement of those personal traits directly concerned with success in teaching. These include the inner feelings and outer manifestations of self-confidence, authority and leadership.

To those students now preparing for careers in the field of instrumental music education, welcome to our profession! We need teaching excellence more than ever before in our history.

We need first-rate musicians who have both teaching and administrative ability, who love children and are willing to work hard. We need teachers who believe in music education as a vital and viable influence in the schools of America. In spite of the seemingly overwhelming day-to-day challenges of our profession, there is great satisfaction to be found in teaching instrumental music. It is much more than merely a job, it is a way of life in which the intrinsic compensations far outweigh the personal expenditures. There is no greater joy than that which results from sharing in a child's growth through music.

In instrumental music education, as in any creative field, imagination is as important as knowledge. The solutions to each day's challenges will not always be found in textbooks. The creative teacher will, therefore, seek and find answers through his or her own ingenuity. Granted *that* premise, the author offers this sourcebook of practical ideas and information in the hope that it will prove helpful to both graduates and undergraduates in the field of instrumental music teaching. It is a distillation of a lifetime of teaching experience, and is offered not only as a product of the mind, but of the heart as well.

CHAPTER I

HISTORICAL PERSPECTIVES

Although the emphasis of this text is on practicality as related to the everyday challenges of instrumental music teaching, one would indeed be remiss not to begin with some mention of our professional heritage. It is impossible to measure distances traveled or to know where we are in the scheme of history without some idea as to our points of origin. For school instrumental music such beginnings may be said to have occurred around the turn of the century and in only a few scattered communities throughout the country.

1900 — 1920

Some of the earliest of the successful instrumental programs were organized in such widespread locations as Los Angeles, CA - Aurora, IL - Wichita, KS and Richmond, IN, to name but a few. Curiously enough, to those of us accustomed to an era of band predomination, these were school *orchestra* programs, organized and directed by either choral supervisors or dedicated amateur conductors possessed of high-intentioned musical standards and unflagging devotion. Most such pioneer programs were not initially considered to be part of the school curriculum however, each sponsoring school serving in the main only as a base of operations. Also, because of a lack of organized beginning programs in the lower grades to feed trained students into the high school ensembles, instrumentation continuity was problematic at best. Lessons on the instruments of the school orchestra . . . winds, strings, percussion and piano . . . were usually available only on a private outside-of-school basis.

Edward Birge,* in his eye-witness account of the school music of those times, describes early orchestra programs thus:

> These early organizations were all extraneous activities, with no settled place in the school program, and were forced to hold their rehearsals after school hours. Their membership was made up of pupils of private teachers. Instrumentation at best was limited to that of the ordinary theatre orchestra, namely, first and second violins, an occasional bass and cello, cornets, trombones, clarinets, flutes, drums, and piano. There were always plenty of violins and cornets, and it was not usually difficult to secure an occasional clarinet and trombone or flute, but basses and cellos were scarce, and there were no violas, French horns, oboes, bassoons or kettle drums.

> With such varying equipment orchestras of twenty or more players began to be fairly numerous early in the century. The purpose of the supervisors who organized these first orchestras did not include teaching instrumental technique, nor even less of starting an orchestra of beginners. They chose boys and girls who already possessed creditable playing ability, and welded them into as perfect an ensemble as the varying capacities of the players permitted. The result was a magnified nine-piece orchestra in a variety of instruments, playing a repertory of marches, waltzes, operatic arrangements and standard overtures.

While the early school orchestra movement was mushrooming throughout the country, the school band movement was getting under way also. Although military, civic and industrial bands (sometimes known as "silver cornet" bands) had been numerous in the latter half of the 1800s, it wasn't until the turn of the century that the school band movement first began and, even then, its potential impetus wasn't to be evinced until a quarter of a century later. Most of the early "academy" or "cadet" bands were organized and taught by local musicians, interested townspeople or musical instrument salesmen.** Despite the fact that the early

---

*Birge, Edward Bailey, *History of Public School Music in the United States*. Reston, VA: Music Educators National Conference, Revised 1966.

**As flamboyantly portrayed by Professor Harold Hill in the stage and screen productions of Meredith Wilson's *The Music Man*.

school bands did not, at that time, have any abundance of quality literature of their own and therefore did not enjoy the cultural esteem of the school orchestra, the band movement did have many inherent factors in its favor, which over the course of the first half of the 20th century, were to contribute to its growth and to the overwhelming prevalence of bands over orchestras in our public schools.

These factors included the power and maneuverability of the wind instruments themselves which made the band adaptable to both indoor and outdoor performance, the allure of colorful band uniforms and the fact that in those days the band, because of its historical roots in the military, seemed more masculine in its character and hence was more appealing to boys. In addition was the fact that the latter half of the 1800's and the early 1900's marked the heyday of professional touring bands. Led by splendid musicians and showmen such as Patrick S. Gilmore and followed by Arthur Pryor, John Philip Sousa and Harold Bachman, these professional bands with their impressive repertoires of classical transcriptions and original works of entertainment, with their brilliant soloists and with that glamorous mystique of the "big name band," had tremendous influence on the embryonic school band movement.

AN EARLY SCHOOL ORCHESTRA
(Photo courtesy of Carl Hulbert)

From such sporadic and makeshift beginnings in the early 1900's both the school orchestra and band movements expanded rapidly throughout the country. Feeder systems for many high schools were developed in the lower grades, thus ensuring a continuing flow of trained students to replace graduating members. School boards gradually came to accept the responsibility for instrumental music funding. School credit was extended in many school systems for participation in and study of instrumental music. Major ensembles in some schools were scheduled for rehearsal during the regular academic day. The rising popularity of band instruments helped to supply complete wind sections for the orchestras, and both orchestras and bands continued to grow in size, numbers and musical quality of performance. It should be mentioned also that along with the regular choral and instrumental ensemble offerings, class lessons in piano as well as courses in music appreciation, history, harmony and counterpoint were not uncommon.

The first two decades of the 1900's provided fertile ground for the inception of instrumental music in the public schools. It was an era of expanding school curricula, an era in which the traditional classic subjects of the 1800's were being supplemented with courses such as home economics and agriculture, and one in which the rigid subject-oriented concept of public education was rapidly being pre-empted by the new child-oriented philosophy. John Dewey's precept of learning-by-doing was perfectly served by instrumental music. Too, it was an era in which the country was seeking a musical culture of its own, separate and apart from the umbilical influences of Europe. Not only were many professional bands active during that particular period of American history, but major symphony orchestras in several cities, including Chicago, Boston and New York were, by that time, well established. School orchestras were deemed cultural, a fact that provided easy justification for their inclusion in school curricula; school bands were considered functional and entertaining, and were eagerly adopted for their public relations potential. That original dichotomy of reason-for-being persisted throughout the remainder of the century.

1920 — 1940

It was during the two decades following World War I that the school instrumental music movement gathered its greatest momentum. The seeds which had been almost experimentally broadcast between 1900 and 1920 took deeper root, the contagion spread, and by 1940 nearly every school system in the country could boast of either a band or orchestra program or, as in the case of many larger and more comprehensive music departments, both.

There were many major milestones during that era which were responsible in part for the tremendous growth of the movement. Prior to the 1920s the Music Supervisors National Conference [parent organization of the Music Educators National Conference (MENC)] had been primarily concerned with music supervision and choral activities. In 1922, however, a committee on instrumental affairs was formed within the conference, thus, not only adding official credibility to band and orchestra programs, but also providing a national coordinating and guiding body to aid in shaping the future of the growing movement.

The year 1923 saw the first national band contest in Chicago, which instituted a tradition of competition in instrumental music. This contest, sponsored by musical instrument manufacturers, was taken over in succeeding years by the committee on instrumental affairs of the Music Supervisors National Conference, which organized, promoted and supervised a system of state, interstate and national contests. Orchestra competitions were instituted in 1928 and resulted in the same high interest and fervor that marked the band contests. It is difficult to assess the total influence which the competition-festival tradition has had on school instrumental music; to say the least, it has been one of the great motivating factors in the upgrading of band and orchestra performance. Richard Colwell neatly sums up the basic reason for its initial success and its continuing popularity by writing:*

*Colwell, Richard J., *The Teaching of Instrumental Music*. New York, NY: Appleton-Century-Crofts, 1969.

The competitive spirit of the American people insured the immediate success of the contests. As with athletic competition and debate tournaments, the American community had a chance to test its superiority against its neighbors in a music contest. The history of the contest became the history of the school band.

AN EARLY "BOYS BAND"   (Photo courtesy of Ken Brainard)

AN ORCHESTRA AND BAND PROGRAMME, TYPICAL OF
THE EARLY YEARS OF SCHOOL INSTRUMENTAL MUSIC

It was in the early 1920s also that instrumental teachers, in addition to their responsibilities as conductors, were becoming increasingly responsible for providing lessons for their students. It had become a matter of efficiency, if not expedience, to devote teaching time to *classes* of students rather than to private lessons during school hours. The method books previously used for private tutelage were not suitable for large class instruction, particularly when the classes were of mixed instrumentation. One of the first of many heterogeneous methods for instrumental class teaching, *The Universal Teacher*, was published by C. G. Conn, Ltd. in 1923. In the years to follow, the band class method became the most popular system for teaching wind instruments, the string class method for teaching strings.

It was not unusual in those early years for local music merchants to provide rental instruments and professionally trained musicians to teach in the area schools. Such teachers organized and directed instrumental ensembles, traveling from school to school and making the most of the talent at hand. While the movement started as a promotional scheme to sell instruments, it also provided an opportunity to learn to play and to participate in a musical activity which appealed to the student, the school administration and the general public. Following is the recollection of Elvin L. Freeman, formerly principal tuba with the Sousa band:*

The period of the 1920s involved the organization of many school bands in New York State. Francis Larkin (music dealer) in Binghamton hired me on the off-season of the Sousa band tours to teach for him in the schools he organized. My first group of towns consisted of Seneca Falls, Clyde, Savannah, Marcellus and Solvay, 1927–28. After the next tour I taught in Waverly, Addison, Painted Post, Dundee and Hammondsport. Following the 1929 season with Arthur Pryor I directed the Syracuse University Band and taught for Clark Music Company. Those towns were Port Byron, Skaneateles, Pulaski, Baldwinsville, Jordan, Elbridge and Boonville.

The band teachers were generally working on a salary guaranteed by the music dealer. Fees were collected by the school administration (50¢ per student) and averaged about $15.00 per

*Excerpted from letters to the author.

day. As the years passed, the school board assumed the guarantee or paid a salary. In some towns the band was organized as a club project (such as Rotary or Kiwanis) and rehearsals were often held at night. Later such groups were taken over by the schools and a full time teacher hired to continue the program.

TYPICAL RURAL SCHOOL BAND OF THE 20's
(Photo courtesy of Elvin Freeman)

In the years 1926 through 1928 the annual performances of national high school orchestras further spurred public interest in school instrumental music. These outstanding ensembles were organized and conducted by Joseph Maddy (founder of the National Music Camp and later, the Interlochen Arts Academy) and not only focused much public attention on the artistic capabilities of school musicians, but also brought to their administrators an awareness of the prestige possibilities inherent in the sponsorship of such performing groups.

Another reason for the escalation of the school instrumental music movement during that particular period was the burgeoning ranks of better qualified music teachers. This was due in part to the fact that hundreds of military musicians, trained and experienced in both music and marching, were mustered out of service after the armistice of 1918 and returned home to seek employment as school music directors. Also, some ten years later, the advent of the "talking picture" preempted jobs from thousands of theatre pit musicians, many of whom turned to public school music teaching as a means of livelihood and sought accreditation through attendance at teacher training institutions.

Over the first decades of its existence and particularly in the 1920s and 1930s, public school instrumental music, including class instruction for both band and orchestra instruments, became firmly entrenched in the curricula of high schools, junior highs and elementary schools. Respectability and credibility were substantiated as instrumental music programs, following in the path of choral music, were given their due proportionate place in the school academic schedule. School credit was proffered in recognition of the artistic and scholarly nature of instrumental music study, and more and more states required certification of their music teachers. From its proud but precarious beginnings, instrumental music had grown to be fully accepted and accredited as a legitimate facet of public schooling, a unique phenomenon of American education.

It is interesting to note certain trends which developed in the course of this particular era, the enigmatic results of which persist to this day. *Professional concert bands* which had been so prevalent in the earlier 1900s, because of societal changes, became almost extinct; *school bands*, because of their functional and entertainment capabilities, drastically increased in numbers. *Professional symphony orchestras*, because of their cultural esteem, continued to proliferate; *school orchestras*, unable to compete with school bands in popularity, began to dwindle in numbers by comparison.

1940 — 1960

By the early 1940s the United States found itself again involved in a world war, and once again it was, to a great extent, military band music which set the national mood of patriotic fervor, stimulating war bond rallies and entertaining troops at home and abroad. The aftermath of World War II marked an era of unprecedented prosperity, the results of which directly benefited school music. New schools were being built to accommodate the "baby boom" of that postwar era, and many of these schools were designed to include acoustically-treated rehearsal rooms and practice suites. Music budgets soared to new heights, resulting in better equipment; few instrumental departments were without at least a token representation of school-owned oboes, bassoons, French horns, alto and bass clarinets, and lower strings and brasses.

WOODWIND QUINTET OF THE 50's (with school-owned bassoon, oboe and French horn.

Improved technology spawned by the war was now directed to civilian purposes, and the electronic age was born. This resulted in several new audio devices being made available to the general public, devices which were of great benefit to music educators and to instrumental teachers in particular. The tape recorder made instant recording and playback a reality, and quickly became a "second teacher" in many rehearsal rooms. The perfection of the long-playing record and improved fidelity of sound systems encouraged a post-war recording boom which yielded a plethora of instrumental recordings of educational value for both home and school record libraries. The stroboscopic tuner, a visual tuning device, also appeared on the market during this era and did much to improve intonation awareness in school orchestras and bands. Another innovation was the electronic piano which made possible entire classrooms of pianos, each privately monitored through earphones to the individual students and through a central monitoring system to the teacher; the old concept of class piano instruction took on new and exciting possibilities.

The early 1940s had marked the height of the so-called swing era of jazz and popular music. Student-organized dance bands (later to be known as stage bands and then jazz ensembles) had been prevalent prior to this time, but had seldom been given official recognition or support by their schools. It was during this period that many instrumental directors, some of whom themselves "moonlighted" in dance bands as a means of supplementing their incomes, began to organize large high school jazz groups. This movement was eventually to lead to the formation of the National Association of Jazz Educators and, later, to its recognition as an associated organization of the MENC. Special jazz clinics given with cooperating professional jazz artists, an expanding repertoire of contemporary arrangements and compositions patterned after the styles of professional groups, and stage band competitions all helped to spark the school jazz movement to life and gave increased legitimacy to this new facet of school instrumental music.

The years 1940 to 1960 also saw a remarkable increase in both quantity and quality of original composition for school concert bands. Although from its inception the school orchestra movement could lay claim to much of the standard symphonic repertoire as being its very own, the school band movement by comparison inherited very little in the way of significant literature, the bulk of its serious program material having consisted of transcriptions of standard orchestral works. The earliest composers of original music for band, whose works were published in editions conforming to American band instrumentation, had been Gustav Holst, Percy Grainger and Ralph Vaughan Williams; their magnificient contributions have always been considered the bedrock of concert band literature.*

During the years 1940 to 1960 however, innovative and prolific composers such as Frank Erickson, J. Clifton Williams, Alfred Reed, Clare Grundman, Robert Russell Bennett, Norman Dello Joio, Vaclav Nelhybel, Gordon Jacob and Vincent Persichetti, well aware of the idiosyncrasies of the school band, began their own contributions of major works, thus filling a long-standing void. The gradual accumulation of such a body of

*For a critical analysis of these works, Frederick Fennell's *BASIC BAND REPERTORY*, published by THE INSTRUMENTALIST, is highly recommended.

prestigious literature gave school bands a new and improved image as purveyors of contemporary culture and did much to dispel the old notion of the concert band being merely a vehicle for entertainment.

In 1952 a new concept, that of *the wind ensemble*, was pioneered and promoted by Dr. Frederick Fennell at The Eastman School of Music. It was Dr. Fennell's purpose to create a complete ensemble of winds and percussion, one player per part, which would be adjustable in instrumentation and hence flexible enough to perform with clarity, elegance and authenticity any of the historic or contemporary compositions originally written for combinations of wind instruments. The acoustical result of the new medium was a departure from the massed sound of the typically large concert band toward the transparent sonorities of the orchestral wind section. The extraordinary wind music possibilities inherent in the new concept were quickly recognized, and the wind ensemble found ready acceptance among both university and high school instrumental music departments, offering new challenges to composers, conductors and performers alike.

THE EASTMAN SCHOOL OF MUSIC WIND
ENSEMBLE OF THE EARLY 50's.
(Photo courtesy of Dr. Frederick Fennell, Conductor)

All told, with the exception of the years of the second world war, the period from 1940 through 1960 was a golden era for school instrumental music. Summer music camps sprang up throughout the entire country, providing additional musical experiences for thousands of children. The MENC and its state affiliates sponsored regional and state performing organizations of near-professional calibre. The musical capabilities of individual school orchestras, concert bands, marching bands, stage bands, and ensembles and soloists of all kinds continued to increase as evinced at hundreds of annual festival-competitions and in thousands of school concert auditoriums across the nation.

1960 — 1980

During the 1960s and continuing, instrumental music programs in the public schools continued to flourish, although not without a certain amount of compromise with the social and economic stresses of the times. In the field of education the era was one of innovation in class structure and scheduling, tightening of school budgets, broadening of curricular offerings, integration of races and general student unrest, the sum total of which had direct bearing on music education and on the condition of instrumental music in particular; the earlier days of easy growth and acceptance of school music were over, and justification and accountability became the twin challenges.

In some communities during this period school budget slashes were responsible for cut-backs in music programs and personnel. This tendency was particularly prevalent in the large impersonal metropolitan areas, the school boards of many of the largest cities nationwide having threatened either drastic reduction or, in some cases, total elimination of their fine arts programs. Although most music departments were, with community support, able to resist such threats, the writing on the wall prompted the entire music education profession to a period of introspection . . . a time to re-evaluate its position in the schools and to justify its existence as a valid and viable facet of public education. In response to the societal and educational changes occurring during this period, the MENC in 1967 created the Tanglewood Symposium, a conference of outstanding laypeople, musicians and music educators charged with taking an in-depth look at the offerings and effectiveness of music education in a changing society. The resultant report of this meeting set in motion waves which had far-reaching effect.*

---

*A full *Documentary Report of The Tanglewood Symposium*, is available from MENC Publication Sales, 1902 Association Drive, Reston, VA 22091.

Despite national trends toward stringent music budget appropriations and cut-backs in programs, instrumental music continued to maintain and reinforce its position of credibility in the public schools. Enrollments in music courses generally, and in instrumental music in particular, were the highest in history. The quality levels of performance also continued to climb, reaching levels of artistry undreamed of by the music supervisors of the early 1900s. Because of the overwhelming percentage of school bands as compared to orchestras, however, certain resultant enigmas did remain to be resolved: while thousands of amateur wind players were graduating from high schools each year with little or no opportunity for continued ensemble performance, the playing opportunities for the small percentage of school-trained string players, by contrast, were widening as community and professional orchestras continued to increase in numbers throughout the country.

One of the strongest trends in popular music of the 1960s was the sudden surge of the so-called rock style which appealed to the youth of the nation just as swing music had captured the fancy of the prior generation. Amateur rock groups were spawned in neighborhoods throughout the country, and the movement was eventually sanctioned by music educators, instruction in this style being offered by many instrumental teachers as a means of reaching students who might not otherwise have become involved in the school music program. Likewise country-western and folk music were idioms of popular musical expression in vogue at the time and, as with rock music, the guitar was the instrument basic to the style. This fact led to a great interest in guitar study and to the introduction of class guitar instruction in the public schools. By the addition of such course offerings instrumental teachers were able to appeal to and reach a broader spectrum of students.

Thus after nearly a century of survival and growth, the term "instrumental music" had come to mean much more than just orchestra and band. Although concert orchestras and bands were still the backbone of instrumental music, in keeping with the trends of general education and the needs of society the instrumental programs of those years offered opportunity for study and participation in class piano and class guitar, jazz band, rock groups, small ensembles, string orchestras, marching band and lessons on all instruments as well. It was a broad and comprehensive program reaching out to attract and serve a maximum number of students, and called for teachers of the highest personal qualifications, the broadest training experiences and the deepest musical sensitivities.

THE YEARS AHEAD

To prognosticate concerning the future of instrumental music education is to be presumptuous at best. Any predictions for our profession in the years to come must be predicated on many variables including the future philosophic, economic and pedagogic trends of both our society and its educational system. Then too, one could not expect to gaze into the crystal ball of our profession without clouding the image with his or her own wishful thinking. Nonetheless the years 1980 through 2000 will mark the cumulation of a century of instrumental music education in this country and, in spite of the obvious vagaries inherent in crystal gazing, the course and content of instrumental music education in the years ahead are intriguing to contemplate.

If parents, school administrators, legislators and the general public can be led to understand the place, purpose and importance of the arts in education, and if support is given accordingly, school music education will not merely survive, but will flourish in the years ahead. But for the public to fully understand our objectives in order to qualify us for their support, the music educators of the future must unify their goals and relate their course offerings to the needs and realities of society.

In the years ahead we might anticipate a renaissance of string and orchestra programs, to better balance our curriculum offerings and to give our children the opportunity to intimately experience the wealth of orchestral literature which is our cultural heritage. We might also hope for a proliferation of small ensembles, both string and wind, which could be continued into adult life as leisure-time hobbies. Too, in the forthcoming decades, we need to foster and develop community bands and orchestras,* to broaden the avocational options of our students beyond high school.

If we are ever to be in a position of setting our own program priorities we must, eventually, break the traditional stranglehold of athletics (football in particular) on our instrumental music education programs. A start in this direction might possibly be the development of brass-percussion marching ensembles, perhaps drum and bugle corps, for parade events, game spectacles and marching competitions, to replace existing "marching concert bands."

We must also continue the encouragement and sponsorship of quality composition from first-rank composers, playable music of substance which reflects the deepest sense and spirit of contemporary society.

Furthermore we must wage a constant and concerted compaign toward erasing the anachronistic image of instrumental music education still held by the general public. We must convince the public, through public relations and by example, that we are no longer the traditionally caricatured town band or amateur school orchestra rendering off-key versions of "light classics." And lastly, we must arrive at a better balance between musical entertainment and music education, one by which we can get on with the true nature and purpose of our professional calling.

---

*For information concerning the community band movement, write Association of Concert Bands of America, Inc., 19 Benton Circle, Utica, NY 13501.

*For information concerning symphony orchestras, write American Symphony Orchestra League, Box 669, Vienna, VA.

ADDITIONAL REFERENCES

Birge, Edward Bailey, *History of Public School Music in the United States*. Reston, VA: Music Educators National Conferences, revised 1966.

Browning, Norma, *Joe Maddy of Interlochen*. Chicago: Henry Regnery Co., 1963.

Bryan, Carolyn, *And The Band Played On, 1776-1976*. Washington, D.C.: Smithsonian Institute Press, 1975.

Colwell, Richard J., *The Teaching of Instrumental Music*. NY: Appleton-Century-Crofts, 1969.

Fennell, Frederick, *Time and the Winds*. Kenosha, WI: G. Leblanc Co., 1954.

Holz, Emil A., and Jacobi, Roger, *Teaching Band Instruments To Beginners*. Englewood Cliffs, NJ: Prentice-Hall, Inc., 1966.

Goldman, Richard Franko, *The Wind Band*. Boston: Allyn and Bacon, Inc., 1961.

Lingg, Ann, *John Philip Sousa*. New York: Henry Holt & Co., 1954.

CHAPTER II

PHILOSOPHICAL PERSPECTIVES

In the several decades of existence of instrumental music in this country's public schools, various philosophies have been in vogue, in keeping with the conditions of society and the educational convictions of the particular times. In the earliest years of our profession the assumption had been that instrumental music study was, by its very nature, cultural and educational (as well as functional and entertaining), and therefore worthy of inclusion in the curricula of the public schools. It was such public presumption which facilitated instrumental music's initial acceptance into the schools and by which instrumental music education was able to establish itself as an educational entity. Whatever "philosophy" may have then existed was, in the main, predicated on a litany of platitudes justifying the "merits" of study and participation in orchestra and band programs.

Some of these justifications, still being echoed in variational form today, included the development of better health (blowing a horn develops the lungs), better brain power (reading music strengthens the mind) and better coordination (playing an instrument quickens the senses). Also stressed were the social merits of instrumental ensemble participation, leading to the conclusion that student musicians, performing together, developed character-building virtues such as cooperation, poise and self-discipline. Also, the moral aspects inherent in musical training were touted, the inference being that participation in school instrumental groups was much more socially elevating than, say, hanging around pool halls. As one instrument manufacturer in the thirties advertised, "Teach a boy to blow a horn and he'll never blow a safe."

19

While none of these claims could be disproved, such simplistic justifications for instrumental music education were scarcely necessary in the first half of the century, so well-accepted and wide-spread were school bands and orchestras. Like varsity teams and glee clubs, such activities were considered to be educationally wholesome because they were, of themselves, "good." Instrumental directors of the era went about their teaching seldom questioning the educational legitimacy of their programs, and seldom being questioned. Philosophy was, for most music teachers, purely academic . . . a subject fitting and proper for college music education seminars, but not necessarily relevant to the real world of teaching.

It was not until the late fifties, in the wake of the first successful earth orbit of Russia's Sputnik, that America's educational system suddenly became the scapegoat for seeming deficiencies in the country's space exploration technologies, and abruptly found itself pressured by public investigation and accusation into a self-evaluation of its effectiveness and relevance to practical society. Although the immediate thrust of the educational reformation was toward the bolstering of mathematics and science courses (resulting at the time in an equal and opposite effect on programs of the arts), the ripples of reform permeated the entire educational establishment and challenged every area of educational thought and practice. Instrumental music education programs found themselves in acute competition for school time, budget monies and, in extreme cases, survival. Band and orchestra programs could no longer be justified in superficial terms or for non-musical reasons, and so began an era of vast and profound professional introspection.

In 1959, during this period of critical examination, the American Association of School Administrators, to reaffirm its support, took the following official position:

> We believe in a well-balanced school curriculum in which music, drama, painting, poetry, sculpture, architecture, and the like are included side by side with other important subjects such as mathematics, history and science. It is important that pupils, as a part of general education, learn to appreciate, to understand, to create, and to criticize with discrimination those products of the mind, the voice, the hand, and the body which give dignity to the person and exhalt the spirit of man.

It was also during this period of stress that the Music Educators National Conference, in 1967, sponsored a unique symposium dealing with Music in American Society, seeking to . . . .

> reappraise and evaluate basic assumptions about music in the educative forces and institutions of our communities — the home, school, peer cultures, professional organizations, church, community groups, and communications media — to develop greater concern and awareness of the problems and potentials of music activities in our entire culture and to explore means of greater cooperation in becoming more effective as we seek new professional dimensions.*

During the period beyond Sputnik, and continuing through the 60s and 70s, other debilitating influences were being felt which plagued education in general and music education in particular. Unstable tax bases and inflation combined to pinch the pocketbook of public education and this, in turn, led to intensified scrutiny of educational programs and policy. The arts were most vulnerable to the harsh and sometimes impulsive assessments made of school course offerings, not only because of their nebulous "artistic" nature, but also because of the inability of arts educators to convince the general public of the value of their programs. Instrumental music programs, because of their relatively high cost as compared to other subjects, were most vulnerable of all.

In response, the American Association of School Administrators once again made a commitment to a balanced curriculum, and to the opposition of selective cutbacks in time of budget difficulty, as stated in a 1973 resolution:

> As school budgets today come under extreme fiscal pressures, trimming or eliminating so-called "peripheral" subject areas from the school curriculum appears often to be a financially attractive economy. The American Association of School Administrators believes that a well-rounded, well-balanced curriculum is essential in the education of American children. We believe that deleting entire subject areas which have value in the total ex-

---

*Documentary Report of the Tanglewood Symposium. Reston, VA: Music Educators National Conference, 1968.

perience of the individual is shortsighted. Therefore, AASA recommends that school administrators declare themselves in favor of maintaining a full balanced curriculum at all grade levels, opposing any categorical cuts in the school program.

Today more than ever before in our history, there is a need for us to be able to define our goals and justify our beliefs, and we must be articulate in the process. As Bennett Reimer has so eloquently stated:

> . . . the individual who has a clear notion of what his aims are as a professional, and who is convinced of the importance of these aims, is a strong link in the chain of people who collectively make a profession. Music education has been fortunate in having leaders who have held strong convictions, who have helped enormously to forge a sense of group identity. But too many convictions have been based on platitudes, on attractive but empty arguments, on vague intimations that music education is important with little in the way of solid reasoning to give backbone to beliefs. So many individuals have enormous dedication to this field but little more to base it on than fond hopes. This is why the profession gives the appearance—of tremendous vitality and purposefulness and goodness of intentions, while at the same time the nagging doubt exists as to whether it all makes much difference. In this situation, individuals who do have convincing justifications for music education, who exhibit in their own lives the inner sense of worth which comes from doing important work in the world, become sort of the profession's most prized possessions. To the degree that individual music educators are helped to formulate a compelling philosophy, the profession will become more solid and secure.*

In formulating one's own personal philosophy of instrumental music education, it is necessary to differentiate between those goals which focus on the development of musically worthy performing organizations and those which develop musically sensitive children. The fact that we have been successful in developing musically attractive bands and orchestras and, in so

*Reimer, Bennett, *A Philosophy of Music Education*. Englewood Cliffs, NJ: Prentice-Hall, Inc., 1970.

doing, have won acclaim from an entertainment-oriented public, has tended to delude us into believing that we have been totally successful music educators. The *esprit de corps* engendered in our performance groups through rehearsing, concertizing, marching, competing and socializing has often misled us to believe that our instrumental programs are educationally sufficient. As Bennett Reimer has so well stated:

> Performance can no longer sell itself on the basis of its contribution to social skills or physical health or moral behavior or citizenship training or the need for rewards such as uniforms, medals, "A" ratings, and the like. If such unsupportable and irrelevant claims are all that performance has to offer, then performance is in deep trouble. At a time when every subject must demonstrate that it can make important contributions to the quality of children's lives, justifications for a large, expensive, time and energy consuming performance program had better be at a high level of educational respectability. That such justifications for performance do in fact exist makes it even more unfortunate to continue to rely on specious arguments.*

What, then, should be included among the objectives on which to base our philosophy of instrumental music education? What contributions can we as music educators make to the quality of children's lives which will carry over into their adulthood? Among all educational disciplines, instrumental music education has the most unique potential for influencing the character and quality of a child's life. The effects of instrumental music study pervade all spheres of a child's learning, experiencing and sensing. Not unlike other academic subjects, playing an instrument and participating in musical ensembles affords a broad base for *cognitive learning*: knowing about music in all its aspects of theory, form, style, texture, composition and history. Not unlike physical education, instrumental music activities develop *psychomotor skills*: honing and refining mental and muscular reflexes to split-second sensitivity. Unlike either academic study or athletic participation, however, and perhaps its most valuable contribution to the educational experience of a child, is the fact that in-

*Ibid

strumental music study, when wisely administered, sensitizes the *affective domain*. In a world filled with non-musical and unmusical sounds, in the audio over-kill environment of our modern-day society, there is still beauty to be experienced in the making of quality music. It is that potential for such *aesthetic experience* which distinguishes our teachings from those of all other school subjects and which, by the same token, places tremendous responsibilities on all instrumental music educators in the complete educational process of our children.

The following, taken from a report by the National Commission on Instruction of the Music Educators National Conference, gives an excellent summation of goals for all music educators . . . a realistic and relevant philosophy for today's world:

> The reasons for including music in the curriculum are many and varied. They tend to be interrelated and overlapping. Their relative importance will vary according to the philosophical views of the individual and the community. A few of the major reasons for including music in the curriculum may be summarized as follows:*
>
> 1. To help each student to develop his or her aesthetic potential to the utmost
> 2. To transmit our cultural heritage to succeeding generations
> 3. To give the student a source of enjoyment he can use throughout his life, and to enhance the quality of life
> 4. To provide an outlet for creativity and self-expression
> 5. To help the student to understand better the nature of man and his relationship with his or her environment
> 6. To provide an opportunity for success for some students who have difficulty with other aspects of the school curriculum, and to make the school a more pleasant place
> 7. To increase the satisfaction the student is able to derive from music, and to enable him to deal with sophisticated and complex music
> 8. To help the student become acquainted with other cultures

---

The School Music Program: Description and Standards. Reston, VA, Music Educators National Conference, 1974.

9. To cultivate one of the major symbolic systems that make man uniquely human

10. To help the student realize that not every aspect of life is quantifiable and that it is important to be able to cope with the subjective

11. To contribute to a balanced program of career education.

It is important that every instrumental music director formulate his or her own personal creed, a practical philosophy which will serve as a subtle directional compass in making the dozens of decisions with which we are confronted in the course of each teaching day. Further, it is important that we make those same beliefs known to the members of our community, not merely as a defensive justification of our professional existence but also as an assertive proclamation of our intents, purposes and beliefs.

ADDITIONAL REFERENCES

ASBDA Curriculum Guide. Pittsburgh, PA: Volkwein Bros., Inc., 1973.

Bessom, Malcolm E., Tatarunis, Alphonse M. and Forcucci, Samuel L., *Teaching Music In Today's Secondary Schools.* NY: Holt, Rinehart and Winston, Inc., 1974.

Glenn, Neal E., McBride, William B. and Wilson, George H., *Secondary School Music.* Englewood Cliffs, NJ: Prentice-Hall, Inc., 1970.

Reimer, Bennett, A *Philosophy of Music Education.* Englewood Cliffs, NJ: Prentice-Hall, Inc. 1970.

The School Music Program: Description and Standards. Reston, VA: Music Educators National Conference, 1974.

CHAPTER III

ADMINISTRATIVE RESPONSIBILITIES

The responsibilities of instrumental music teachers go far beyond those activities which are basically musical . . . teaching, conducting and rehearsing. Indeed, the non-musical aspects of any instrumental teaching position, unless properly and efficiently organized and administered, can take on overwhelming and unwarranted proportions of physical and mental preoccupation, thus draining the director's time and energy which might better be allocated to the teaching of music. Many inexperienced teachers, unaware of the importance of control and organization of the mundane facets of their job, either become completely engulfed with unexpected administrative complexities or muddle through their first teaching years oblivious to the possibilities of a smoothly running operation. This chapter deals with many of the more common organizational needs and considerations to be found in the average instrumental music department; other major administrative concerns will be found in special chapters of this book. Although the solutions will vary according to the situation and the ingenuity of the teacher (imagination often being of more importance than knowledge) the significant facts of the matter are that (1) wise and well-organized administration is essential to the efficiency and effectiveness of any instrumental music department and (2) such administration is definitely the responsibility of the instrumental music teacher.

SYSTEMS OF CONTROL AND INVENTORY

Music Library

The instrumental music department library should be considered one of the most important centers of activity, for it is there that all music is categorized for handy reference, mended, inventoried and channeled in and out for use. Although such a library may also include reference books, magazines and recordings, these items are usually considered to be the responsibility of the general school library. Whenever space allows, the departmental library deserves to be housed in a room of its own, preferably adjacent to the rehearsal hall and, ideally, with slots for distribution through the wall between. The minimum working equipment needed for such a set-up will consist of a table and chairs, large filing cabinets of appropriate size, small filing cabinets with 3 x 5 cards, filing boxes or envelopes, paper cutter or scissors, transparent mending tape, and a stamp pad and rubber stamp imprinted with name of department and school. Other optional equipment may include a sorting rack and a wide-carriage typewriter.

The key to a successful library is, of course, the librarian and whatever additional staff is needed. Reliability and accuracy are the key traits necessary, and fortunate is the director who can relegate the library responsibilities to such students. Very often students other than the first-chair performers, the most socially active or those of the highest academic rank, take great pride and satisfaction in such methodical work. The adage "too many fingers spoil the pie" is well-taken when it comes to school music libraries, and stringent rules must be enforced regarding who is to have access to the library room; the library should not become a haven for those students merely escaping from other academic requirements.

Parkinson's law concerning the expansion of the job to fill the available time certainly applies to library filing. The systems of possible indexing and cross-indexing are limited only by one's imagination. However, for practical everyday usage, a title index crossed with a composer-arranger index should serve admirably. Beyond that, a third index by category might prove helpful in the case of music for large concert ensembles. Each area of performance including solo, small ensemble, string orchestra, stage band, marching band, concert orchestra and concert band should have its own file. Filing by numerical sequence is the simplest method of achieving maximum flexibility. Shown below is a well-organized library system with music filed in separate boxes.

SAMPLE INDEX CARDS

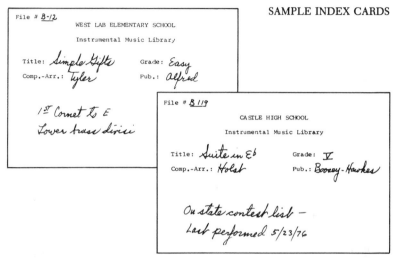

File # *B-12*

WEST LAB ELEMENTARY SCHOOL

Instrumental Music Library

Title: *Simple Gifts*   Grade: *Easy*
Comp.-Arr.: *Tyler*   Pub.: *Alfred*

1ˢᵗ Cornet to E
Lower brass divisi

File # *B 119*

CASTLE HIGH SCHOOL

Instrumental Music Library

Title: *Suite in Eᵇ*   Grade: *V*
Comp.-Arr.: *Holst*   Pub.: *Boosey-Hawkes*

On state contest list —
Last performed 5/23/76

MUSIC FILE BOXES
(Photo courtesy of The Instrumentalist Co.)

It is the librarian's responsibility to see that every folio contains a complete set of parts for each rehearsal, and that the folios are made available to students entering the rehearsal room. If a slot system is not available, folios can be systematically laid out on a distribution rack or placed directly on the music stands. A system should be instituted also for checking out individual folios for private practice. Library check-out cards are useful for keeping such daily records. Here again stringent regulations concerning such procedures are most important. Once the entire library system is working in an orderly and efficient manner, one facet of the director's workload will be eased and his rehearsals more efficiently run.

Uniforms

One of the larger financial investments made by any instrumental music department is in uniforms for its major concert and marching ensembles. For that reason alone it would behoove a director to keep a careful system of control and inventory to guarantee that the uniforms are kept clean, in good repair and properly fitting (Amidst fast-growing teenagers the last-mentioned may be an impossibility!). The basic questions are whether the uniforms are to be stored at home or school, and whether the parents or the school are to be financially and otherwise responsible for their upkeep.

These are questions which must be answered on the basis of the individual school situation and administrative philosophy. Generally speaking, however, matters of control and inventory are greatly expedited by keeping the uniforms at school, numerically marked piece by piece, and hung in a proper storage space. In this way the director and/or student in charge can make periodic checks on the condition of the uniforms, reassign components as necessary, look after tailoring needs to see to it that they are regularly dry-cleaned when necessary. Such dry-cleaning is usually less expensive when done in quantity lots than when done individually. The monies for such maintenance may come from the school budget, the instrumental department fund or from a special assessment to the parents. Since uniforms are usually considered to be school property, they should warrant school budget appropriation for their upkeep.

A card file or large chart of all available pants, jackets, hats, belts, etc., should by kept, showing the sizes, the code numbers and the students to whom they are currently assigned. A tagboard will serve as a flexible means for quick inventory. Tags can be kept on the coat hangers of the components when not assigned, and reassignment records are easily kept by switching the tags to and from the hooks.

SAMPLE TAGBOARD FOR KEEPING INVENTORY OF
UNIFORM COMPONENTS

NAME	PANTS	JACKET	BELT	HAT
Barbara Allen	21	17	10	44
Chas. Bickel	13	33	49	51
Norma Hubbard	10	44	35	52
Phil Hyatt	19	59	18	60
Tom McMillan	42	62	37	32
Ray Premru	61	28	22	17

Equipment

In today's rehearsal rooms equipment, including expensive electronic devices, can be a problem in terms of control and safe storage. The director should keep an up-to-date inventory of all electronic equipment, including such items as make and model, serial number, the date of purchase and original cost. Music stands and chairs should be stenciled with the name of the department and identification numbers. Storage racks should be provided for all instruments and small percussion equipment should be stored in special cabinets or storage cases. A large lockable storage space within the rehearsal room itself will be of great help in keeping an orderly rehearsal environment and in discouraging the tampering with or theft of valuable equipment. Inventory checks should be made at least once each school year and careful records kept.

Perhaps the greatest factor in the maintenance and preservation of rehearsal room equipment is the conditioning of the students to a hands-off policy. Since the director is unable to supervise at all times of the school day, and since some teachers don't believe in an unfriendly locked-door policy during school hours, the problem of student tampering can be annoying and can sometimes lead to destruction of property. Stringent rules must be formulated, agreed to by the students, then enforced as strictly as possible. A neat and orderly room with a minimum of loose equipment about is a good basis for setting an atmosphere conducive to respect for other people's property.

School-Owned Instruments

All modern instrumental music departments have large inventories of school-owned instruments, and these too are the administrative responsibility of the director. Records must be kept itemizing each instrument, its make and model, manufacturer's serial number, date of purchase and original price, along with space for a record of repairs. If the instrument is one which is to be loaned or rented for home use, then additional records must be kept which will form the basis of agreement between the school and the parents. Such agreement forms must stipulate the limits and conditions of responsibility. In addition to the usual items such as name of student, address, phone number, and the make, model, serial number and value of the instrument, matters relating to the return date, obligation for repair bills and liability in event of loss must be explicitly spelled out.

Each instrument case should carry stenciled markings which provide easy identification of the contents. One such coded system might be:

100 through 199	=	flutes
200 through 299	=	clarinets
300 through 399	=	saxophones
400 through 499	=	oboes
500 through 599	=	bassoons
600 through 699	=	cornets-trumpets
700 through 799	=	French horns
800 through 899	=	trombones
900 through 999	=	baritones and basses
1000 through 1099	=	violins
1100 through 1199	=	violas
1200 through 1299	=	cellos
1300 through 1399	=	basses

Many variations of this system are possible. Of most obvious advantage is the fact that with only three digits any instrument can be classified and identified by family and number.

If a rental system for school-owned instruments is in effect, the director would do well to absolve himself from the role of fee collector by putting the matter in the hands of the school business office. In fact this is a good policy to follow whenever and for whatever reason it becomes necessary to collect money in any substantial amount. In matters of insurance on school-owned instruments and equipment, the director should check with the business office to ascertain the coverage, if any; because of soaring rates within recent years, the trend has been away from blanket coverage.

Student Records

A file of student record cards, as with any accumulated data, will be advantageous in direct proportion to the amount of reference use it receives. If such a system merely duplicates personal data already available in the regular school records, the director will be adding unnecessary work to his already busy routine by maintaining his own separate file of student records. Information concerning each music student which might be kept in a departmental file and which might be of permanent reference value would include such items as:

> Parents' name, address and phone number
> Music aptitude test scores
> Music achievement test scores
> Records of solo performances
> Records of solo contest ratings
> Records of special music awards and all-state memberships

It may be possible to incorporate aptitude and achievement scores into the regular school records system. Other information which might be of use on a more temporary basis includes:

> Current class schedule
> Name and telephone number of private instructor (if any)
> Code number of assigned instrument (if rented)
> Code numbers of assigned uniform components

Below are samples of various record cards.

```
                OCEANA HIGH SCHOOL
         INSTRUMENTAL MUSIC DEPARTMENT

Name:                  Watkins-Farnum Scores:
                          9th Grade -
Parent:                  10th Grade -
                         11th Grade -
Address:                 12th Grade -

Phone:                 Solo Contest Ratings:
                          9th Grade -
Homeroom:                10th Grade -
                         11th Grade -
                         12th Grade -
```

```
                PHILIPPI HIGH SCHOOL
         INSTRUMENTAL MUSIC DEPARTMENT

      Name:             Aptitude Test Scores:
                           Pitch  -
      Parent:              Rhythm -

      Address:          Free Periods:

      Phone:            Homeroom :

      School Instrument #
```

SPECIAL ACTIVITIES

Concerts

The organization of school concerts is a recurring responsibility of all instrumental directors. Despite the extra planning and preparation involved, each concert should be considered an opportunity rather than merely an obligation in line of duty. Concerts, at any level of technical ability, are of great motivational value to both performers and conductor, providing a challenge to everyone concerned to perform at an artistic level above and beyond that of the day-to-day rehearsal. The experience of such intensification of musical efforts results in both personal and musical maturation. By the same token, however, concerts should not be so severe in preparation and nerve-wracking in performance that they result in totally stilted and conditioned musical responses. Although music-making is a discipline, as with athletics it requires a certain amount of relaxation for the best possible performance.

Another opportunity afforded by public concerts is that of community enlightenment, the chance to reveal not only the musical progress and prowess of the students, but also the opportunity to show, if only by inference, the true significance of music education within the school system. In these times of questioning the disparate values of general education, we instrumental music teachers are indeed fortunate that our art is basically that of both creation and re-creation and that, unlike other academic subjects, it requires sharing through public performance.

Among the many items of concert pre-planning will be the following:

(1) *Place and date*: These must be selected well in advance and thoroughly checked out to avoid possible conflicts with other school activities.

(2) *Performing groups*: It must be decided whether it is to be a concert of combined choral and instrumental, band and orchestra, various levels of ensembles or only one major organization. Generally speaking, more than one group will add interest and variety to the program. The total concert time, however, should not ordinarily exceed ninety minutes.

(3) *Numbers to be performed*: The kind of music depends to a large extent on whether it is to be a special occasion (e.g. Christmas) or a regular concert. Whatever the type of program and whatever the musical maturity of the students, the selections should be of good musical substance. Even though entertainment begets easy applause, education is our true business; in formulating the program the two must always be kept in balanced proportion. The list of selections should have variety and balance in matters of style, duration, interest and technical challenges. Soloists and/or small ensembles will add variety to the occasion and relieve whatever tedium might result from too much sameness of sound. The numbers on the program should be representative of the day-to-day musical abilities and ambitions of the students.

(4) *Publicity*: This depends on the size of the school community, and may vary from a poster in the local drugstore window to spot announcements through local radio and television stations. Local newspapers, especially in smaller communities, are always interested in school events and will usually cooperate in giving free promotional space if the information is presented in factual form. It is important that a reliable person or group be assigned to such publicity solicitation, and that the assignment be carried out with logical timing.

(5) *Programs*: These must be printed, either on school equipment or by a commercial printing shop. They should be neat, attractive and accurate, and if possible, should include succinct program notes of general interest and educational value. Whenever space allows, the personnel of the performing ensembles should be listed with special identification of officers and/or section leaders. Attractive covers can be designed by talented art students or stock designs can be procured commercially. Very often local merchants are agreeable to underwriting program costs in return for a modicum of advertising.

(6) *Ticket sales*: If tickets are to be sold, a strict accounting must be kept of tickets issued vs. monies collected. Reliable and mature students can be assigned to this detailed chore. A tickets-at-the-door policy may save a lot of unnecessary problems with the collection of money. Whatever the system, it would be most politic to send pairs of complimentary tickets to school board members and administrators.

(7) *Other considerations*: These include assignment of ushers and ticket-takers, designation of warm-up rooms and supervisors, directions for stage and lighting crews and, if the occasion warrants, recruitment of a special introductory speaker.

Trips

A fringe benefit of membership in any secondary school musical organization is that great get-away . . . the trip. It may be occasioned by an exchange concert, an away game involving a half-time show, a visit to a cultural center to hear a professional performance or participation in a solo-ensemble competition. Whatever the occasion, the transportation, meals and overnight accommodations, if any, are the direct responsibility of the director. Within recent years administrators have taken a wary view of such trips, not necessarily because of disinterest in the traveling activities of the music department but because of the legal liability considerations. Nonetheless, occasional travel is a necessary and important aspect of instrumental music education, and it is the director who must usually take the responsibility for all arrangements. The main considerations and concerns are that all students travel together in a common vehicle, that they are legally covered by insurance, that they are adequately supervised and that, when necessary, their meals and lodging are provided for.

Under ordinary circumstances involving relatively short trips, school buses can usually be made available as long as the schedule does not conflict with the regular bus runs. On longer trips it may be necessary to hire commercial buses and drivers, the cost to be defrayed either by departmental funds or by the school itself. Here again, if such a trip is considered to be truly educational, the cost should be considered a school budget item; if the trip does not qualify as being educational, it shouldn't be undertaken in the first place. If there is ever doubt as to the insurance liability, signed waivers of school responsibility should be obtained from the parents.

When students are excused from regular academic classes for purposes of music trips, it is advisable that the director insist that the school work missed be made up by the students on their own time. This attitude will certainly be looked on with approval and appreciation by the classroom teachers, and it may help soften any possible administrative resistance to future trips.

Overnight lodging reservations must be booked well in advance and will probably require a substantial deposit. The hotel or motel should be located as close to the center of the musical activities as possible. Eating accommodations, too, should be available within easy access. Needless to say, without strictly enforced rules of conduct, overnight trips can become a nightmare for the director. Any infractions of agreed-upon regulations must be dealt with at once and with authority, even if it should mean on-the-spot dismissal of a key member of the organization.

Trips, reasonably scheduled, should be encouraged, for there is no better way to build a cohesive spirit within a musical organization than by traveling together and performing before an alien audience. Successful concert trips engender pride within the group and provide a pleasurable reward for the many hours of individual practice and rehearsal preparation.

Fund Raising

Fortunate is the instrumental music department which is totally underwritten by the school. Such situations, however, have become the exception rather than the rule. Because of the unusual cost of such basic items as instruments, equipment and travel, most secondary school instrumental music departments are forced to rely on their own resourcefulness in providing funds for at least part of their operating expenses. Such fund raising, as time and energy consuming as it can be, is one more responsibility of the instrumental director.

The methods of raising money run the gamut from out-and-out soliciting in front of busy supermarkets to peddling merchandise door to door, to rendering services for a fee. None of these three money-making schemes are dishonorable, although the first-mentioned (begging) does not have any redeeming educational virtue. The selling of magazine subscriptions, personalized calendars, candy, cook books, Christmas cards, oranges, fruit cakes and the like can be highly profitable, but the venture must be well organized and entered into with zealous ambition on everyone's part if it is to succeed. Of increasing popularity and less time-consuming in its administration is the selling of services. This might include such various enterprises as washing cars, baby sitting, mowing lawns, shoveling snow or cleaning out garages. Whatever fund raising system is decided upon, it is important that it be sanctioned by the school administration. It is best to confine the drive to a limited time so that a maximum of concerted publicity and effort can be focused on the project.

Listed below are companies which specialize in the sale of fund raising products:

Better Homes and Gardens
Locust at 17th Street
Des Moines, IA 50336

The Dimension Weld Organization
84 Commerce Road
Stamford, CT 06902

International School Supply Corp.
2001 Boston Post Road
Larchmont, NY 09593

Key Specialties
P.O. Box 24
Elk Grove Village, IL 60007

Boise Knitting Mills
P.O. Box 7383
Boise, ID 83707

Weaver Popcorn Co., Inc.
P.O. Box 395
Van Buren, IN 46991

Gold Medal Products Co.
1825 Freeman Avenue
Cincinnati, OH 45214

Langdon Barber Groves
Box 4428
McAllen, TX 78501

Best Citrus of Florida, Inc.
Box 3333
Ft. Pierce, FL 33454

Crest Fruit Company
P.O. BOX 517
Alamo, TX 78516

Cumberland Cabin Candies
Box 4739
Nashville, TN 37216

Fresh Picked Fruit Services
Box 2266
Orlando, FL 32802

Kathryn Beich Candies
Front & Lumber Street
Bloomington, IL 61701

S.W. Smith & Co.
716 East Thrush Avenue
St. Louis, MO 63147

Mr. Z's Fund Raising Corp.
P.O. BOX 324
Cedarburg, WI 53012

Sweet Note Chocolate
P.O. Box 165
York, PA 17405

Sunsweet Fruit, Inc.
Box 3264
Vero Beach, FL 32960

Velva-Sheen Co.
3860 Virginia Ave.
Cincinnati, OH 45227

Q.S.P. Inc.
P.O. Box 301
Pleasantville, NY 10570

Wisconsin Blueribbon Foods
39 Walmar Drive
Sun Prairie, WI 53590

For other fund raising ideas and case histories of successful plans refer to Chapter VIII of Selmer's *How To Promote Your Band* booklet, available in their educational kit. See also *Fund Raising Facts* by Sue Bradle, The Instrumentalist, May, 1979.

SUMMER PROGRAMS

Many successful instrumental departments sponsor summer music programs. For beginning students it is the most feasible time of year for those very first lessons. With more lesson and practice hours available during the vacation months, and away from the hustle and bustle of normal school life, summertime beginners can usually make more rapid progress than ordinarily possible during the regular school year. To be sure, family vacation plans sometimes interfere to knock the lesson schedule askew, as do conflicting summer recreation programs such as playground activities, Little League baseball and scout camp. Nonetheless, well-organized and well-taught summer music activities can do much to bolster the entire instrumental program. For more advanced groups, a summer series of rehearsals and public performances will provide not only extra training and experience for the students, but also perfect opportunities for enhancing public relations. For those organizations anticipating an active autumn marching season, even a two-week late-August band camp can take much of the pressure off both the director and his students by providing relaxed but intensive cram sessions before that first halftime appearance.

Most school boards, administrators and community leaders readily understand the benefits of summer recreation programs carried out by the physical education department, and are usually willing to provide facilities and funds for such purposes. Instrumental teachers should expect the same sort of backing, and with the very same justifications. Summer programs result in:

1 — worthy use of student leisure time

2 — on-going development of student skills and understanding

3 — more efficient use of school facilities and equipment

4 — gainful employment of specialist teachers

5 — teaching experience for advanced high school and college music majors

If, however, total school board funding is not available, there are several options which, with the approval of the administration, can be undertaken by the instrumental director. The program can be underwritten by charging a reasonable tuition to the parent, or it is possible that costs can be partially covered by scholarships donated by local merchants and civic groups. In any event, the resourceful and enterprising director who really wants to institute a summer program can usually bring such a plan to fruition by using a bit of political maneuvering and administrative psychology. Whatever the methods of accomplishment, once the summer program is in operation, the results will certainly justify the efforts.

WORKING RAPPORT WITH SPECIFIC GROUPS

School Administrators, Faculty and Staff

The successful operation of any instrumental music department is highly dependent on good working relations and communications with every other department of the school. Never a teaching day passes in which some sort of cooperation isn't called for between the instrumental music teacher and his colleagues. Maintaining an open rapport with one's fellow professionals and staff members is not only a personal obligation of the music teacher . . . it may be the determining factor between success and failure in the administration of his department. It is true that some of our associates may sometimes see us from a jaundiced point of view; the principal may view our department as an expensive luxury (but worth our weight in public relations!), our fellow teachers may see us as noisy competitors vying for class time and use of the auditorium, and the custodial staff may think of us in terms of the extra work involved in moving chairs and shuffling equipment. But lest the aforesaid be misconstrued, it should be added that in any school system the instrumental music director, when he is friendly, considerate and cooperative where his associates are concerned, will usually receive all possible support from administrators, fellow teachers and general staff members.

Administrators in today's schools are busy professionals, beseiged on all fronts with all manner of challenges, many of which, although school related, extend far beyond the bounds of school. Most principals are very much interested in the smooth functioning of their instrumental music department, but do not have time for petty problems which can well be solved within the music department itself. Instrumental directors are hired for their administrative ability as well as their musical capability, and are expected to be able to run their own show with a minimum of assistance from the front office. On the other hand it is necessary to apprise the appropriate administrative officer of all out-of-the-ordinary plans and to solicit approval for all major projects to be undertaken. Administrators are interested in facts and figures, but in concise and graphic form . . . enrollment data, financial reports, schedules, projected plans *and* costs, instrument and equipment inventories and, of course, superior rating statistics. Directors new to a school would do well to make an appointment with the principal before the school year begins in order to clarify traditional policies and establish official procedures which relate specifically to the instrumental department.

The importance of a friendly and cooperative rapport with one's fellow teachers cannot be over-emphasized. Scheduling complexities coupled with a general shortage of facilities in our crowded schools require much give and take among faculty members. The instrumental director who is not amenable to occasional compromise will not find much cooperation in return. In addition to relationships with our colleagues is our rapport with custodians, secretaries, bus drivers and many other specialists, all of whom we depend on for special services in the course of the school year. Professional considerations are usually in keeping with personal courtesies.

Parents' Organizations

Parent groups can be a help or a hindrance, depending on purposes and personalities. The most prevalent parents' organization to be found in school communities is the Parent-Teacher Association. Although some teachers question the PTA as being composed of a bunch of parent busybodies meddling in the professional affairs of teachers, in most schools the cooperation and attitude shared by the two factions are excellent and lead to much constructive communication concerning the mutual welfare of the children. Whatever the instrumental director's personal feelings, he should keep in mind that there is no better public forum for selling and promoting the instrumental music program than through the PTA. Parent-teacher meetings are opportune occasions for displaying departmental endeavors to an interested and concerned segment of the community. By the same token, the PTA can often be of great assistance to the instrumental music department by undertaking special projects to raise funds for summer camp or private lesson scholarships, trips or purchases of uniforms or instruments.

Another organization which can be very helpful, particularly to school bands, is what is generally known as the Band Booster Club. Such a special parent group, if well organized and wisely directed, can be of immense assistance to the instrumental director in matters of fund raising, publicity, transportation and chaperonage. To be successful such organizations should be structured on a formal basis with very clear-cut delineation between the areas of responsibility of the parents and those of the director.

Music Dealers

Fortunate is the instrumental director with a local school

music dealer knowledgeable about and empathetic to the special needs of his department. In some small communities that kind of dealer is extremely rare, many merchants specializing in home appliances and stocking but a few dusty instruments and perhaps a bit of sheet music in what might loosely be called "the music section." What every instrumental music teacher needs is dependable service in matters of purchase of music, supplies and instruments, repairs, instrument rentals, new music for perusal and, ideally, pickup and delivery service. Purchase discounts, if offered, may be considered an extra bonus, but certainly no substitute for good service. Most music stores will order and stock whatever method books and instrument models the teachers recommend for their students. Directors new to a community should become acquainted with the area music dealer and apprise him of their department's service needs. If the local music store cannot provide a full range of services, it may be necessary to seek out a dealer in a neighboring community who can. Instrumental teachers rely heavily on their music dealers, almost on a day-to-day basis, and they need salespeople who are knowledgeable, reputable and reliable.

Private Teachers

One of the most important factors in the development of strong performing groups is the availability of private music teachers. This fact is readily recognized when one considers some of the outstanding school bands and orchestras throughout the country, many of which are situated in near proximity to large metropolitan areas where artist-teachers abound. Students should be encouraged to study with private teachers; some school systems offer school credit for this type of study. But private teachers can be a bane as well as a blessing to the instrumental department, depending on their teaching methods and motives, and on the attitudes they engender in their students. The instrumental department should keep a list of approved area private teachers, and should be aware of each one's credentials and teaching abilities. While it is a responsibility of the school director to be able to recommend fine private teachers, it is equally his responsibility to advise his students against study with unqualified instructors.

Civic Organizations

Instrumental music teachers are often eagerly and innocently besought by civic and community organizations to provide music, usually of an entertainment or functional nature, for all sorts of occasions . . . Rotary Club meetings, church socials, business banquets, American Legion parades and Little League games, to name but a few possibilities. Such invitations are a credit to the department and flattering to the director but, if the requests reach undue proportions, steps must be taken to regulate the number of non-school appearances. All such requests should be channeled through the proper administration office which then can act as a discreet buffer between the director and the general public.

Reasonable rules should be established which will serve as a guide in determining the validity and practicality of the requests. Generally invitations to affairs that affect the entire community can be considered legitimate and proper (and politic) for school participation; private club affairs should not be so considered. Of course it is impossible to suggest hard and fast rules which will apply fairly to all school-community relations; those matters must be decided between the administration and the music department according to the type and frequency of requests, the philosophy of the directors and the traditions of the school. Repeated appearances before civic-minded clubs by representative school instrumental groups *can* be of great value. They not only afford the students opportunity for the experience of public performance, but they are a splendid gesture for developing community interest and pride in the instrumental music activities. Very often such community organizations can be induced to help support the instrumental department financially, by providing summer camp scholarships, purchasing instruments or helping out when special funds are needed. Directors who regularly cooperate in supplying musical entertainment to civic groups should feel unabashed in requesting occasional reciprocation in the form of financial support.

ADMINISTRATIVE PLANNING

Curriculum Development

Music curriculum, in the broadest sense of the term, refers to all the course offerings and experiences in music made available to the students in a given school system. As instrumental specialists it is our responsibility to see to it that our own courses of study contribute with logical content and in orderly sequence to such a total school music program. In order to accomplish this it is primarily necessary that all music teachers within the system collectively determine and structure their objectives, including their goals in the development of skills, attitudes, appreciation and understanding, into a cohesive and comprehensive master plan applicable to students from primary grades through high school. All too often, there is a propensity among music staff members toward an every-man-for-himself approach which results in conflicting directions of educational theory and practice or, worse, no directions at all. Although it is the direct responsibility of the music department chairman to develop and coordinate the total curriculum, it is the responsibility of each individual teacher to be aware of his role in the total plan and to carry through on the philosophical consensus of the department.

The instrumental curriculum, in and of itself, should make possible a logical ladder of musical development from the very first lesson on through the senior year. It is the administrative responsibility of every director to formulate courses of study consistent with his own teaching principles but which are, at the same time, in conformity with the chain of learning established by the total music department. The fact that most instrumental methods designed for beginners are preplanned into a progressive course of lessons is of immense advantage to teachers of beginning instrumental music. Such logically sequenced lesson plans spare the director much personal planning time. As students develop and matriculate from beginning classes into the major ensembles, however, that type of system of structured lessons is often either neglected or completely terminated, leaving the students to mere chance improvement through participation in the band or orchestra. All students, whatever their level of accomplishment, should be given home practice assignments which provide the challenge to improve and the motivation to practice, even if such assignments must be administered within the tight time frame of the major ensemble rehearsal period. Individual practice and accomplishment of ensemble literature, no matter how beneficial to the musical effectiveness of the group, are never a completely satisfactory substitute for the progressive development attainable through structured lesson assignments. If private or class lessons are not possible, there are many ensemble technique books available from which regular assignments can be made on an individual or group basis. Students should be tested periodically on these behavioral objectives, the results of which can be used as a partial determinant in the process of grading.

The planning of courses should not be confined only to the area of skills; the teacher, whether in the classroom or on the podium, must be much more than a mere drillmaster. Written exams which reflect the general learning about music style, theory and history, and which may have been either casually absorbed in the course of rehearsals or acquired through outside reading assignments or research projects, should be systematically administered. All teaching objectives, whether in the area of skills or understanding, should be preconceived and structured to challenge and stimulate the abilities and imagination of each child . . . to guarantee his or her continuing musical growth. Such programmed instruction takes high priority on the long list of administrative responsibilities of the instrumental music director.

SCHEDULING

Scheduling, in this age of the computer, may seem very much beyond the control of the instrumental music teacher. The impersonal quality of computerization coupled with new concepts and procedures in scheduling have become, within recent years, factors of frustration for many instrumental directors. This is particularly true at the secondary level where overcrowded schools have been forced into split sessions, or where quinmester plans, modular scheduling systems and other innovative schemes have been put into effect. Such trends in scheduling, which initially may appear as subversive to our program, need not necessarily be considered incompatible with our scheduling needs. Much depends on the liaison between the instrumental department and the administrative office in charge of the schedule programming. Communication is a prerequisite for cooperation in matters of favorable scheduling, and it is the director's responsibility to make known his department's needs. The scheduling of instrumental class lessons and ensemble rehearsals can be very complex since, as opposed to most academic subjects, it cuts across class levels and involves matters of instrumentation and student proficiency.

For secondary schools with the traditional system of scheduling, the major problem remains the student conflict of options between music courses and required academic courses. If it is necessary to have students excused from other classes in order to facilitate lesson scheduling, a system of rotation can easily be devised wherein the same students will miss the same classes only every few weeks. Such a revolving schedule must, of course, have administrative approval. The instrumental music teacher with the tact and patience to pursue these problems with the proper authorities will, in the long run, find the most satisfactory compromises. There are no pat solutions to modern-day scheduling problems in our public schools. Each director must appraise his or her own situation and diplomatically stand up for the needs of his or her own department.

Lesson and ensemble scheduling in the elementary grades is generally easier than at the upper levels. The classrooms are more or less self-contained and there is more flexibility to accommodate the needs of teaching specialists. It must be remembered however, that by the same token, there are many special teachers who during the course of the school week impose on the regular teacher's classroom time. The instrumental music teacher can, with the sanction of the administration, work directly with the classroom teachers to develop a fair and feasible schedule for lessons. The band or orchestra rehearsal schedule should be planned bilaterally by the principal and the music teachers. In all such negotiations the key word is TACT.

LONG RANGE PLANNING

The instrumental director is responsible not only for the day to day operation of his department, but also for its year to year planning. It is possible to become so engrossed with daily duties and commitments that, as the saying goes, we are unable to see the woods for the trees. Whatever the director's personal intentions are concerning his future tenure in his present position, he owes it to his school and to himself (or his successor) to formulate long-range plans of acquisition and growth. Although it is possible for an instrumental department, like a garden, to grow haphazardly, it is through well-planned and calculated expansion that the department will have the best chance of achieving its ultimate objectives. The director who is business-like and communicates his step-by-step goals to the school administration will have a better chance of success than the director who makes requests in helter-skelter fashion. School boards are more willing to provide funding when the budget request is backed with facts, figures and forethought.

The director must, first of all, take stock of his present equipment and instruments, perhaps also of facilities and staff. Then he must project his departmental needs and his plans of expansion over, say, a five-year term. The costs must be estimated and itemized, and then broken down into a methodical year-to-year sequence of budget requests. The entire plan should be organized in chart form, giving a graphic picture of growth comprehensible to even the most non-musical of school board members, most of whom may be businessmen who have understanding and empathy for well-organized, long range plans.

Planning must include, of course, much more than annual funding requests. Departmental expansion must be projected also in terms of increasing enrollments and added ensembles and courses, all of which will have bearing on and substantiate the need for budget monies, increased staff and facilities. This sort of planned growth, when kept within the bounds of realistic possibility, is vital to the viability of any music department.

Another area of growth consideration, other than those of equipment and enrollment—and one absolutely essential to any and all other areas of growth—is that of respectability and credibility of the department itself. This is an area which cannot be calculated in dollars and cents, nor in terms of equipment, enrollment, facilities or size of staff. Its growth can be fostered only by the director himself, and can be only a direct reflection of his personal abilities and sincerity of purpose.

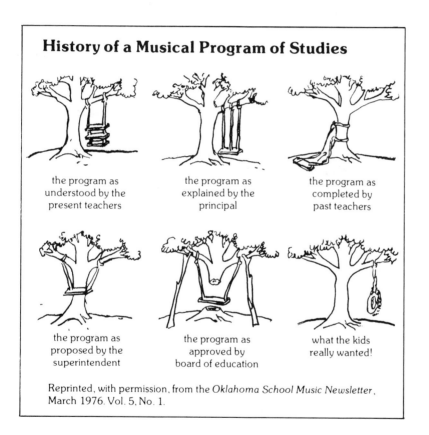

History of a Musical Program of Studies

the program as understood by the present teachers

the program as explained by the principal

the program as completed by past teachers

the program as proposed by the superintendent

the program as approved by board of education

what the kids really wanted!

Reprinted, with permission, from the *Oklahoma School Music Newsletter*, March 1976. Vol. 5, No. 1.

ADDITIONAL REFERENCES

American School Band Directors Association, *The ASBDA Curriculum Guide*. Pittsburgh, PA: Volkwein Bros. Inc., 1973.

Bessom, Tatarunis and Forcucci, *Teaching Music In Today's Secondary Schools*. NY: Holt, Rinehart and Winston, Inc., 1974.

Colwell, Richard J., *The Teaching of Instrumental Music*. Englewood Cliffs, NJ: Prentice-Hall, Inc., 1969.

House, Robert W., *Administration in Music Education*. Englewood Cliffs, NJ: Prentice-Hall, Inc., 1973.

Hovey, Nilo W., *The Administration of School Instrumental Music*. Melville, NY: Belwin-Mills, 1952.

Leblanc, Albert, *Organizing The Instrumental Music Library*. Evanston, IL: The Instrumentalist Co.

Neidig, Kenneth L., *The Band Director's Guide*. Englewood Cliffs, NJ: Prentice-Hall, Inc., 1964.

Neidig, Kenneth L., *Music Director's Complete Handbook Of Forms*. West Nyack, NY: Parker Publishing Co. Inc., 1973.

Robinson, William C. and Middleton, James A., *The Complete School Band Program*. West Nyack, NY: Parker Publishing Co. Inc., 1975.

CHAPTER IV

THE BEGINNING BAND CLASS

The basic training system of the school band movement, since its inception in the early decades of the century, has been the beginning band class. Although there are many instrumental directors who are proponents and practitioners of teaching by private lessons and/or classes of like instruments, the feeder system for many, if not most, successful band programs is based on the precepts of heterogeneous grouping. Despite the lessening of individual attention sometimes necessitated by teaching large classes of mixed instrumentation, the benefits of the band class system, at the hands of an expert teacher, can far outweigh the advantages of smaller homogeneous classes. Some of the advantages of the beginning band class are:

1. The students experience a musical and social relationship with the total band ensemble from the very beginning.

2. Pride in band membership, coupled with peer pressure, results in greater motivation toward practice.

3. Scheduling is facilitated since the class is large enough to warrant a designated band rehearsal period.

4. Teaching time, when utilized for larger classes, is more efficiently used and better justified.

5. The students, despite the differences in playing techniques required for various instruments, learn from each other's mistakes and accomplishments, since the learning problems are more common than disparate.

The success of any instrumental music class lies with the teacher, and this is particularly true in large, mixed instrument classes. Although private lessons and small classes of like instruments are relatively easy to manage, the large band class, not unlike a seven-ring circus, requires much control and expertise in its supervision. The successful band class teacher must be well organized, thoroughly grounded in instrumental techniques, able to hold the attention of many children concomitantly and capable of motivating the students' desire to work toward improvement.

THE BEST AGE TO BEGIN

There will always be differences of opinion among music teachers as to the ideal age at which children should begin band training. Considering the normal variations in physical aptitude, there can be no universal age level best for beginning instrumental study. Wind instruments, as opposed to string instruments, do not come in 1/2 and 3/4 sizes, and therefore a certain degree of physical maturation is a prerequisite for early success. If children are started too young, the attrition rate reflected in drop-outs will run at an impractical high. The national range for starting instrumental beginners runs from third grade through ninth, the most popular grades being the fifth and sixth. There are, however, many successful beginning band programs throughout the country which enroll students in the fourth grade and lower. The critical factor between success and failure in such programs is the number of lessons scheduled per week; very young instrumentalists need almost daily supervised practice if they are to maintain any practical amount of progress.

SELECTIVITY

Another important consideration in the beginning band program is the degree of selectivity to be used in admitting students to the program. Sometimes it is necessary, because of inadequacies of staff size or facilities, to limit enrollments to manageable proportion by means of a screening process. A more prevalent reason for such selectivity is that it is felt that some beginning band applicants are not suitable candidates for such study because of either personal immaturity or musical ineptitude. Many directors feel that they are doing such children (and themselves) a service by sparing the students the frustration and disappointment of inevitable failure. While it is undoubtedly true that not all students should be recommended for band instrument study, the criteria upon which such recommendations are based must be as valid as possible.

Some of the devices used to estimate students' potential for success include informal and standardized music tests (see chapter on *Testing and Grading*), academic records, pre-band instrument classes and classroom teacher consultations. Research has shown that evaluation based solely on standardized music tests is not reliable enough to be used as a factor for prediction. The academic achievement record usually offers a more valid prediction as to a child's probability of success in instrumental music but, here again, it is not always a foolproof factor when used as the only criterion. Pre-band instrument classes (tonette, flutophone, recorder) are excellent for teaching certain basic skills of music and wind performance. Of equal importance is the fact that such classes give the teacher an opportunity to observe individual work habits and attitudes, both of which are critical to success in instrumental music study. Consultations with classroom teachers regarding individual students can provide insights concerning special problems or handicaps which might be detrimental to a child's progress; some children may not be able to cope with an additional activity. If the music teacher, whether for practical or philosophical reasons, is to devise a screening procedure for beginning band applicants, the process should include a combination of predictive factors. And whatever the determined probability for success of the individual child, the results should be conveyed to the parents in the form of a discreet recommendation only.

ORGANIZATION

Recruitment of beginning band students is seldom a problem, depending of course on the stature and popularity of the existing instrumental department. Departments which enjoy a tradition of positive instrumental programs never have to "drum up business" beyond sending announcements to the parents and sponsoring an informal assembly concert or recital to demonstrate the various instruments in solo and combination. New programs, or those which have not as yet earned the confidence and respect of the school community, may have to be promoted more broadly and with greater political intensity.

Early in the initial recruitment activities, a general meeting of interested parents should be held to discuss the program. A typical invitational letter might read:

Dear fifth-grade parents:

A new beginning band class is now being organized to commence the first week of the fall semester. A demonstration will be given by the Junior High Band at an elementary school assembly concert on May 23rd at 2:00, to better acquaint the students with the various band instruments. This informal concert will also be open to the public.

On the evening of June 1st at 8:00, in the music room of the Lincoln Elementary School, a general meeting will be held for all interested parents and their children. At that time the entire band training program will be discussed, and all questions you may have concerning such matters as instruments, rental fees and home practice will be answered.

The Lincoln Elementary School has a proud tradition of excellent band programs, and we hope that you will consider the opportunities of membership for your child. If you are interested, kindly return the attached section of this letter to the school office.

Sincerely,

, Band Director

, Principal

* *

We are interested in having our child, _____
participate in the band program.

We will be able to attend the meeting.

We will not be able to attend the meeting.

Our telephone number is _____

(Signed) _____

INSTRUMENT PROCUREMENT

There are various systems of providing instruments for beginning band students. Some schools own all such instruments and rent them to the students at a modest charge. This is a commendable system although it requires extra time and effort for inventory and record keeping, upkeep of instruments and rental fee collection. Another system is the dealer rental plan which allows the parents to rent an instrument for a limited time through a cooperating music store. The rental fee is usually applicable toward the purchase price of the instrument although the parents are never under any ultimate obligation to buy. This system has the advantages of,

(1) providing the student with an instrument of good quality

(2) providing a trial period of time in which the student can prove to both the teacher and the parents his seriousness purpose

(3) relieving the director of involvement in the business of procuring instruments.

Within recent years some major instrument manufacturers have begun offering leasing plans, providing schools with those kinds of instruments ordinarily school-owned but which might be, for reasons of stringent budget, not affordable by direct purchase. In some situations, especially with new programs, leasing may be a feasible solution by which to provide an immediate balanced instrumentation at a relatively reasonable cost.

Not to be overlooked is taking advantage of those used instruments which may be gathering dust in the attics, basements and storage closets of the community. While sometimes such secondhand instruments may be of poor basic quality and/or playing condition, frequently they turn out to be quite serviceable. An ad of solicitation in the local paper, church bulletins or PTA announcements can turn up surprising results. The market value of the instrument is tax deductable by the donor, of course!

Most elementary school bands are composed of so-called basic instruments including flute, clarinet, alto saxophone, cornet or trumpet, trombone and percussion. Occasionally school-owned instruments such as oboe, bassoon, French horn, baritone and tuba may be available for more mature elementary students. Usually, however, such instruments are not offered until junior high age, after the student has proved himself by showing some ability on a basic instrument. The director must keep in mind that eventually many of the beginning students will be transferring to other instruments, and must plan the beginning ensemble balance accordingly. B$\flat$ clarinet players may switch to alto and bass clarinet, alto saxophone players can transfer to tenor and baritone sax, and cornet players sometimes change to French horn, baritone and tuba.

The question of what instrument to choose for study is predominant in the thinking of most beginning band applicants, and it is not always an easy question to answer. Although some children, for one personal reason or another, are highly predisposed toward a certain instrument, other students and their parents rely solely on the teacher for advice and a final decision. The instrumental director must then consider what the child may best be suited for physically and temperamentally, as well as what may be needed to maintain a balance of instrumentation in the eventual ensemble. There are all sorts of "rules of thumb" upon which directors base their decisions concerning the matching of student and instrument. In addition to such obvious considerations as finger and hand size and length of arms is the more nebulous matter of facial characteristics. Although these factors are discussed in the chapter on Basic Techniques for Teaching Band Instruments, suffice to say here that among successful performers there are as many exceptions to the rules as there are rules. Generally speaking a child who decides on his own what instrument he wishes to play, and is highly determined, should be allowed the freedom of his choice. Other children will need closer consultation and empathetic guidance.

TEACHING PROCEDURES

The very first lesson is the most important one, for it is from this initial point that playing habits and practice attitudes are established. The first lesson, therefore, deserves much careful planning and organization. Every move from the opening of instrument cases to the assembling of instruments, to the first efforts at tone production (as discussed in detail in the chapter on beginning techniques) must be deliberately systematized. Nothing should be left to whim or chance. The military method of "by the numbers" applies perfectly, for the secret of teaching young children is to take but one small step at a time in ordered sequence.

Most teachers agree that the first lessons should be limited to rote learning. Although music reading is one of the most important aspects of band training, it should be delayed until the young student has had opportunity to play by ear and to orient himself to producing the beginning pitches of his instrument. The emphasis in the early lessons should be on tone production, which presupposes correct playing position, embouchure and breathing. After the students have developed some control of their normal starting tones, the teacher can sing or play short and simple phrases which the ensemble can then echo back on their instruments. A student may be chosen to write the phrases on the chalkboard in musical notation.

Once past the initial rote learning stage (which may continue from one to three weeks, depending on the maturity of the students and the frequency of the lessons), the ensemble will be ready to begin the lesson sequence as structured in their band method book. It is important that an assignment be given for each successive lesson, and that every future assignment be thoroughly explained before it is taken home for practice. It is good policy also to give only assignments which, with reasonable practice, will be achievable by the majority of students. Pride in the musical accomplishment itself, no matter how small the step, is a strong motivational factor necessary for continuing progress.

The process most necessary for musical improvement, at any level of proficiency, is that of *repetition*. Young children have a natural propensity toward practicing their lessons exercise to exercise, seldom repeating a line or passage once it has been read through in reasonable (or sometimes *un*reasonable!) musical fashion. There are many "game" activities which can be improvised by the teacher in order to bring fun and freshness to what otherwise might be dull and boring practice routine.

With lesson book duets, for instance, the teacher might suggest "the girls take the melody this time, the boys the harmony part." Or, the "blue eyes" can be assigned the top line, the "brown eyes" the bottom. The possibilities for such simple but imaginative devices are endless. With single-line exercises the class can be divided into "soloists," each individual player being responsible for his own two measures of the exercise. The first soloist plays his two-bar phrase, the second soloist plays the next two bars and so on around the class and through the exercise. This technique is excellent for matching tones and intonation player to player, for developing rest counting abilities, and for putting each class member momentarily in the spotlight as well as "on the spot."

PRESENTING NEW RHYTHMS

There are many ways of teaching new rhythms, and each director must find the system which works best for him in a given situation. The prime consideration is not the system itself but, rather, the consistency of its use. Most directors teach their students to foot tap, each down-up cycle corresponding to an equal eighth-note subdivision of the beat. Since the beat can be expressed overtly, this is a good system for most children (if later they can substitute their big toe for their foot during concert performances). Some teachers prefer a more direct rote process, and such a "do as I do" method of teaching rhythms may, in some instances, be as effective as any other.

Many teachers use a mnemonic system of word association such as:

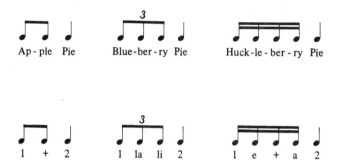

The foregoing are merely sketches of rhythmic teaching ideas and methods used by most instrumental directors. The creative teacher will develop his or her own system through experience and experimentation, the principle objectives being to 1) help the student to feel and physically manifest the pulse of the music and 2) give the student a consistent system with which to solve rhythmic problems on his own. For a more detailed analysis of the teaching of rhythm, Daniel Kohut's *Instrumental Music Pedagogy* is highly recommended.

MOTIVATION

After the intrigue and excitement of the first weeks of endeavor have ebbed, and it is discovered that accomplishment on a musical instrument is a matter of expenditure of time and effort, many children will gravitate into a behavioral slump. Having been born into a world in which appliances, guaranteed to work, can be bought, it often comes as a rude surprise to some students that the same principle doesn't apply to musical instruments. The teacher must find appropriate persuasive tactics by which to motivate each child to practice. Games, competitions, solo recitals and practice records (signed by the parent) are among the most popular devices employed by instrumental teachers for impelling students in their instrumental progress (see chapter on *Motivation*). Once past this psychological hump, however, when the student has gained some control of his instrument, when his own sound is satisfying to himself, and when he can play by ear and read music with some degree of fluency, he will be forever converted to the cause of music making.

As has been so well stated by Holz and Jacobi,

> If learning depends on wanting to learn, then *teaching is the art of making students want to learn*. In the beginning instrumental class, then, teaching is *not* conducting, *not* lecturing, *not* judging. Teaching *is* motivating, explaining, demonstrating, encouraging, suggesting, organizing and evaluating.[*]

The role of the parents as home supervisors cannot be overemphasized. Instrumental directors sometimes assume that parents are aware of the necessity for regular home practice and attendance at lessons, when indeed they are not. Students, especially those inclined to backsliding, can easily hoodwink their parents into believing that progress is being made in their instrumental studies when, in reality, they may be falling far behind the class level of accomplishment. Whether the child is doing well or poorly, some sort of consistent communications should be in effect among the student, teacher and parents. This can be accomplished by phone calls, form letters or special grading cards. Parents should be encouraged to phone the music office and/or set up personal appointments with the instrumental director whenever they wish to discuss their child's musical progress or problems.

BAND METHODS

Great care should be taken in choosing the band method to be used, for it represents the basic course of study upon which the

---

[*]Holz, Emil A. and Jacobi, Roger E., *Teaching Band Instruments To Beginners.* Englewood Cliffs, NJ, Prentice-Hall Inc., 1966.

beginning band program is predicated. As with any textbook, it should be selected only after a comparative study has been made among several class method folios. A teacher is ill-advised to use a particular method merely because it is the only one stocked by the local dealer or simply because it has been the traditional one used in a school system. All band methods for mixed instrumentation have certain similar pedagogical compromises. On the other hand, each different method has its own merits, and it is the responsibility of the instrumental director to choose the one which is best suited for the particular needs of his or her class. Points of consideration include:

(1) Does it begin with whole notes (good for setting embouchures) or with quarter notes (good for establishing a rhythmic feeling)?

(2) Are rhythm and range developments practical in keeping with the maturity of the students and the frequency of the lessons?

(3) Are new problems isolated and presented in understandable fashion?

(4) Is the print clean and are the pages uncluttered?

(5) Are pictures included and are they of value to the student?

(6) Are comprehensive fingering charts included?

(7) Is a full score with helpful reminders available? Is a piano accompaniment available? Is a demonstration record or cassette available for home study?

(8) How many volumes are in the complete series and how many pages are in each book?

(9) Does it teach musicianship as well as music?

(10) Does it include interesting songs and harmonizations?

Published band methods are almost invariably unison methods and, of necessity, the learning problems indigenous to each different instrument are presented in compromise form. Of the basic beginning instruments, the clarinet and cornet players are favored in matters of range and key signature. The flute players, by contrast, are immediately confronted with problems of flatted note fingerings, crossings between the upper and lower registers, and raising the left index finger on D and Eb. By the same token the alto saxophone players must execute the register break and the trombone players must acquire quick agility to manipulate between first, third, fourth and sixth positions. Instruments other than the basic ones—the oboe, bassoon and French horn in particular—each have their own idiosyncracies. The teacher must be empathetic toward these individual instrument problems and not expect all students to progress in lock-step. The band method should be considered only as a progressive series of lesson plans which serve as a core curriculum. Along with such a course of study the teacher should make use of supplementary materials which will review and reinforce those learning steps already accomplished. Such tangential teaching will serve as a "holding pattern," providing an opportunity for the slower members to keep up with the class while, at the same time, affording the more advanced students the challenge of "new" music.

As the class proceeds lesson to lesson, a great diversity in the rates of progress among the students will be evident. This natural disparity is the result not only of the varying aptitudes and attitudes among the students, but also of the differences in playing techniques required for the various instruments. It is not uncommon for clarinet and cornet players to be able to play simple tunes within the first few days, while the flute players are still striving to produce a tone or the trombone players are still uncertain of slide positions. Keeping all members of the ensemble motivated *despite* such differences is the greatest challenge facing teachers of beginning bands. The successful teacher must have the patience, skill and ingenuity to hold the ensemble together, to be able to sustain the interest of the rapid achievers while at the same time motivating the students of slower pace. *The secret of successful music teaching is to generate enthusiasm for tasks which require patience.*

THE INITIAL CONCERT

As soon as feasible, probably by the end of the first semester of study, the beginning band should present its initial concert.

Although the materials used for training and concert both serve the same purposes, the concert music per se should never be considered a substitute for the progressive sequence of learning incorporated in the lesson book. The concert music should parallel in difficulty the instructional material, reinforcing those skills of reading and performance already accomplished. It is not ordinarily desirable for the students to take their concert music home for practice. Not only does drilling on parts negate practice of the regular lesson assignment, but also such practice leads to an over-familiarity and complacency concerning the concert music in rehearsal. There should be very little concert music, if any, which cannot be read at sight.

The transition from lesson performance to concert rehearsal will be an uncomplicated procedure providing the teaching techniques for each are consistent with one another. Beginners, accustomed to the relatively short exercises of their instruction book, soon become accustomed to "playing a whole page" and counting extended rests. Concert performance, as compared to the unison playing of lesson material, requires much more independence in the reading of individual parts. Children who have been taught to "hold their own" on contrapuntal parts, as in the playing of rounds, will be better prepared for concert work. A more prevalent problem is that of the students "following the stick," giving some visual attention to the conductor. If the performers have had the previous experience of being conducted during their band lessons, the carry-over in training will serve them well in the concert band.

There is no more exciting and satisfying experience than starting a band class of rank beginners and developing and unifying their talents to culminate in a concert. The total achievement in terms of the personal and musical growth of the children is almost beyond estimation. The satisfaction of working for a common goal, the pride of accomplishment, the thrill of making music together . . . these are intangibles which deeply touch the affective domain of every band member. Many of the students will go on to greater musical achievements, a few will drop by the way. Whatever their future, the band experience will have added a new and meaningful dimension to the life of each child.

METHODS FOR BEGINNING BAND CLASSES
(listed in order of publication date)

Easy Steps To Band (1942)	Taylor	Belwin-Mills
Belwin Band Builder (1953)	Weber	Belwin-Mills
Guide To The Band (1955)	Sawhill-Erickson	Bourne
Master Method For Band (1958)	Peters-Yoder	Kjos
First Division (1962)	Weber et al	Belwin-Mills
MPH Band Method	Kinyon	Witmark (1962)
Play Now (1968)	Phillips	Silver Burdett
Basic Training Course (1972)	Kinyon	Alfred
Learning Unlimited (1973)	Jensen	Hal Leonard
Alfred's New Band Method (1974)	Feldstein	Alfred
Sessions In Sound (1976)	Buehlman-Whitcomb	Heritage Music Press
Band Today (1977)	Ployhar	Belwin-Mills
Building Tomorrow's Band—Today (1977)	Burden	Columbia Pictures
Alfred's Basic Band Method (1977)	Feldstein-O'Reilly	Alfred

ADDITIONAL REFERENCES

American School Band Directors Assn., *The ASBDA Curriculum Guide*. Pittsburgh, PA: Volkwein Bros., 1973.

Duerksen, George L., *Teaching Instrumental Music*. Reston, VA: Music Educators National Conference, 1972.

Holz, Emil and Jacobi, Roger, *Teaching Band Instruments to Beginners*. Englewood Cliffs, NJ: Prentice-Hall Inc., 1966.

Robinson, William C. and Middleton, James, *The Complete School Band Program*. West Nyack, NY: Parker Publishing Co., 1975.

Kohut, Daniel L., *Instrumental Music Pedagogy*. Englewood Cliffs, NJ: Prentice-Hall, Inc., 1973.

CHAPTER V

BASIC TECHNIQUES FOR TEACHING BAND INSTRUMENTS

No other responsibility of instrumental music teaching is as vital and directly related to professional success as is knowledge and skill in instrumental techniques. Instrumental music education majors about to enter the teaching field owe it to themselves and to their students to be thoroughly grounded in the playing techniques of all instruments, for such expertise is fundamental to the workaday world of band and orchestra directors.

Many undergraduates, deeply committed to their major instrument, tend to shy away from involvement with minor instruments not realizing that, once in the field as a professional teacher, a playing familiarity with all instruments will be of critical importance. This is not to imply that the teacher must achieve a high degree of artistry or be a master of every instrument but rather, *at the very least,* that he or she be able to demonstrate a legitimate tone, be absolutely positive of all fingerings, have a basic knowledge of strings, reeds and mouthpieces, and be familiar with the acoustical properties and tone production principles of each instrument. While the accomplishment of these multifarious requirements may seem to be an awesome task, there are many family similarities which, if understood, can be helpful in assimilating the required knowledge and skills.

BREATH CONTROL

In order to produce a full, focused tone on any wind instrument it is essential that the breath be pressurized (supported) by the large abdominal muscles. Once the air column is thus activated, it must flow through an open throat to be focused and intensified in the oral cavity into a faster moving stream which will efficiently activate the reed or lips, thus setting the instrument's tone column in motion. This set of conditions is sometimes a difficult concept to convey to young performers. The sensation of narrowing the air stream in the oral cavity can be demonstrated by the act of whistling. As the student raises the pitch from low to high, the action and correct position of the tongue will be realized. Many beginners tend to blow broadly in an unfocused manner, as if they were merely blowing up an empty bag or toy balloon. A comparison, especially meaningful to young children, can be made between trying to blow out all the candles on a birthday cake at once by puffing the cheeks as compared to concentrating on only one candle by keeping the cheeks in and arching the tongue. Once this "jet stream" action is realized, the sensation must be that of directing the air stream *through* the instrument rather than merely at it.

OPENING UP THE THROAT

A prevalent problem among beginning wind students, and sometimes also among more advanced players, is the tight throat syndrome, a choking off of the air stream. This muscular reaction is comparable to a kink in a garden hose resulting in little force at the nozzle despite full pressure from the tap. Such inhibited air flow is most noticeable when young students, especially brass players, attempt the higher register. The throat tightens in a psychological reaction to *trying* to play higher whereas, in direct contradiction, the opposite effect is induced and the student merely frustrates his own efforts by literally choking himself. Since the tongue and throat muscles are inseparably connected, any exercise which loosens the tongue will result in a more relaxed throat. One way of accomplishing this is to have the student practice sustained flutter tongue action (trill an R). This action will automatically open up the throat and give the player the sensation of relying on an uninhibited breath flow activated by the abdominal muscles. For more advanced brass students, this practice technique can be applied to the instrument itself.

TONGUEING

The tongue acts as an air valve in playing all wind instruments. The tongue tip lightly touches the upper teeth or palate, or the tip of the reed, temporarily blocking the air and/or damping the reed. When the tongue tip is pulled back in a short, quick stroke (similar to saying "ta"), the air rushes through to start and sustain the tone until being again blocked by the tongue. It is of extreme importance that the air pressure be generated while the tongue is in the blocking position in order to ensure a firm attack when the "ta" action occurs. It must be emphasized also that the stroke of the tongue, while positive, must be short and light, retracting only far enough to provide a channel for the air stream. Although teachers disagree as to whether to teach tongueing along with the student's initial efforts at tone production, it is an essential technique which must be instituted as soon as possible in the early lessons. As the student progresses, and with brass players in particular, more subtle articulations must be introduced, such as substituting "da" for "ta" in legato passages, and, eventually, teaching the use of the explosive syllable "ka" for purposes of double (ta-ka) and triple (ta-ta-ka) tongueing.

THE BREATH IMPULSE METHOD

A relatively new concept, especially applicable to beginning wind students, is the Breath Impulse Method, commonly referred to by the acronym, BRIM. Basically this technique involves the use of diaphragmatic breath pulsations to establish a feeling of musical pulse while, at the same time, reinforcing the sensation of breath support. Initially the young student is taught to sustain whole notes which are subdivided by four equal breath accents from the diaphram. As the student progresses, further subdivisions of beat are generated, thus quickening the action of the breathing muscles and ensuring positive diaphragmatic control of the air stream while, at the same time, giving physical feeling to the rhythmic flow. Carrying the process to the ultimate results in the establishment of a diaphragm vibrato. Advocates of the BRIM technique contend that it "accelerates the development of rhythmic concepts and provides a psychological basis for improved breath support which, in turn, aids tone quality and intonation."*

THE WOODWINDS

Fingering Similarities

All woodwind instruments have certain common fingering characteristics, the basic principles of which are exemplified in the recorder. When all holes are covered, the lowest fundamental tone of the instrument will be sounded, the tonal wavelength being equal to the total length of the instrument.

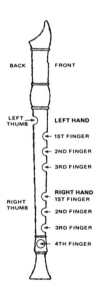

As holes are opened sequentially from bottom to top of the instrument, the wavelength is progressively shortened, thereby raising the pitch of the instrument to correspond to its closed-hole length. The C recorder fingerings given on pg. 73 are almost identical to those for flute, oboe and saxophone, and they correspond also to the clarinet fingerings for notes written an octave above.

*For a more detailed analysis of the BRIM method, refer to *The Complete School Band Program* by William Robinson and James Middleton, published by Parker Publishing Co. Inc., 1975.

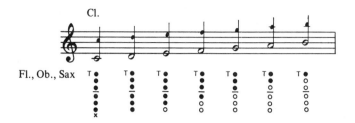

The F recorder fingerings given below are almost identical to those for clarinet written an octave below and the bassoon written two octaves below.

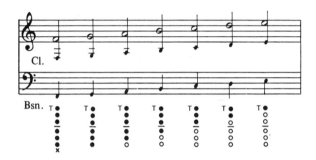

Although we are speaking here of *basic* fingering similarities among the various woodwind instruments, each instrument does have its own system of hole placement, keys, rings and connecting devices. On some woodwinds the majority of holes are covered by means of padded keys; these are called *plateau* systems. On other woodwinds the majority of holes must be covered by the fingers themselves; these are called *open hole* systems. Major differences occur also according to the positioning of the hole governed by the first finger of the right hand in relation to the hole governed by the third finger of the left hand. On the oboe and bassoon this distance results in a half-step; on the flute, clarinet and saxophone this distance results in a whole-step. Another basic fingering difference among woodwinds is that the oboe and saxophone, unlike the others, do not have a thumb (T) hole.

Activating the Upper Partials

Another characteristic common to all woodwinds is that the fundamental tone row can be repeated at the octave above by means of *venting* (opening a hole near the top of the instrument) or by *overblowing* (increasing the intensity of the air stream). The only exception to the rule of the octave differential is the clarinet which, because of acoustical idiosyncracies, is capable of sounding only its odd-numbered partials and therefore first repeats its fundamental row at an interval of a *perfect twelfth*. The primary venting device used in generating upper partials is called the register key (RK) and it is found on all woodwind instruments except the flute. Venting or overblowing results in the fundamental wavelength being divided into two or more equal subdivisions, thereby producing the upper harmonics of the natural overtone series.

FLUTE   OBOE

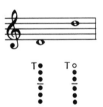   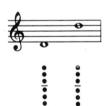

The flute has no register   The oboe has a half-hole
key. Upper partials are   device for venting plus
activated by venting   two register (octave) keys.
and/or overblowing.

CLARINET   SAXOPHONE

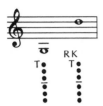   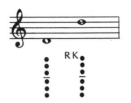

The clarinet produces the   The sax has a register (oc-
upper partials by means   tave) key for playing the
of a register key.   upper register.

BASSOON

The bassoon makes use of
half-holes and a whisper
(W) key.

REEDS

   In matters of tone production, the reed itself is the heart of the
tone; no student will play better than his reed allows. The best
reeds are made of cane, and single reeds are available in strengths
ranging from #1 (extremely soft) to #5 (extremely hard). Most
beginners on clarinet and saxophone can perform satisfactorily
on #2 reeds. However, as their embouchure muscles strengthen
and their playing ranges extend, young performers should be en-

couraged to adapt to reeds of 2½ or 3 strength. Reeds which are too soft tend to collapse under any extra pressure exerted from the lower lip, resulting in poor intonation and undependable tonal response, especially in the high register.

Double reeds, whether commerically manufactured or handmade, usually need at least a modicum of "personalization" in keeping with the individual student's embouchure strength and characteristics. Many professional oboists and bassoonists make and sell reeds and, if the teacher is not adept in this area, he is advised to seek out such a reed source, either locally or through the advertisements which appear regularly in the music education magazines. Although it takes much experience to handcraft consistently good reeds, the teacher who is not an oboe or bassoon principal will find that, with a few simple tools and supplies, a good text on the subject and a bit of patience, double reed making is not the mysterious art that it may first seem to be. There are many books which cover the subject most explicitly, some of which are listed at the end of the sections on oboe and bassoon.

THE FLUTE

It is customary for the beginning flute student to work with the head joint alone until a fairly intense "oo" sound can be obtained with some degree of consistency. One technique for establishing the correct position of embouchure hole on the lower lip is to start from a kissing position in which the hole is flush to the center of both lips, then to roll the head joint a quarter turn down and away from the upper lip, leaving the inside edge of the plate resting across the center of the red of the lower lip. This procedure will give an approximate correct position. Enough lower lip must be against the plate and covering the hole to allow for control of the tone, yet not enough to block or divert the air stream away from the outer edge of the embouchure hole. The narrow jet of air must focus on and split against the outer rim. The teeth must be slightly apart, the corners of the mouth drawn slightly down and firm, and the jaw relaxed and in a natural position. (See Figure 1 on pg. 78.)

Much experimentation may be required in order to find the exact embouchure formation needed. Common problems of poor tone (or no tone at all) can usually be remedied by rolling the flute in or out, changing to a higher or lower position on the lip, or by shifting the instrument right or left. In an effort to achieve a small enough aperture between the lips, many teachers recommend that the student let the air stream push the lips apart as if saying "poo."

Beginning flutists require much patience and understanding from the teacher, especially in classes of mixed instrumentation where it is easy to become lost in the shuffle of the louder instruments. With constant attention, however, and home practice tenacity, most children can learn to produce a satisfactory flute tone. Students who have a pronounced dip in the upper lip may have on-going problems of not being able to properly direct the air stream and focus the tone, and it may be necessary to blow off-center or, in extreme cases, change to another kind of instrument.

Once a satisfactory tone can be produced on the head joint, the student is ready to learn to hold the instrument and play the first notes. The flute is supported among three points—the *Right thumb*, the base of the *index finger of the left hand* (see Figure 2) and the *lower lip*. Additional balance will be provided by keeping the little finger of the right hand on the E♭ key most of the time. Young students sometimes have a tendency to allow the right arm to drop too low, thus precluding the best possible angle of the air stream across the outer edge of the embouchure hole. The teacher must check to make certain that the flute is held fairly straight across and that cramped conditions in the class don't force the player into bad posture habits (see Figure 3).

HELPFUL IDEAS

1. A mirror should be kept handy for classroom use. It is especially helpful for beginning flutists.

2. Demonstrate the principle of air stream direction by having the student blow against the back of his or her extended hand.

The slightest adjustment of the lower jaw position will show the greatly affected angle of the air flow.

3. A small cocktail straw held between the lips can be used to demonstrate air focus and the required smallness of the embouchure aperture.

4. Encourage the students to practice with the head joint alone, even as a warm-up procedure after study of the total instrument has begun. Make a game of it by attaching the head joint directly to the foot joint, and encouraging the students to make up their own tunes.

5. Attach bits of colored tape to the correct thumb and finger keys to prevent fingering confusion in the early lessons.

6. A light pin scratch on the head joint will give a guide mark for beginners to expedite their initial efforts at tuning to a standard pitch.

PLAYING POSITIONS*

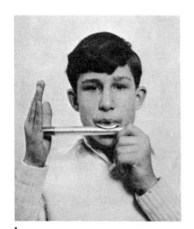

1

2

*All of the photos and fingering charts in this text are taken from the *Learn to Play* instrumental series published by Alfred Publishing Co., Inc. used with permission of the publisher.

FINGERING CHART

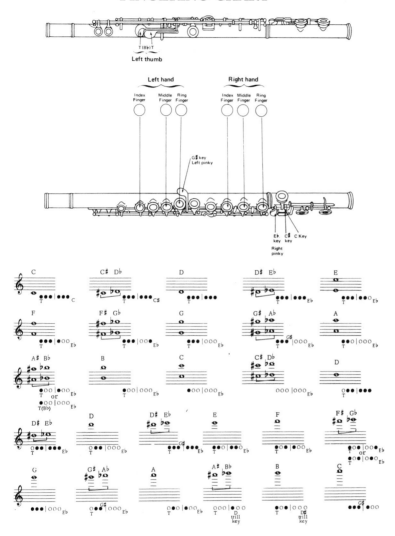

BEGINNING METHODS FOR CLASS OR PRIVATE FLUTE INSTRUCTION

Adventures in Flute Playing— VanBodegraven	Staff
Breeze Easy Method for Flute— Anzalone	Warner Bros.
Eck Method for Flute—Eck	Belwin-Mills

Learn to Play the Flute—Jacobs	Alfred
Rubank Elementary Flute Method—Peterson	Rubank
Universal Fundamental Flute Method—Melnick	Pro-Art

SOLO AND ENSEMBLE COLLECTIONS FOR YOUNG FLUTISTS

Basic Solos and Ensembles—Feldstein/O'Reilly	Alfred
Breeze Easy Recital Pieces for Flute—Kinyon	Warner Bros.
Chamber Music for Three Flutes—Voxman	Rubank
Flute Sessions—Gearhart & Wilkins	Shawnee
Folk Songs for Flute—Silverman	Chappell
Forty Little Pieces in Progressive Order for Beginner Flutists—Moyse	Schirmer
Selected Duets for Flute (Vol. I)—Voxman	Rubank
The Young Flautist—Lawton	Oxford University

PUBLICATIONS CONCERNING FLUTE PEDAGOGY

The Woodwinds—Timm	Allyn & Bacon
Woodwind Ensemble Method—Westphal	Wm. C. Brown Co.
Woodwind Anthology—	The Instrumentalist Co.

BOOKLETS AVAILABLE

Woodwind Tone Production Chart—Gower	Educational kit available from G. Leblanc Corp.
A Brief Compendium of Woodwind Embouchure Errors—Hilton	
A Teacher's Guide to the Flute—Delaney	Educational kit available from Selmer, Inc.

THE CLARINET

Once the reed has been slightly moistened, fitted to the mouthpiece and lightly secured in position with the ligature, the student is ready for the very first attempts at tone production. It is customary teaching procedure to have the young clarinetist produce a satisfactory sound with the mouthpiece and reed alone before attempting to hold and finger the assembled instrument. The correct embouchure can be established by bringing the lower lip back *to* the lower teeth in a combination of a slight outward thrust of the jaw coupled with a firm bunching of the muscles at the corners of the mouth. This will give a *rounded* feeling to the embouchure with the lower lip forming a firm, *narrow* cushion over the lower teeth. The mouthpiece should be held lightly but securely by the *lower lip*, the *upper teeth* and with a snug, *round-mouth feeling*.

The mouthpiece should be inserted into the mouth at a rather downward angle. The proper amount of mouthpiece to be taken into the mouth (the bite) can be ascertained through experimentation (see Figure 1). Too big a bite will produce a raucous, uncontrolled sound while too small a bite will result in a stifled sound or, at the extreme, no sound at all. The tip of the reed must be free to vibrate, unhampered by the lower lip.

Once the beginner has acquired the knack of producing a fullblown squawk on the mouthpiece alone, the clarinet can be assembled and the correct holding position demonstrated. It is essential, from the very first lessons, that the weight of the instrument be borne by the *nail-joint of the right thumb* (see Figure 4) rather than by the lower lip. The fingers of both hands must be slightly arched and relaxed, poised in a position of readiness over the appropriate holes and keys. Holes must be covered by the padded portion of the fingers rather than the extreme tips (see Figures 2 & 3).

HELPFUL IDEAS

1. A tiny piece of foam rubber attached to the thumb rest will alleviate the "hurt" sometimes experienced by tender right thumbs.

2. Colored tape stuck onto the appropriate "pinky-finger" keys can be a good "memory aid" in the beginning student's home practice efforts.

3. Reversing the customary sides in first learning the F/C and E/B fingerings may bring those notes within easier reach of short fingers (see fingering chart—L5 and R7).

4. Pushing up with the right thumb (taking the pressure off the reed) may be helpful, especially in the first efforts at playing above the break in the higher register.

5. In order to provide the sensation of blowing a full tone for those students who have trouble completely covering the holes, teachers can finger the instrument while the student blows. Turning the clarinet upside down in relation to the mouthpiece will facilitate this process.

6. When needed in an emergency, wrapped strips of paper, or better, waxed dental floss can substitute for loose or missing joint corks.

7. Although cardboard and plastic cases are available, a clean flat surface for preserving reeds in between playings can be made from a small pocket mirror and a rubber band.

PLAYING POSITIONS

1

2

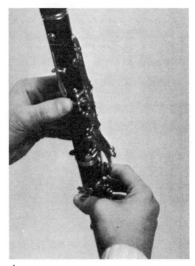

3   4

FINGERING CHART

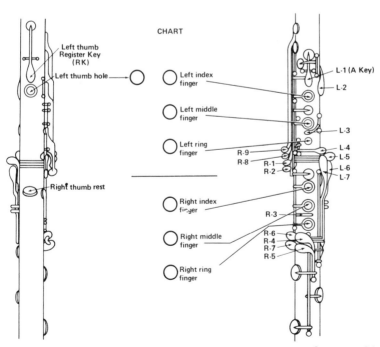

CHART

Left thumb
Register Key
(RK)

Left thumb hole

Left index
finger

L-1 (A Key)

L-2

Left middle
finger

L-3

Left ring
finger

R-9

L-4

R-8

L-5

R-1

L-6

R-2

L-7

Right thumb rest

Right index
finger

R-3

Right middle
finger

R-6
R-4
R-7
R-5

Right ring
finger

continued on pg. 84

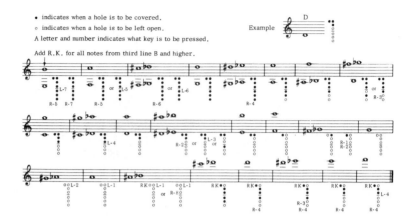

BEGINNING METHODS FOR CLASS OR PRIVATE CLARINET INSTRUCTION

Adventures in Clarinet Playing— VanBodegraven	Staff
Breeze Easy Method for Clarinet— Anazalone	Warner Bros.
Learn to Play the Clarinet—Jacobs	Alfred
The Clarinet Class—Phillips	Summy-Birchard
The Clarinet Instructor—Heim	Kendor
Rubank Elementary Clarinet Method— Hovey	Rubank
Play the Clarinet—Tschaikov	Chappell

SOLO AND ENSEMBLE COLLECTIONS FOR YOUNG CLARINETISTS

Basic Solos and Ensembles— Feldstein/O'Reilly	Alfred
Breeze Easy Recital Pieces—Kinyon	Warner Bros.

Duet Sessions—Gearhart	Shawnee
Chamber Music for Three Clarinets (Vol. I)—Voxman	Rubank
First Pieces for B♭ Clarinet—Benoy & Bryce	Oxford Univ. Press
Selected Duets for Clarinet—Voxman	Rubank
The Young Clarinetists—Lawton	Oxford Univ. Press
Chalumeau Canons for Clarinets—Brown	Chappell

PUBLICATIONS CONCERNING CLARINET PEDAGOGY

The Art of Clarinet Playing—Stein	Summy-Birchard
The Clarinet: Excellence and Artistry—Mazzeo	Alfred
The Woodwinds—Timm	Allyn & Bacon
Woodwind Anthology	The Instrumentalist Co.
Woodwind Ensemble Method—Westphal	Wm. C. Brown Co.

BOOKLETS AVAILABLE

Woodwind Tone Production Chart—Gower	Educational kit available from G. Lebanc Corp.
The Clarinet Embouchure—Kruth	
A Brief Compendium of Woodwind Embouchure Errors—Hilton	
A Teacher's Guide to the Clarinet—Hovey	Educational kit available from Selmer, Inc.
Chart of Regular and Trill Fingerings for B♭ Clarinet—Hovey	
The Teacher's Guide to the Alto, Bass and Contrabass Clarinets—McCathren	

THE SAXOPHONE

The first efforts at embouchure formation and tone production should be with the mouthpiece and reed alone. The saxophone embouchure, although somewhat more relaxed than that required for the Bb clarinet, deserves equal attention from the teacher. Basically the two lip formations are the same in that the lower lip is rolled *to* the lower teeth, enough lip rolling over to form a firm narrow pad between the teeth and the reed. The upper teeth are in light contact with the top of the mouthpiece, and the sensation of embouchure to mouthpiece is *round* with equal pressure being applied from all sides. The major difference in embouchures stems from the fact that the angle of entrance of the saxophone mouthpiece is more straight on. With a modicum of experimentation the student should be able to produce a substantial sound on the mouthpiece alone before attempting tone production on the instrument itself (see Figure 1).

PLAYING POSITIONS

1

The weight of the saxophone is supported by means of a neckstrap (carefully adjusted in length for the individual student) and additional support comes from the right thumb at the nail-joint. As with the clarinet, if the right thumb crotch is used (a common position of comfort and convenience found among beginners), the right hand will be out of position for maximum finger accessibility to the keys. It is important also that the saxophone be held slightly to the right of the body, not directly in front or angled too far back. The mouthpiece and neck of the instrument should be positioned to accommodate this slight off-center position. The fingers should be naturally arched and the left thumb in a position where it can be easily tipped to the register key in a rolling motion (see Figures 2 and 3).

2   3

FINGERING CHART

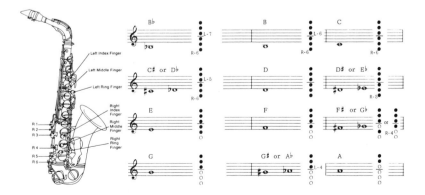

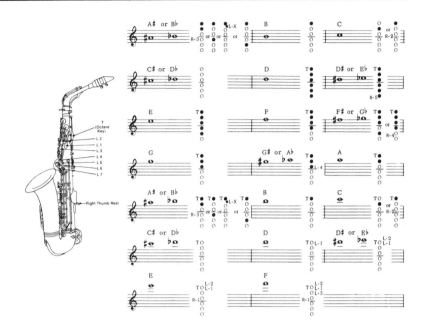

BEGINNING METHODS FOR CLASS OR PRIVATE SAXOPHONE INSTRUCTION

Adventures in Saxophone Playing—   Staff
VanBodegraven

Breeze Easy Method for Saxophone—   Warner Bros.
Anzalone

Learn to Play the Saxophone—Gouse   Alfred

Rubank Elementary Saxophone   Rubank
Method—Hovey

Foundation To Saxophone Playing—   Carl Fischer
Vereecken

SOLO AND ENSEMBLE COLLECTIONS FOR YOUNG SAXOPHONISTS

Basic Solos and Ensembles   Alfred
Feldstein/O'Reilly

Breeze Easy Recital Pieces—Kinyon   Warner Bros.

Chamber Music for Three Saxophones—Voxman (2 altos & tenor)	Rubank
Saxophone Ensembles for Young Performers—Kinyon (2 altos & tenor)	Alfred

PUBLICATIONS CONCERNING SAXOPHONE PEDAGOGY

The Art of Saxophone Playing—Teal	Summy-Birchard
The Woodwinds—Timm	Allyn & Bacon
Woodwind Ensemble Method— Westphal	Wm. C. Brown Co.
Woodwind Anthology	The Instrumentalist Co.

BOOKLETS AVAILABLE

Woodwind Tone Production Chart— Gower	Educational kit available from G. Leblanc Co.
Teacher's Guide to the Saxophone— Hemke	Educational kit available from Selmer Inc.
Chart of Regular and Trill Fingerings for Saxophone—Hovey	

THE OBOE

Before the student commences the initial attempts at tone production, the reed tip must be lightly soaked in order to make it soft and pliable. This can be accomplished either by holding the reed in the mouth or, as is the more common custom, by letting it stand momentarily in a glass of water. Only the tip portion should be moistened.

As with all wind instruments, it is standard practice to have the beginner achieve a tone on the mouthpiece or reed only before attempting tone production on the instrument itself. The reed tip should be placed on the lower lip and then the lip rolled inward so that approximately a quarter inch of the reed tip extends into the mouth beyond the red of the lip, free to vibrate. The feeling is one of roundness, the lips being drawn around the reed with enough firmness to support the reed without restricting its vibration. The embouchure for oboe corresponds to the clarinet embouchure except that *both* lips cushion the reed and in a puckered formation (see Figures 1, 2 and 3). The student may have to experiment until the proper crowing sound is achieved. This reed-alone sound should be a raucous buzzing rather than a pure single high pitch. Too much reed in the mouth will cause an uncontrollable sound, too little will result in a stifled tone or no tone at all.

Once a proper crowing sound has been achieved with the reed alone, the student is ready to begin with the instrument. As with all reed instruments, the weight is supported at the thumbnail joint of the right hand. The fingers should be arched and held at a slight angle to the instrument (see Figures 4 and 5).

PLAYING POSITIONS

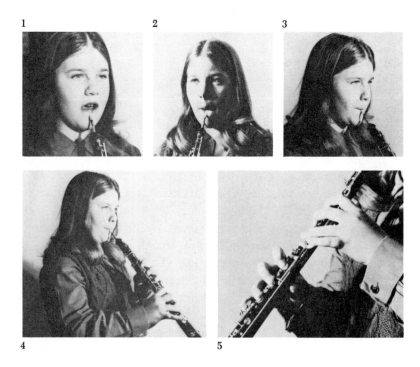

FINGERING CHART

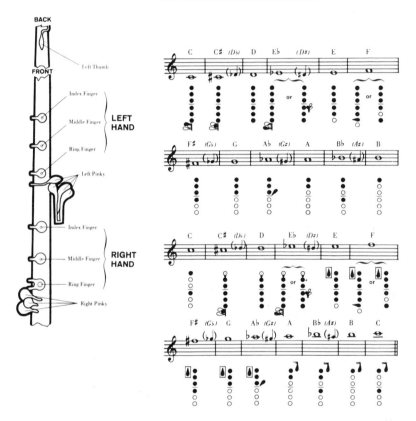

BEGINNING METHODS FOR CLASS OR PRIVATE OBOE INSTRUCTION

A Method for Oboe—Mueller	University Music Press
Breeze Easy Method for Oboe—Anzalone	Warner Bros.
Gekeler Method—Gekeler	Belwin-Mills
Learn to Play the Oboe—McBeth	Alfred

Method for Oboe—Carey	Carl Fischer
Oboist's Companion—Rothwell	Oxford Univ. Press
Rubank Elementary Oboe Method— Hovey	Rubank

SOLO AND ENSEMBLE COLLECTIONS FOR YOUNG OBOISTS

Basic Solos and Ensembles Feldstein/O'Reilly	Alfred
A Tune Book for Oboe—Rothwell	Oxford Univ. Press
Seventy-Two Oboe Solos	Belwin-Mills
The Young Oboist—Lawton	Oxford Univ. Press

PUBLICATIONS CONCERNING OBOE PEDAGOGY

Oboe Reeds—Mayer & Rohner	The Instrumentalist Co.
Oboe Technique—Rothwell	Oxford Univ. Press
The Art of Oboe Playing—Sprenkle & Ledet	Summy-Birchard
The Woodwinds—Timm	Allyn & Bacon
Woodwind Anthology	The Instrumentalist Co.
Woodwind Ensemble Method— Westphal	Wm. C. Brown Co.

BOOKLETS AVAILABLE

Woodwind Tone Production Chart— Gower	Educational kit available from G. Leblanc Corp.
Teacher's Guide to the Oboe—Lehman	Educational kit available from Selmer, Inc.

THE BASSOON

Before the initial attempts at tone production, the reed must be soaked for a very few minutes in a glass of water to make it manipulative and better responding. Soak only the tip to the first wire, and only in moderation.

As with all woodwind instruments, the customary procedure in bassoon teaching is to have the student achieve a sound with the reed only before attempting tone production on the instrument itself. Place the reed on the lower lip and bring the lip to and slightly over the teeth. The upper lip will close about the reed from the top, forming a rounded cushion around the double-lip embouchure. Normally the lower jaw will be in a natural receded position with more lower lip than upper being in contact with the reed. The embouchure must form a firm cushion without restricting the vibration of the reed. Of all the woodwind embouchures, the bassoon must be the most relaxed. By experimenting with the amount of reed in the mouth, the student should easily find a position which, with adequate breath application, will produce the typical double-crow effect.

Once the student can produce a consistent raucous crowing sound on the reed alone, he is ready to attempt tone production on the bassoon itself. The weight of the instrument must be supported by a strap or a floor spike. If a neckstrap is used, a right hand thumb crutch for balancing the instrument may be desirable, especially for young students. The most popular method for instrument support, however, is the seat strap which takes all the weight off the body, leaving the hands relaxed and free to control the comparatively complex system of fingerings (see Figures 4 and 5).

PLAYING POSITIONS

 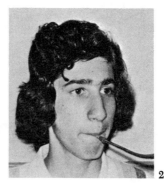

1 2

4

3

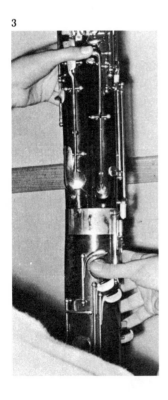

5

FINGERING CHART

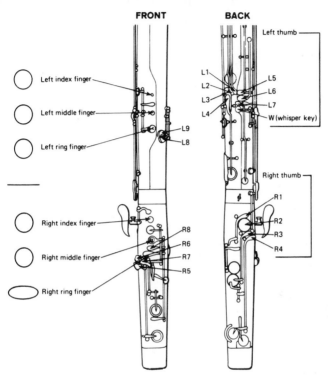

FRONT

BACK

Left thumb

Left index finger

Left middle finger

Left ring finger

L9
L8

L1
L2
L3
L4

L5
L6
L7
W (whisper key)

Right thumb

Right index finger

Right middle finger

Right ring finger

R8
R6
R7
R5

R1
R2
R3
R4

BEGINNING METHODS FOR CLASS AND PRIVATE BASSOON INSTRUCTION

Breeze Easy Method for Bassoon—Anzalone	Warner Bros.
Gekeler-Hovey Bassoon Method	Belwin-Mills
Learn to Play the Bassoon—Eisenhauer	Alfred
Lentz Method for Bassoon—Lentz	Belwin-Mills
Practical Method for Bassoon—Weissenborn	Carl Fischer
Rubank Elementary Method for Bassoon—Skornicka	Rubank

SOLO AND ENSEMBLE COLLECTIONS FOR YOUNG BASSOONISTS

Basic Solos and Ensembles Feldstein/O'Reilly	Alfred
First Pieces for Bassoon—Benoy	Oxford Univ. Press
50 Standard Bassoon Solos—Hudadoff	ProArt
A Classical and Romantic Album for Bassoon—Phillips	Oxford Univ. Press

PUBLICATIONS CONCERNING BASSOON PEDAGOGY

Bassoon Reed Making—Popkin & Glickman	The Instrumentalist Co.
Essentials of Bassoon Technique—Cooper & Toplansky	Howard Toplansky 559 Winthrop Rd. Union, N.J. 07083
The Art of Bassoon Playing—Spencer	Summy-Birchard
The Woodwinds—Timm	Allyn & Bacon
Woodwind Ensemble Method—Westphal	Wm. C. Brown Co.

BOOKLETS AVAILABLE

Teacher's Guide to the Bassoon—Pence   Educational kit available
from Selmer, Inc.

THE BRASSES

The Overtone Series

All brass instruments share the same basic principles of fingering (or slide positioning), embouchure and breath control. An understanding of these similarities can be of great advantage to the instrumental teacher in learning the performance techniques of the different instruments of the brass family. Tone production is inseparably linked with the natural overtone series, historically all brass instruments having evolved from open (valveless) horns.

The intervals of the natural overtone series in approximate pitch:

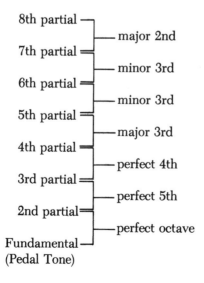

8th partial ─┐
               ├── major 2nd
7th partial ═┤
               ├── minor 3rd
6th partial ═┤
               ├── minor 3rd
5th partial ═┤
               ├── major 3rd
4th partial ═┤
               ├── perfect 4th
3rd partial ═┤
               ├── perfect 5th
2nd partial═┤
               └── perfect octave
Fundamental ─┘
(Pedal Tone)

The following notations of the open tones of the various brass instruments, in written pitch, illustrate this relationship:

Note: (1) The fundamental tone (1st partial) is not generally of practical use except on large bore instruments such as bass trombones.

(2) The 7th partial is too flat on all brasses to be used per se.

Fingerings and Slide Positions

All three-valve instruments are similarly constructed in that the first valve adds enough tubing to lower the instrument's open pitch a major second, the second valve adds enough tubing to lower the open pitch a minor second and the third valve adds enough tubing to lower the open pitch a minor third. Hence through a series of seven valve combinations the intervals between the natural overtones can be bridged chromatically. The seven trombone positions correspond to these valve combinations identically and serve the same pitch changing functions by extending the length of tubing.

Descending Half-Steps

```
Fingering combinations          1 2 1 1
for three-valve instruments:  0 2 1 2 3 3 2
                                        3
```

```
Corresponding trombone
positions:                      1 2 3 4 5 6 7
```

The following example illustrates descending chromatic scales for both cornet and trombone:

Further study will reveal that many alternate fingerings and positions are possible. The fourth note of the scale above, for example, could be fingered 1-2 on the cornet or played in the 4th position on the trombone.

Embouchure

There are as many different brass embouchures as there are players, for each brass performer has his or her own individual jaw structure, dental information and set of facial muscles. There are, however, certain general principles of performance which apply to all brass students. The upper and lower teeth must be very slightly apart so as not to obstruct the air flow. The lower jaw may be thrust forward slightly in order to compensate for any natural occlusion which tends to block the free flow of the air stream. The tension of the "pucker" muscles (corners pushed forward) must counteract the "smiling" muscles (corners of the lips pulled back) to create a firm pad upon which to set the mouthpiece. The center of the upper lip must be free to vibrate and the lower lip free to control the direction of the air stream into the mouthpiece. Although some modest pressure of mouthpiece-to-lip is necessary for most brassmen, any extreme pressure will be self-defeating. Adequate breath support and focusing of the air stream will negate to a great degree the necessity for excessive pressure in matters of range and endurance.

The mouthpiece itself should be horizontally centered on the mouth as nearly as possible. Most players, adapting to their own "natural" embouchure, prefer a vertical setting of 1/2 or 2/3 of the mouthpiece on the upper lip, thus allowing for a maximum area of vibration. At the same time, however, enough of the lower lip must be on the mouthpiece to give an adequate cushion area against normal pressure, the lower lip being somewhat tougher and more resilient than the upper. French horn players should set the lower rim of the mouthpiece on the red portion of the lower lip, thus keeping the mouthpiece in a high position. Trumpet and lower brass players, on the other hand, should avoid any extreme position which causes the mouthpiece to rest on the red portion of either lip. As with woodwind embouchures, the feeling must be one of roundness, with equal muscle support from all sides. Although there is an on-going difference of opinion among brass players, the majority seems to find that wetting the lip with the tip of the tongue before placing the mouthpiece to the lip is an aid in embouchure manipulation during performance.

MOUTHPIECES

Every brass instrument manufacturer has its own graded line of mouthpieces, and most of these are consistent in quality and specifications. There are also several companies which specialize in both stock and individualized mouthpiece production, and whose advertisements appear regularly in music magazines. Any extravagant claims of "easy high notes" and "increased endurance" must be taken with a grain of salt, however, for although it is easily possible to make a mouthpiece which will support the claims, it is often at the sacrifice of tone quality. Generally speaking, most mouthpieces which are issued with new American-made instruments are quite adequate for beginners. These stock mouthpieces are "average" in rim shape, cup depth and diameter, throat size and back-bore taper. The pioneer in the standardization of brass mouthpieces was Vincent Bach.* Among the most popular models from the Bach line are:

Cornet or trumpet—	7-C
French horn—	11
Trombone—	12
Baritone—	11
Tuba—	18

ORTHODONTICS

One of the most discouraging inconveniences for young wind instrument students, and particularly for brass players, is in trying to continue practice efforts while wearing orthodontic appliances. Although it may be possible to circumvent the area of sensitivity with the larger mouthpiece instruments such as trombone, baritone and tuba, the effects can be painful for cornet and trumpet players because the normal playing pressure is concentrated on such a relatively small lip area. Recent investigations have shown that the pressure applied in normal wind performance does not necessarily negate the long-range effectiveness of the orthodontia. As has been stated by Wiesner, Balbach and Wilson,**

> While some orthodontists may suggest outright that the patient stop playing his wind instrument, the possibility nevertheless exists for adjustment to the appliances with either the same or a different wind instrument. A member of a different family of instruments also may be considered, such as a string instrument or percussion. However, one or both of these families of instruments may not be available, and choice of instrument must be determined largely by player interest.

*For an in-depth discussion of brass mouthpieces refer to *Embouchure and Mouthpiece Manual* by Vincent Bach, available from Selmer Corp., Box 310, Elkhart, IN 46514.

**Wiesner, Glenn, R., Balbach, R., and Wilson, Merrill A.__*Orthodontics and Wind Instrument Performance.* Reston, VA, Music Educators National Conference, 1973.

Comfort and ease of performance are more important than the natural force tendencies of specific instruments with certain types of malocclusions. This is true because the force and effect of the appliances on movement of teeth is many times greater than those of any particular instrument.

Double reeds, saxophones, flutes and larger brass instruments, while providing very little help or hindrance in the correction of any type of malocclusion, can be played with relatively good comfort and natural embouchure adaptation with a fairly wide variety of malocclusions.

The writers also give many suggestions for protective coverings which can be devised by orthodontists to enable the wind player to continue his or her study and performance during this otherwise awkward and sometimes painful period of embouchure adjustment.

THE FIRST TONES

Beginning brass students who are able to demonstrate a substantial buzzing sound and some degree of pitch flexibility on the mouthpiece alone will seldom have a problem in producing an acceptable tone through the instrument. For this reason most brass teachers routinely have their beginners start by vibrating their lips together and/or buzzing into the mouthpiece (see Figures 1 and 2 for each instrument). With minimal experimentation most students will easily achieve the knack. Students having problems may be:

1 — puffing their cheeks and not focusing the air stream

2 — clenching their teeth

3 — not getting enough upper lip into the mouthpiece

4 — holding their lips too far apart

5 — pinching their lips too tightly together

6 — not blowing with enough force

7 — blocking the air with their tongue or lower teeth

The concept of blowing *through* rather than *at* the instrument is most important. Whatever time is taken in the early lessons to teach proper embouchure set and correct concepts of breathing will pay off many times over in the student's performance future. Tongueing, as described earlier, is a basic skill which must not be neglected. Although teachers disagree as to whether it should be taught in the very first lesson, it should certainly be stressed as early as possible.

THE CORNET (TRUMPET)

The entire weight of the instrument should be supported by the left hand and arm, leaving the right hand and wrist perfectly relaxed. The fingers of the right hand should be arched in a natural position over the valves with the right thumb bent forward and resting under the leadpipe. The fourth finger will normally be hooked around the finger ring although some teachers prefer that their students leave the fourth finger free to move with the third. The angle of instrument-to-body should conform with the natural angle of the jaw; most trumpeters play with a slight downward tilt of the horn (see Figures 3 & 4). Although manipulation of the third valve slide for purposes of flattening the naturally sharp 1-3 and 1-2-3 combinations is usually postponed until the student has achieved some basic control of the instrument, this tuning reflex should be developed sometime within the first months of study.

PLAYING POSITIONS

1

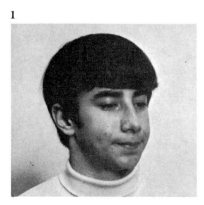

2

3   4

FINGERING CHART
(Alternate fingerings are given in parenthesis)

BEGINNING METHODS FOR CLASS OR PRIVATE CORNET (TRUMPET) INSTRUCTION

Breeze Easy Method for Cornet—Kinyon	Warner Bros.
Learn to Play the Cornet—Gouse	Alfred
Rubank Elementary Cornet Method—Robinson	Rubank
Method for Cornet—Beeler	Warner Bros.
Universal Fundamental Cornet Method—Pease	Pro-Art
First Book of Practical Studies (For supplementary study)—Getchell	Belwin-Mills
Physical Approach to Elementary Brass Playing—Gordon	Carl Fischer

SOLO AND ENSEMBLE COLLECTIONS FOR YOUNG CORNETISTS

Basic Solos and Ensembles—Feldstein/O'Reilly	Alfred
Breeze Easy Recital Pieces—Kinyon	Warner Bros.
Duet Sessions—Gearhart	Shawnee
Fifteen Folk Tunes—Meyer	Shawnee
Selected Duets for Trumpet (Vol. I)—Voxman	Rubank
Ten Trios—Knight	G. Schirmer
The Young Trumpet Player—Lawton	Oxford Univ. Press
61 Trumpet Hymns and Descants—Smith	Hope Pub. Co.

PUBLICATIONS CONCERNING CORNET PEDAGOGY

Brass Anthology	The Instrumentalist Co.
Essentials of Brass Playing—Fox	Volkwein Bros.

Playing and Teaching Brass Instruments—Winslow & Green	Prentice-Hall
The Brass Ensemble Method—Hunt	Wm. C. Brown Co.
The Brass Instruments—Winter	Allyn & Bacon
The Trumpeter's Handbook—Sherman	Accura Music

BOOKLETS AVAILABLE

Teacher's Guide to the Brasses—Getchell	Educational kit available from Selmer, Inc.

THE FRENCH HORN

The traditional holding position for the French horn is away from the body, with the instrument supported by the left hand with the right hand in the bell. With young students, however, it is usually necessary that the bottom rim of the bell rest on the thigh at a point that will bring the mouthpiece in a comfortable position to the lip. This position can be varied slightly according to the angle of the right leg from the chair. Under no circumstances of expediency should the young performer be forced to hunch in an awkward stance which will impair breathing or force the mouthpiece angle from a natural downward slant. The mouthpiece must be brought to the lip, not the lip to the mouthpiece. The right hand position is extremely important in that the right hand controls both tone and intonation. Despite the fact that rank beginners seldom achieve a true French horn sound, nonetheless the correct right hand position must be established in the first lessons. The hand should be slightly cupped, with the back of the hand resting at the far side of the bell (see Figures 3 and 4).

The controversy of the single F horn vs. the single B♭ horn for beginning students has abated within recent years, the F horn purists seeming to be in the majority. However, those who have taught elementary school hornists (the author included) will be aware that the B♭ horn has many advantages in relation to beginning ensemble concert pitch ranges, and that the less mellow tone qualities associated with the B$^\flat$ horn (for whatever the difference in tone may be at the beginning stage!) can be a worthwhile "sacrifice" in view of the relatively high attrition rate among young horn players.

Good solo and study material for beginning horn players is relatively scarce but, in other than ensemble performance, any of the standard trumpet literature can be used to good advantage.

PLAYING POSITIONS

1   2

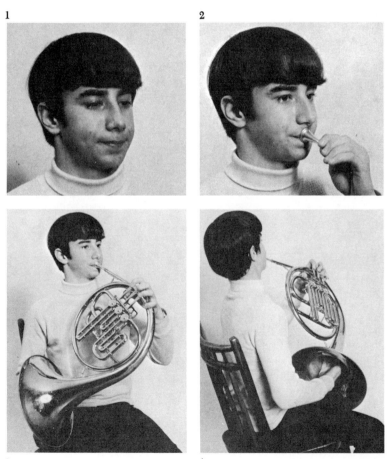

3   4

FINGERING CHART

The fingerings for the B♭ horn are shown in parenthesis.

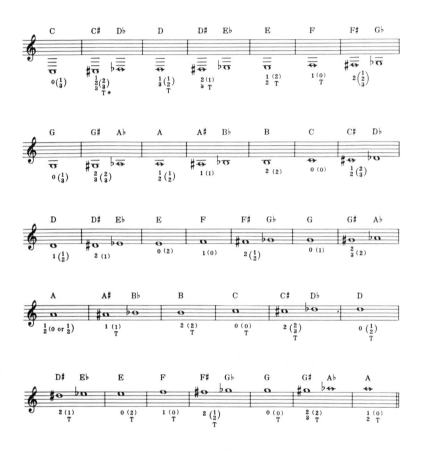

*When playing the double (F-B♭) horn, the B♭ fingering is accomplished by pressing the thumb valve (T). In this chart the letter T appears only under those B♭ fingerings that are most suitable for the double horn.

BEGINNING METHODS FOR CLASS OR PRIVATE FRENCH HORN INSTRUCTION

Breeze Easy Method for French Horn—   Warner Bros.
Kinyon

Learn to Play the French Horn—Eisenhauer	Alfred
Method for the French Horn—Howe	Warner Bros.
Play Away—Beeler	G. Schirmer
Rubank Elementary French Horn Method—Skornicka	Rubank
First Book of Practical Studies (for trumpet) (for supplemental study)—Getchell	Belwin-Mills
Illustrated Method for French Horn—Robinson	Southern Music

SOLO AND ENSEMBLE COLLECTIONS FOR YOUNG FRENCH HORNISTS

Basic Solos and Ensembles—Feldstein/O'Reilly	Alfred
Breeze Easy Recital Pieces—Kinyon	Warner Bros.
Everybody's Favorite French Horn Solos	Amsco
First Solos for the Horn Player—Jones	G. Schirmer
Three Easy Solos for Horn and Piano—Brightmore	Taurus Press

PUBLICATIONS CONCERNING FRENCH HORN PEDAGOGY

Brass Anthology	The Instrumentalist Co.
Essentials of Brass Playing—Fox	Volkwein Bros.
Horn Technique—Schuller	Oxford Univ. Press
Playing and Teaching Brass Instruments—Winslow & Green	Prentice-Hall
The Art of French Horn Playing—Farkas	Summy-Birchard
The Brasses—Winter	Allyn & Bacon

BOOKLETS AVAILABLE:

Teacher's Guide to the Brasses—Getchell	Educational kit available from Selmer, Inc.
Teaching the French Horn—Why All the Mystery—Robinson	Educational kit available from Leblanc Corp.
Breathing and Breath Control— Neilson	Leblanc Corp.

THE TROMBONE

The entire weight of the instrument must be supported by the left arm, leaving the right fingers, wrist and arm perfectly relaxed. Normally the trombone is held between the thumb and the last three fingers of the left hand with the index finger extended upward and over the mouthpiece. For young students of small stature this position may be modified in keeping with the size of the hand. The slide should be held lightly at the brace, between the right thumb and the first and second fingers at the nail-joint. A flexible wrist is essential to eventual slide technique since it acts as a facile second lever to the arm itself, enabling the trombonist to change positions with a minimum of arm action. The instrument should be held at a slight downward tilt, conforming to the natural angle of the jaw.

One of the first problems confronting the beginner is finding the correct positions. Although visually guiding on the bell ("3rd is just above, 4th just below") and letting the right hand index finger extend and tick the bell in passing may lend a feeling of security, there is no substitute for finding the exact slide position *by listening*. A popular rote exercise for finding the 4th position is the "walking bass" line -

OR

The legato style requires special consideration and diligence on the part of the young trombonist (and his teacher). A tip-of-the-tongue TU is necessary for initial attacks but, when connecting tones in a legato phrase, a DU articulation will serve to broaden the sound and connect the notes. Perfect slurs can be made between tones of the same overtone series such as

although, in song style

playing, most trombonists would nonetheless use some subtle tongueing action. Other than the use of lip slurs where possible, the general rule is that a smooth slur can be made when the note goes up and the slide goes down or vice versa.

A facility with alternate positions is essential to every trombonist, and the beginning months of training are by no means too early for their study. The most common such positions for young trombonists and exercises to help intonation are as follows:

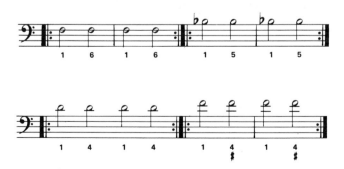

PLAYING POSITIONS

1

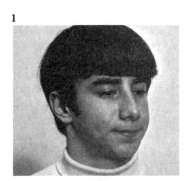

2

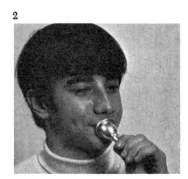

3

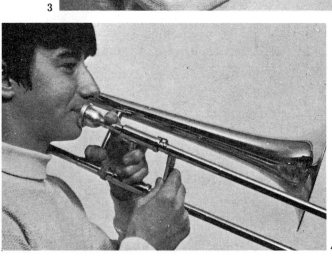

4

POSITION AND FINGERING CHART

Trombone position is shown above the note; baritone fingering below. Alternates are shown in parentheses.

BEGINNING METHODS FOR CLASS OR PRIVATE TROMBONE (BARITONE) INSTRUCTION

Breeze Easy Method for Trombone— Kinyon   Warner Bros.

Learn to Play the Trombone—Gouse   Alfred

Method for the Trombone—Beeler   Warner Bros.

Rubank Elementary Trombone Method—Long	Rubank
221 Progressive Studies—Cimera (For supplementary study)	Belwin-Mills

SOLO AND ENSEMBLE COLLECTION FOR YOUNG TROMBONISTS

Basic Solos and Ensembles— Feldstein/O'Reilly	Alfred
Breeze Easy Recital Pieces—Kinyon	Warner Bros.
First Solos for the Trombone Player— Smith	G. Schirmer
Old Masters for Young Cellists—Moffat	Associated
78 Easy Trombone Solos—Arnold	Amsco
The Young Trombonist—Lawton	Oxford Univ. Press

PUBLICATIONS CONCERNING TROMBONE PEDAGOGY

Brass Anthology	The Instrumentalist Co.
Essentials of Brass Playing—Fox	Volkwein Bros.
Playing and Teaching Brass Instruments—Winslow and Green	Prentice-Hall
The Art of Trombone Playing— Kleinhammer	Summy-Birchard
The Brasses—Winter	Allyn & Bacon

BOOKLETS AVAILABLE

Teacher's Guide to the Brasses— Getchell	Educational kit available from Selmer, Inc.

THE BARITONE AND TUBA

Most young baritone players hold the instrument in their lap, with the left arm in a cradle position around the horn. The right hand and wrist should be relaxed, the fingers naturally arched as in playing trumpet (see Figure 3). Although players switching from trumpet will find it expedient to read treble clef parts, all baritone students should be required to learn to read bass clef baritone music. Some directors start their young players on the baritone, reading directly from tuba instruction books. Within a year or so, when the student has grown large enough to be able to handle the larger instrument, the switchover is relatively easy to make.

Young tuba players can rest the weight of the upright tuba directly on the chair and, like baritone players, cradle the left arm around the instrument for balance and support (see Figure 3). Small students will find it an advantage to sit on an added short stack of books or a cushion in order to achieve the proper level of lip to mouthpiece. With both baritone and tuba it is important that the mouthpiece be brought to the lip rather than the lip to mouthpiece. Sousaphones can sometimes be utilized to advantage with beginners because of their handling flexibility and the fact that sousaphone chair-holders are available. Too, those many light-weight model sousaphones from the senior marching band may be put to good use at the elementary school level during the spring semester or during the summer months when the marching band may be inactive.

PLAYING POSITIONS

1

2

3

PLAYING POSITIONS

1

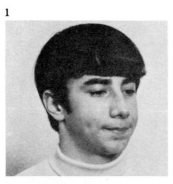

2   3

FINGERING CHART
(Alternate fingerings are given in parentheses)

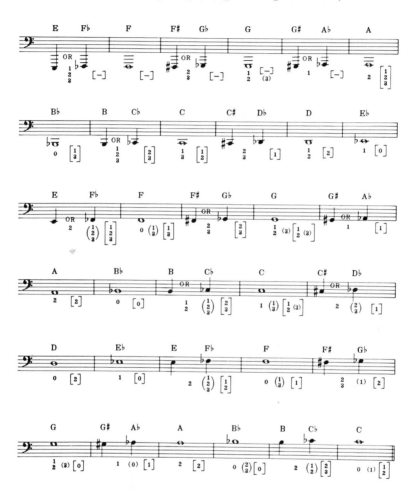

BEGINNING METHODS FOR CLASS OR PRIVATE TUBA INSTRUCTION

Breeze Easy Method for Tuba—Kinyon   Warner Bros.

Learn to Play the Tuba—Gause   Alfred

Method for Tuba—Beeler   Warner Bros.

Rubank Elementary Tuba Method—   Rubank
Hovey

SOLO AND ENSEMBLE COLLECTIONS FOR YOUNG TUBISTS

Basic Solos and Ensembles— Feldstein/O'Reilly	Alfred
Breeze Easy Recital Pieces—Kinyon	Warner Bros.
8 Bel Canto Songs—Phillips	Shawnee

PUBLICATIONS CONCERNING TUBA PEDAGOGY

Brass Anthology	The Instrumentalist Co.
Essentials of Brass Playing—Fox	Volkwein Bros.
Playing and Teaching Brass Instruments—Winslow & Green	Prentice—hall
The Brasses—Winter	Allyn & Bacon
The Tuba Handbook—Mason	Sonante Publications
Tuba Music Guide—Morris	The Instrumentalist Co.

BOOKLETS AVAILABLE

Teacher's Guide to the Brasses— Getchell	Educational kit available from Selmer, Inc.

THE PERCUSSION

Unlike the school drummer of bygone days who was judged primarily on his ability to execute the 26 standard snare drum rudiments, today's percussionist is expected to be versatile and flexible with expertise in many areas of percussion performance including not only the traditional snare drum, bass drum, and cymbals, but keyboard mallet instruments and timpani as well. The contemporary music performed by school bands, orchestras, and wind and percussion ensembles requires a battery of multiple percussion instruments and percussionists of high creativity and sensitivity, as well as consummate skill. Not only have the required techniques of "drumming" expanded within recent years, but also the *teaching* responsibilities have increased accordingly. For the modern-day school instrumental teacher (seldom a percussion major) the challenges are many and varied.

As with any other kind of instrument, basic percussion concepts include the development not only of skills but of attitudes as well. The once popular notion that percussion instruments are not to be taken as seriously as other instruments or that their playing requires less musical intelligence and effort than wind or string instruments is anachronistic to the modern world of school music. For that reason beginning drummers should be selected judiciously with at least the same degree of selectivity as candidates for other instruments. A grounding in piano study which will have provided the serious young student with an understanding of the elements of rhythm and melody as well as a familiarity with both treble and bass clefs may well serve as a major qualification.

THE SNARE DRUM

Although a practice pad will suffice during the initial stages of home practice, students showing promise should be encouraged to own their own snare drums. As with any kind of instrument, pride of ownership will contribute toward practice motivation. In snare drum classes where many students are involved, the music room should be equipped with one snare drum and several mounted practice pads of adjustable height. This set-up will allow for a system of rotation, each student being able to have his turn at the drum, while at the same time keeping the overall sound confusion to a minimum. The standard model drum stick, 2-B, is of good heft for young beginners.

The following sketch shows practice pads mounted on a slanted board (or long table with one end propped) which will accommodate a class of students of various heights.

Fundamental considerations when teaching beginning snare drum techniques are as follows:

MATCHED VS. TRADITIONAL GRIP—The traditional grip (right palm down, left palm up) originated as the most practical position for military marching drummers, the drum having been slung so as to necessitate a relatively high left hand posture. Today for the same reason, most school marching band drummers find the traditional grip to be natural and necessary. Loose but secure stick-in-hand positions and flexible working wrists are fundamental to good snare drumming. The left stick is secured by and pivots in the crotch between the thumb and index finger, the right stick is balanced between the ball of the thumb and the index finger.

The matched grip, finding favor among many young professional drummers, features the left hand in a mirror position to the right. This method of stick holding is excellent preparatory training for percussionists who eventually will be doubling on timpani and other mallet instruments. Either the traditional or matched grip is considered to be correct and acceptable; most teachers teach the system they themselves were taught.

REBOUND VS. STROKE-TAP METHOD—Although many of the old-time rudimental drummers were products and proponents of the stroke-tap method whereby rolls were executed entirely by separate impulses from the wrists, most present-day teachers advocate the less discouraging method of letting the rebound from the original thrust serve as the tap of the stroke-tap combination. Thus in the traditional "Ma-ma Dad-dy" which serves as the basis for all double-stroke rolls, the first syllable of each pair represents the thrust and the second the natural rebound. To help the student get the feel of rebounding, most teachers suggest the practice of promiscuous multiple bounces until the knack of controlling each stroke with but one accompanying bounce is acquired.

ALTERNATE STICKING VS. RIGHT HAND LEAD—Sticking refers to the sequence of right and left hand usage, invariably notated R and L. While sticking is usually indicated in instructional methods, actual snare drum parts for ensemble performance are not ordinarily so marked, leaving the choice of hand alternation to the performer. It is for this reason that snare drummers should be taught to develop a system which not only gives a balanced feeling between the two hands but one which will also serve as a guide in choosing stick patterns with consistency.

Proponents of the alternate system of sticking believe in the development of ambidexterity by which notation can be performed hand-to-hand, alternating right and left sticks. While practitioners of this style of snare drumming seldom use a *strict* system of alternation, the basic emphasis is on kinesthetic balance achieved through alternation of hands. The proponents of the system of right hand lead, on the other hand, believe that the right stick should be used for strong beats, leaving the left stick for beats of less musical emphasis. The theory is that the right hand is stronger by nature and that, through application and habit, the student will develop a more natural and consistent playing style.

Beginning snare drummers should be assigned lessons which include both reading exercises and rudimental drill. Despite a more casual attitude within recent years concerning the importance of rudiments per se, they still remain the "scales of drumming" and provide the young drummer with the basic techniques necessary to his or her art. In teaching rolls to young students it is both physically and psychologically helpful to start from the relatively short 5-stroke roll and, that having been achieved, to proceed to the longer rolls and ultimately to the long roll rather than to follow the traditional reverse order of procedure. The use of recorded musical backgrounds will provide a beat and pleasant accompaniment to many drill-type exercises which can of themselves become boring routine to youngsters. Marches and other kinds of recordings which set up a steady pulse can serve as a stimulating "metronome" for home practice.

The Percussive Arts Society (110 South Race Street, Room 205, Urbana, IL 61801) has many publications and much information available designed to assist the public school percussion teacher.

PLAYING POSITIONS

There are many different ways of holding snare drum sticks, but all have three things in common.

1. There is a point where the stick is firmly gripped (called the fulcrum).
2. All of the fingers are around the stick in a position where they can be used.
3. The main motivating force of each stroke is the wrist.

The right stick is gripped between the thumb and the first joint of the index finger. The other fingers are wrapped around the stick.

The left stick is gripped in the crotch of the left hand between the thumb and index finger. Two fingers are placed above the stick and two below.

The sticks may also be gripped in the matched-grip or like-hand style. Both sticks are gripped between the thumb and the first joint of the index finger.

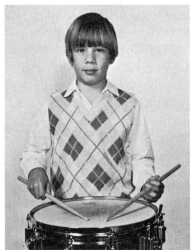

The position on the drum is the same for traditional and matched-grip performance.

THE STROKE is produced by a turn of the wrist in a down-up motion.
1. Place the tip of the snare stick or ball of the bass drum beater on the head.
2. Turn the wrist so the tip of the stick or the ball of the beater is as far away from the head as possible.
3. Play the stroke (down-up) striking the head and returning immediately to the up position.

KEYBOARD MALLET INSTRUMENTS

A lightweight and inexpensive bell kit will provide the beginning percussionist with a means of introduction to keyboard mallet instruments which, later on in his or her career, may include xylophone, marimba, vibraphone and glockenspiel. Many teachers program such elementary mallet instruction as an adjunct to the students' snare drum studies. Scales plus any easy melodic material such as found in beginning oboe, flute and recorder books will suffice as lesson material. Mallets are held similar to the matched snare drum grip and the basic stroke is the same . . . the mallet action is "like putting one's finger on a hot stove." The study of single stroke rolls, used for sustaining tones, should be introduced early on, the initial objective being control rather than speed.

PLAYING POSITIONS

There are various ways of holding Keyboard Percussion mallets, but all have three things in common.

1. There is a strong point where the stick is firmly gripped (called the fulcrum).
2. All of the fingers are around the stick in a position where they can be used.
3. The main motivating force of each stroke is the wrist.

Both sticks are gripped between the thumb and the 1st joint of the index finger. The other fingers are wrapped around sticks.

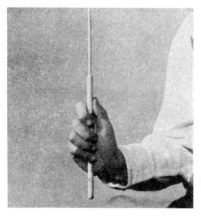 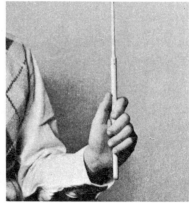

POSITION AT THE INSTRUMENT

For most playing the left mallet is positioned in front of (closer to the accidental keys) the right mallet.

THE KEYBOARD PERCUS-SION SOUND is produced when the keyboard bar (key) is set into vibration. The mallet should remain in contact with the bar for as short a time as possible. Strike the center of the natural keys. The accidentals should be struck at the edge nearest the player.

Note: When practicing at the Bell Lyra, lay the instrument down in a horizontal position rather than in the vertical marching position.

THE STROKE is produced by a turn of the wrist in a down-up motion.

1. Place the head of the mallet on the keyboard bar.
2. Turn the wrist so the head of the mallet is as far away from the bar as possible.
3. Play the strike (down-up) striking the bar and returning immediately to the up position.

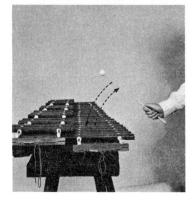

TIMPANI

Although many fifth and sixth grade percussionists are not too young to begin the study of timpani, it is well that they first prove both their musicianship and maturity through snare drum and keyboard mallet study before directing their time and efforts to timpani. The ideal age for beginning timpani study is probably the 8th, 9th or 10th grade, and only after the candidate has attained other musical proficiencies. Although private sessions are necessary for the teaching of tuning, sticking, damping and interpretation of timpani parts, students generally tend to acquire and polish these fundamental skills through actual band and orchestra playing experience.

The successful timpani student must have an acute sense of pitch discrimination, a knowledge of scales and intervals, and much musical sensitivity. A pitch pipe is essential for the setting of the pitch of one of the drums (usually, but not always, the lowest); from that given pitch the other drum(s) should be tuned by interval. A matched grip, similar to that used on snare drum, is usually used in playing timpani although some prefer a "thumbs up" grip. The appropriate choice of sticks for a given musical situation is always a consideration, and students should experiment with soft, medium and hard mallets in order to know what effect is possible from each different pair.

PLAYING POSITIONS

There are various ways of holding timpani mallets, but all have three things in common.
1. There is a strong point where the stick is firmly gripped (called the fulcrum).
2. All of the fingers are around the stick in a position where they can be used.
3. The main motivating force of each stroke is the wrist.

Both sticks are gripped between the thumb and the 1st joint of the index finger. The other fingers are wrapped around sticks.

The position of the hands above the drum may be either with the palms down or with the thumbs up. In both cases, the grip is the same.

PALMS DOWN   THUMBS UP

POSITION AT THE INSTRUMENT

THE TIMPANI SOUND is produced when the head is set into
vibration. The mallet should remain in contact with the head
for as short a time as possible.

THE STROKE is produced by a turn of the wrist in a down-up
motion.
1. Place the ball of the timpani mallet on the head of the drum.
2. Turn the wrist so the ball of the mallet is as far away from the
   head as possible.
3. Playing the strike (down-up) striking the head and returning
   immediately to the up position.

The mallet should strike the drum 3″ to 5″ from the rim.

BEGINNING METHODS FOR SNARE DRUM INSTRUCTION

Breeze Easy Method for Snare Drums— Kinyon	Warner Bros.
Class Percussion Method—McMillan	Pro-Art
Haskell Harr Drum Method—Harr	Cole
Learn to Play the Snare and Bass Drum—Gilbert	Alfred
Pro-Art Drum Method—Pease	Pro-Art
Rubank Elementary Method for Drum—Yoder	Rubank
The Drum Student—Feldstein	Belwin

BEGINNING STUDIES FOR MALLET INSTRUMENT INSTRUCTION

Fundamental Studies for Mallets— Whaley	Kendor
Learn to Play the Keyboard Percussion—Gilbert	Alfred
Masterpieces for Marimba—McMillan	Pro-Art
Music for Marimba—Jolliff	Rubank
Percussion Keyboard Technique— MacMillan	Pro-Art
The Mallet Student—Feldstein	Belwin

BEGINNING STUDIES FOR TIMPANI INSTRUCTION

Basic Timpani Technique—McMillan	Pro-Art
Fundamental Studies for Timpani—Whaley	Kendor
Learn to Play the Timpani—Gilbert	Alfred
Rubank Elementary Method for Tympani—Whistler	Rubank
The Tympani Student—Feldstein	Belwin

PUBLICATIONS CONCERNING PERCUSSION PEDAGOGY

Guide to Teaching Percussion—Bartlett	Wm. C. Brown Co.
Percussion in the School Music Program—Payson/McKenzie	Payson Percussion Products
Playing and Teaching Percussion Instruments—Collins & Green	Prentice-Hall
Teaching Techniques for the Percussion—Buggert	Belwin-Mills
The Percussion—Spohn	Allyn & Bacon

BOOKLETS AVAILABLE

Ludwig Industries	Slingerland Drum Company
Premier Drum Company	

CHAPTER VI

THE BEGINNING STRING CLASS

The school orchestra movement which began with such a positive surge in the early years of this century is now, in many school systems across the country, relegated to "playing second fiddle" to the seemingly more glamorous and public-relations oriented band movement. Indeed, some school systems in which string programs once flourished now have no string offerings at all. Yet there *are* dedicated pied-pipers of our profession who, year after school year and in spite of such competition, continue to nurture and develop enthusiastic young string players and splendid school orchestra programs. Such teachers are highly competent, dedicated, aggressive and able to compete successfully for schedule time, budget monies, student loyalties and public recognition on the basis of their own quality teaching and the resultant positive program.

There is no valid reason, either musical or educational, why string programs shouldn't be encouraged and supported in our public schools. One of the strongest arguments in favor of string and orchestral training is its carry-over into adult life. College, community and professional orchestras offer on-going opportunities for qualified string players of all ages. Furthermore, the wealth of great literature available for smaller ensembles makes this medium of musical expression ideal for family and neighborhood string quartets. Indeed, as leisure time becomes more prevalent in our society, and as the percentage of retirees among our population continues to increase, participation in amateur string groups could well serve many as an ideal hobby.

Although most successful programs are taught by string specialists, there exist many fine school orchestras throughout the country which have been developed by woodwind or brass principals. Unfortunately however, most band directors have shied away from promoting and teaching strings, either out of feelings of incompetence, because of lack of time, or for fear that an orchestra program would detract from or lessen the effectiveness of the band program. Given proper consideration in matters of budget, scheduling and teaching staff, neither program need conflict with the other. If each is equally supported and administered, the two will but serve to enrich each other. If our commitment as instrumental directors is to serve the community through the teaching of music, we owe our constituents well-rounded programs which include orchestras as well as bands. Indeed, if given a fair opportunity, many children of high sensitivities will opt for string study *rather* than winds or percussion.

Stringed instruments lend themselves well to mixed class instruction, far more naturally than do winds, and although it may be feasible to hold the initial lessons in small groups of like instruments, the full, heterogeneous class will provide a more efficient teaching set-up and should be organized early in the childrens' training. Not only do the violin, viola, cello and bass share certain open strings of the same pitch (disregarding ranges), but also the bowing and fingering considerations are reasonably similar. In addition are the advantages to the student of being early immersed in a harmonious orchestral environment, learning to accept a personal share of the responsibility for the total string section sound and of being made aware of the importance of individual tone, intonation and phrasing in relation to the combined ensemble. As with beginning band classes, the *social* aspects of belonging to the string ensemble cannot be denied. Indeed, such a positive factor of motivation may be quite essential to the success of the program. Finally, it goes without saying that the added efficiency made possible through the teaching of larger mixed classes as opposed to private lessons or small homogeneous groups is an important consideration in defending the string program in matters of budget and teaching staff.

RECRUITMENT

The fourth or fifth grade is, generally speaking, the ideal time for beginning the study of stringed instruments. Although Shinichi Suzuki* and his disciples have proved to us that children, given the right environment and vigilant parental supervision, are capable of developing prodigious violin skills at an extremely early age, teachers are in general agreement that the age of nine or ten is a propitious time for the average elementary school child to begin. Obviously much depends on the personal maturation and motivation of the individual student.

In those situations where the band program predominates the orchestra program, in order to avoid direct competition between the wind and string recruitment, a practical policy might be to allow the strings a head start of a semester or a year. This not only gives the string teacher an equitable "pick of the crop" where talent is concerned, but also allows the string students additional time in which to "get their feet on the ground" and adjust to the idiosyncrasies of their instruments. Much of the initial appeal of wind instruments lies in the fact that, almost from the very beginning, it is possible to play simple yet recognizable tunes. By contrast the string students are confronted with problems of left hand finger positionings and right arm bowing techniques, all of which take considerable practice before they can be coordinated and applied to music making. A year's differential in starting times could help bridge this natural gap in technical skills between the strings and winds, thus paving the way for a well-balanced elementary school orchestra.

The degree of selectivity used in choosing future string players will depend on the teacher's philosophy and the school's administrative policy. Of further concern is the matter of availability of teaching time and classroom space which may govern the number of students who can be accepted for study. However, of more critical importance than any of these factors in the selection of students, is the consideration that string players must possess a good sense of pitch and be well coordinated physically. This is not to imply that young wind and percussion players need not

---

*For further investigation of the Suzuki methods in this country see John Kendall's *Suzuki Violin Method in American Music Education* (1973), published by Music Educators National Conference.

possess these same aptitudes but, rather, to emphasize that such natural talents are necessary for any reasonable degree of success in the study of a stringed instrument. There are many standardized tests available (see chapter on *Testing and Grading*) which, within certain limits of reliability, will aid the teacher in determining the student's pitch sensitivity. Other than that sort of prognosis, the child's overall academic record will give some indication of his or her alertness and competitiveness in matters of classwork and home study, characteristics which usually carry over into the study of instrumental music. The personal traits of extroversion or introversion should not be misinterpreted as being indicative of any particular degree of musical aptitude or measure of future success. Often it is the "quiet" child who is most persevering and for whom music study means the most. Although a moderate degree of selectivity *is* necessary in choosing future string students, there is no reason why, with sufficient motivation, the "average" child cannot develop to become a competent school string player.

A preliminary but critical part of the string recruitment process should be a demonstration of the various stringed instruments, either through informal classroom visitations or by means of a general assembly program. It is important that the violin, viola, cello and bass each be demonstrated in a positive musical manner, either by the teacher or by capable high school performers. Young children are easily prejudiced, positively as well as negatively, and a superior or inferior demonstration can quickly sway the attitude of potential students concerning their preference of instrument for study. Given the advantage of a choice among half, three-quarter and full size instruments, most children of average build are able to adapt to any of the stringed instruments. However, in order to give the student with unusually large or small hands the best possible opportunity for success, the teacher must not be hesitant to suggest to the parent the particular instrument best suited for the child's physique.

PROCURING INSTRUMENTS

Quality in stringed instruments for beginners is every bit as important as it is in wind instruments, and despite the common notion concerning vintage stringed instruments, *old* does not necessarily guarantee *good*. Although it is generally true that stringed instruments, when properly cared for, "improve with age," it does not follow that stringed instruments of original poor quality will, like wine, mellow with the years. Solicitation of used instruments through advertisements in local papers, PTA announcements and church bulletins will seldom fail to turn up old instruments of varying qualities, some of which may even bear the "Stradivarious" label—meaning, of course, that the instrument is merely a *copy* of a model originally made by that famous craftsman. Used instruments which come from attics and storage closets must be thoroughly checked and approved by the teacher and/or local repairman before being placed in the hands of eager young children. Of first consideration, of course, is the tone quality potential inherent in the instrument, a factor which can only be ascertained by having the instrument played by a competent performer. Beyond that, the components to look for include a set of good quality strings, a full-haired and balanced bow matched to the size of the instrument, a comfortable chin rest, a properly set soundpost, a well-fitted bridge, easily adjusted tuning pegs, workable metal string adjusters where necessary and a fingerboard nut which allows for optimum height and spacing of strings.

Unlike the earlier years of school string programs when most stringed instruments available for purchase through music dealers were of varied and often questionable quality, today's teachers can recommend with confidence standard-line new instruments, most of which will have been professionally adjusted and thoroughly inspected at the factory. Quality control in stringed instrument manufacturing has vastly improved over the years, due in large part to basic standards established by the MENC through its Minimum Standards for Stringed Instruments in Schools, adopted in 1957.

Some school systems own a large inventory of stringed instruments for loan or rental to beginning students. This is an advantage in meeting the need for less-than-full size instruments since many parents may be hesitant to invest in a half or three-quarter size, in the knowledge that a larger model will become necessary within a very few years. Most instrument dealers have rental plans whereby it is possible to trade up when it becomes necessary for the student to transfer to a larger size. The teacher must keep in mind the importance of balanced instrumentation at the beginning level since this, to a large degree, will affect orchestral balance at the eventual advanced level. In order to encourage children to play stringed instruments other than the violin, it may prove to be practical policy in some situations for the school to furnish *only* violas, cellos and basses.

CONSIDERATIONS IN METHODOLOGY

There are currently several different approaches to string class teaching as advocated and practiced by well-known teachers and authors of methods for mixed-class string instruction. The primary consideration has to do with separating the initial problems of music reading, finger placement and bowing, introducing these three totally different techniques one step at a time. As with the wind instruments, rote playing is generally advocated in the earliest lessons, giving the student opportunity to concentrate on tone production and aural awareness before diverting attention to the printed page.

In the matter of initial attempts at left hand finger placement, many teachers and authors advocate pizzicato playing, either with the instrument in traditional position or, with the violin and viola, sometimes at a guitar-holding position. Another consideration of methodology in the teaching of fingerboard skills has to do with the choice between what are commonly called the key of C and the key of D fingering patterns. The crux of the difference between the two systems lies in the fact that the C approach involves the student in several different finger patterns while the D approach (D and A strings) utilizes the first, second and third fingers in a whole-whole-half spacing, a setting that is then extended to the key of G utilizing the G and D strings, and to the key of A utilizing the A and E strings. Although valid arguments can be given for each of the two approaches, most modern class methods follow the D system.

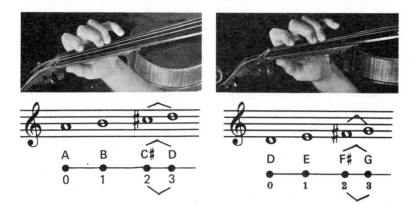

The third consideration, bowing technique, is also presented initially as a separate entity, permitting the student's full attention to the right hand finger holding position and wrist-arm movements. Unlike the traditional long-bow approach demanded by teachers of the past, many modern-day teachers and authors advocate a shorter, middle-bow approach in the earliest lessons, expanding to whole bow movement as the young student acquires better control.

One of the great influences of our times in the field of string teaching has been the innovations of Shinichi Suzuki. The Suzuki concept is based on the principle that very young children can learn to play violin in much the same way that they learn to assimilate and understand their native language . . . within the setting of their own home and by imitating their parents. Other key elements of the system are the exclusive use of rote learning for an extended period of time, the involvement of parents as partners in learning, the acceptance of instrument practice as a natural part of family life, learning by listening to others and total physical, mental and emotional involvement in the learning experience. In Suzuki's native Japan, his talent education program often includes children as young as two years of age. While performing, the children walk and move to the music, thus developing a responsiveness to the rhythms. Through a highly structured course of study which includes listening to and imitating recorded sounds, the students progress to works such as the

Vivaldi concertos and the Bach double concerto. The Suzuki movement has had great influence on and given much impetus to the revival and interest in strings in this country. Although the differences between Japanese and American home cultures are significant, there are many highly successful string (and piano) teachers in this country who base their teaching approach and methods on the concepts of Suzuki. For more information, the following books are recommended:

Suzuki, Shinichi, *Nurtured By Love*, New York: Exposition Press, 1969

Starr, William, *The Suzuki Violinist*, Knoxville: Kingston Ellis Press, 1976

Mills-Murphy, *Suzuki Concept*, Berkeley, CA: Diablo Press, 1973

Suzuki Violin School, books 1–10, Princeton, NJ: Summy-Birchard Co., 1973

Kendall, John, *Suzuki Violin Method in American Music Education*, Reston, VA: Music Educators National Conference, 1973

METHOD BOOKS AND SUPPLEMENTARY MATERIALS

Many methods designed for heterogeneous string classes are available. College students who intend to teach stringed instruments will do well to investigate some of the following, making a comparison study of such considerations as the methodology, score format, eye appeal, rate of progress, availability of piano accompaniment, use of harmonized song materials and comprehensibility (to children).

String Class Methods

A Tune A Day	Herfurth	Boston Music Co.
Belwin String Builder	Applebaum	Belwin-Mills
Bornoff's Finger Patterns	Bornoff	Big 3
Breeze Easy Method	Dilmore	Warner Bros.
Fun For Fiddle Fingers	Bornoff	Big 3
Learning Unlimited String Program	Wisniewski	Hal Leonard
Learn To Play A Stringed Instrument	Matesky & Womack	Alfred
Listen And Play	Kendall	Summy-Birchard
Muller-Rusch String Method	Muller & Rusch	Kjos
String Class Method	Waller	Kjos
Unison String Class Method	Feldman	ProArt
Visual Method For Strings	Gordon & Beckstead	Highland
Ward-Stephen Beginning String Method	Ward & Stephen	Kendor

Supplementary String Class Folios

Advancing Strings	Miller	M. M. Cole
Basic Scales and Two-Part Inventions	Muller & Rusch	Kjos
Beginning String Musicianship	Cheyette & Salzman	Bourne

Building Technique With Beautiful Music	Applebaum	Belwin-Mills
Early Etudes For Strings	Applebaum	Belwin-Mills
Etudes And Ensembles	Muller & Rusch	Kjos
Etudes For Strings	Muller	Belwin-Mills
First Position Etudes	Applebaum	Belwin-Mills
Funway To Fiddletown	Martin	ProArt
Intermediate Etudes And Ensembles	Muller & Rusch	Kjos
Intermediate String Musicianship	Cheyette & Salzman	Bourne
Learn To Play In The Orchestra	Matesky	Alfred
Orchestral Bowing Etudes	Applebaum	Belwin-Mills
Patterns in Positions	Bornoff	Big Three
Rhythm and Rhythmic Bowings	Muller & Rusch	Kjos
Scales for Strings	Applebaum	Belwin-Mills
String Builder	Applebaum	Belwin-Mills
Third and Fifth Position String Builder	Applebaum	Belwin-Mills
22 Studies for Strings	Reese	Belwin-Mills
Waller Vibrato Method	Waller	Kjos
Well Tempered Stringed Player	Matesky	Alfred

LESSON PROCEDURES

The classroom should be equipped with chairs and stands of appropriate height and arranged in a semi-circle with adequate spacings to permit the teacher to walk among the students. From the very beginning it is important that the children understand the kind of behavior expected of them; it is of equal importance that the teacher enforce such rules of conduct. In the course of the first class meetings much time and attention must be devoted to discussing and demonstrating care and handling of the instrument and bow. Stringed instruments, unlike comparable school-line wind instruments, cannot be built to be relatively "kid proof" and whatever time is devoted to the subject of careful handling will be a worthwhile investment.

The following pages taken from the LEARN TO PLAY A STRINGED INSTRUMENT method for class string instruction by Matesky and Womack, illustrate the initial stages of teaching proper holding positions and bow placement for violin, viola, cello and bass.

PENCIL EXERCISE

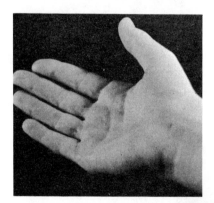

1a
Hold your right hand
in front of you
with the palm up.

1b
Place your thumb
(with the thumb knuckle
bent out) at the
top joint on
your longest finger.

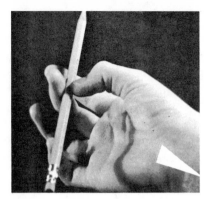

1c
Slip a pencil between
the thumb and finger
at the place where
they come together.

1d
Let the two other
long fingers curl
around the pencil.

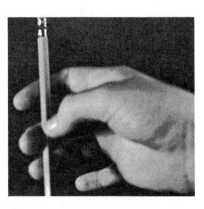

1e
Let the tip of
the little finger
touch the pencil.

1f

In this same position
turn your hand over,
relaxing your elbow
and your wrist.
Don't raise your elbow.
Don't raise your hand.

1g
Keep your arm still;
gently wave the hand
up and down.

HOLDING THE BOW

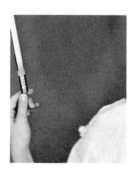

2a
With your left hand
hold the bow by the
screw end with the
hair up.

2b
Put the tip of your
right thumb on the
little bump at the
bottom of the bow.

2c
Fix the rest of your fingers as you did on the pencil.

2d
Balance the bow straight up and down on your right knee.

BOW AND WRIST EXERCISE

Take the position you had holding the bow on your knee. (See 2d)

3a
Place your left hand on the tip of the bow.

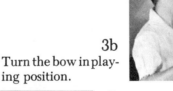

3b
Turn the bow in playing position.

3c
Now slowly move the right wrist up and down gently. *Be sure you move only the wrist and not the arm.*
Don't grab the bow tightly.
(See 1g)

HOLDING THE VIOLIN

4a
Be sure your shoulder pad
is attached correctly.
(Get the kind that is most
comfortable for you.)

4b
With the violin
on your left knee
and the strings turned
away from you,
place your *left* hand
on the *left* shoulder
of the violin.

4c
Bring the violin up against
your neck with your left arm
directly under the violin.

Check your position in a mirror and practice standing and walking
around so you get used to this correct position.

SETTING THE BOW ON THE D STRING

5a

Take the correct bow position.
(See 2d)
Take the correct playing position
with the violin.
(See 4c)

Set your bow on the "D" string
(the 2nd string from the left).
Place it about one inch from the
bridge. Be sure your elbow is
relaxed and neither too high nor
too low. Also, be sure your bow
is straight with the bridge.
Tilt the bow stick slightly away
from you. Check your position
in the mirror.

PLAYING THE D STRING

Take the correct playing position of the violin and the
bow on the "D" string. (See 5a)

Count out loud, evenly,
"1-2-3-4," while you draw the
bow down to the right and
away from your body. This is
called DOWN BOW and is used
when the sign ⊓ is written in
the music. Use the whole bow.
As you near the tip, tilt the stick
gradually towards you so more
of the hair touches the string.
*Don't press the bow into the
string.*

Count out loud, evenly, "1-2-3-4," while your bow *rests on the string.* During this rest, carefully check your position and see that your bow is straight.

Count out loud, evenly, "1-2-3-4," while you push the bow all the way up to the left. This is called UP BOW, and is used when the sign V is written in the music. Relax your shoulder, elbow and wrist. Use the whole bow and be sure to return to the same position from which you started. Tilt the bow slightly away from you at the frog.

Repeat this exercise many times before a mirror. Be sure to have the correct tilt of your bow at the frog and the tip.

HOLDING THE VIOLA

4a
Be sure your shoulder rest is attached correctly. (Get the kind that is most comfortable for you.)

4b
With the viola on your left knee and the strings turned away from you, place your *left* hand on the *left* shoulder of the viola.

4c
Bring the viola
up against your neck
with your left arm
directly under
the viola.

SETTING THE BOW ON THE D STRING

5a

Take the correct bow position.
(See 2d)
Take the correct playing posi-
tion with the viola.
(See 4c)

Set your bow in the "D" string
(the 3rd string from the left).
Place it about one inch from the
bridge. Be sure your elbow is
relaxed and neither too high nor
too low. Also be sure your bow is
straight with the bridge.
Tilt the bow stick slightly away
from you. Check your position
in the mirror.

PLAYING THE D STRING

Take the correct playing position on the viola and the bow on the "D" string. (See 5a)

Count out loud, evenly, "1-2-3-4," while you draw the bow down to the right and away from your body. This is called DOWN BOW and is used when the sign ⊓ is written in the music. Use the whole bow. As you near the tip, tilt the stick gradually towards you so more of the hair touches the string. *Don't press the bow into the string.*

Count out loud, evenly, "1-2-3-4," while your bow *rests on the string.* During this rest, carefully check your position and see that your bow is straight.

Count out loud, evenly, "1-2-3-4," while you push the bow all the way to the left. This is called UP BOW, and is used when the sign ⋁ is written in the music. Relax your shoulder, elbow and wrist. Use the whole bow and be sure to return to the same position from which you started. Tilt the bow slightly away from you at the frog.

Repeat this exercise many times before a mirror. Be sure to have the correct tilt of your bow at the frog and at the tip.

HOLDING THE CELLO

4a

Set your cello floor-board under the left front leg of the chair. (Rock-stop front center)

4b
Pull out the
end-pin on your cello
and tighten it.
Be sure it is
tight enough so that
it does not slip
when you start to play.

4d
Never let
the cello rest
against the chair.

4c Set the end-pin of your cello
in one of the board holes (or use
rock-stop) so that the back of
the cello rests against your chest.
The cello neck should cross your
left shoulder.

4e
Place your left hand on
the left shoulder of the cello.
Your feet must be on the floor
with your knees against the side
of the cello. Keep your knees
back far enough so that
the bow doesn't hit them
when you play.

The right knee may be back a little
farther than the left one.

SETTING THE BOW ON THE D STRING

5a

Take the correct bow position.
(See 2d)
Take the correct playing posi-
tion with the cello.
(See 4e)

Set your bow on the "D" string
(the 3rd string from the left).
Place it about two inches from
the bridge. Be sure your elbow
is relaxed and neither too high
nor too low. Also, be sure your
bow is straight with the bridge.
Tilt the bow stick slightly
toward you. Check your position in the mirror.

PLAYING THE D STRING

Take the correct playing position of the cello and the bow on
the "D" string. (See 5a)

Count out loud, evenly,
"1-2-3-4," while you draw the
bow down to the right and
away from your body. Keep the
bow parallel to the floor. This is
called DOWN BOW and is used
when the sign ⊓ is written in
the music. Use the whole bow.
As you near the tip, tilt the stick
gradually away from you so more
of the hair touches the string.
*Press the bow firmly but not too
hard into the strings.*

Count out loud, evenly, "1-2-3-4," while your bow *rests on the string*.
During this rest, carefully check your position and see that your bow
is straight and your arm relaxed.

Count out loud, evenly, "1-2-3-4," while you push the bow all the
way up to the left. This is called UP BOW, and is used when the sign

V is written in the music. Relax your shoulder, elbow and wrist. Use the whole bow and be sure to return to the same position from which you started. Tilt the bow slightly toward you at the frog.

Repeat this exercise many times before a mirror. Be sure to have the correct tilt of your bow at the frog and the tip.

HOLDING THE STRING BASS

4a
Adjust the end-pin of the bass to the proper length (out 3 to 5 inches).

4b

The lowest turning peg should be about level with the top of your head. When your bow arm hangs at your side, your thumb and fingers should be half way between the bridge and the end of the fingerboard.

4c

Hold the bass firmly with your *left* hand on the *left* shoulder of the bass. Let the right side of the bass rest on the inside of your *left* knee. The inside of your *left* knee should rest lightly against the bass. The neck of the bass should be tilted slightly toward you.

Check your position carefully (end-pin, left knee, and tilt of bass).

HOLDING THE BOW

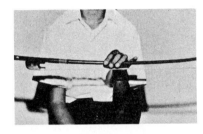

2a

French bow
With your left hand hold the bow at the middle of the stick with the tip pointing left.

German bow
With your left hand hold the bow at the middle of the stick, the tip pointing left and the hair turned toward you.

2b

French bow
Put the tip of your right thumb at the side of the little bump at the bottom of the bow.

German bow
Put your stick between your first finger and thumb. Bend the thumb and rest it on top and slightly inside the stick. The tip of your little finger touches the bottom of the frog.

2c

French bow
Place your other fingers in a hanging position over the bow: ring finger in the curve of the frog; little finger slightly over the bow; other fingers curved gently around the bow stick.

German bow
Put your first two fingers along the stick, slightly bent; ring finger just inside the frog near the hair of the bow.

BOW AND WRIST EXERCISE

Take the position you had holding the bow. (See 2c)

3a

French bow
Place your left hand on the tip of the bow.

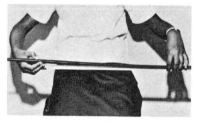

German bow
Place the tip of the bow in your left hand.

3b

French bow
Turn the bow in playing position (the hair toward you).

German bow
Turn the bow in playing position
(the hair toward you).

3c

French bow
Now *slowly* move your right
wrist up and down gently. *Be
sure you move only your wrist
and not your arm. Don't grab the
bow tightly.*

German bow
Now *slowly* move the fingers of
your right hand so that they are
curved as you *pull* the bow to
your right, and then gradually
return to the extended position as
you *push* the bow back to your
left.

SETTING THE BOW ON THE D STRING

5a

Take the correct bow position.
(See 2c for both French and
German bows.)
Take the correct playing posi-
tion with the bass. (See 4c)

Set your bow on the "D" string
(the second string from the
right). Place it about three
inches from the bridge. Be sure
your elbow is relaxed and the
bow in a straight line with the
bridge. Turn the bow stick
slightly toward you. Check your
position in the mirror, if
possible.

PLAYING THE D STRING

Take the correct playing position of the bass and the bow on the "D" string. (See 5a)

Count out loud, evenly, "1-2-3-4," while you draw the bow down and away from you. Keep the bow parallel to the floor. This is called DOWN BOW and is used when the sign ⊓ is written in the music. Use the whole bow. Tilt it gradually away from you so more of the hair touches the string as you near the tip. *Press the bow firmly into the string to start the tone.* Then let up a little on the starting "bite" and follow through easily.

Count out loud, evenly, "1-2-3-4," while your bow *rests on the string.* Check your position and see that your bow is straight and your arm relaxed.

Count out loud, evenly, "1-2-3-4," while you push the bow all the way up to the left. This is called UP BOW, and is used when the sign ⋁ is written in the music. Relax your shoulder, elbow and wrist. Use the whole bow and be sure to return to the same position from which you started. Tilt the bow slightly toward you at the frog and use the same starting "bite" of the bow.

Repeat this exercise many times before a mirror. Be sure to have the correct tilt of your bow *at the frog and at the tip.*

Once the string class is under way and normal lesson book progress is being made, an informal concert should be planned sometime within the first year of study. If available, select woodwind, brass and percussion players can be added to expand the string class to a full-fledged orchestra. The pitch stability of the winds will be of help to the string players while, in turn, the challenge of playing in sharp keys will broaden the musicianship of the wind players. There are available many series and collections of orchestra and string orchestra concert materials for young performers in which the string parts remain in the first position, thus ensuring correlation with the first year lesson materials.

Not unlike beginning band concerts, the first public concertizing by the young string orchestra will give the students an added sense of pride and confidence in themselves, and will serve to strengthen the esprit de corps of the ensemble. Such feelings of musical accomplishment, reinforced by parental acclaim, will motivate the students to further work and progress, thus ensuring a positive, self-renewing string program year after year.

ADDITIONAL REFERENCES

Green, Elizabeth, *Orchestral Bowings and Routines.* Ann Arbor, MI: Ann Arbor Publishers, 1957.

Green, Elizabeth, *Teaching Stringed Instruments in Classes.* Englewood Cliffs, NJ: Prentice-Hall, Inc., 1966.

Kuhn, Wolfgang, *Principles of String Class Teaching.* Melville, Melville, NY: Belwin-Mills, Inc., 1957.

Kuhn, Wolfgang, *The Strings.* Boston, MA: Allyn & Bacon, 1967.

Lamb, Norman, *Guide to Teaching Strings.* Dubuque, IA: Wm. C. Brown, Co., 1976.

Matesky, Ralph and Rush, Ralph, *Playing and Teaching Stringed Instruments.* Englewood Cliffs, NJ: Prentice-Hall, Inc., 1963.

Trzcinski, Louis, *Planning the School String Program.* Melville, NY: Belwin-Mills Co., 1963.

CHAPTER VII

THE SELECTION
OF PROGRAM MUSIC

One of the most consequential responsibilities of instrumental music directors is the selection of music for their performing ensembles. When one considers the vast repertoire of works presently published, not to mention the plethora of publications which become newly available each year, the job of sifting and sorting looms as a formidable one. Yet the hours spent in score study and program planning are as important as the time devoted to the rehearsal of the music itself.

The college instrumental music education student should give thought to and compile selective lists of standard works in the course of the undergraduate years, for membership in college ensembles provides a most fertile opportunity for becoming acquainted at first hand with quality repertoire. The development of a card index of selections for concert band, orchestra and wind ensemble, at all levels of difficulty, should be an on-going process. Such cards should be notated with the title of the composition, the name of the composer and/or arranger, the publisher, the grade of difficulty, program notes and personal annotations concerning interpretation, instrumentation and special inherent technical problems of performance. Such a card file will prove to be invaluable when the student matriculates to the professional world of instrumental music teaching.

The instrumental director assuming a new teaching position will inherit a library reflective of the tastes and requirements of the previous directors and which may be, or may not be, of sufficient quantity or quality. Whatever the situation, it is the new director's responsibility to continue to add to the existing library according to the needs of the department and in keeping with his or her own sense of musical value. The process of selecting quality music and building a musically respectable library is a continuing one and the considerations are many.

The primary consideration in choosing program music must always be that of *quality*. Living in a society in which mundane music is the rule rather than the exception, we owe to our students the experience of performing, studying and sensing exceptional music of aesthetic potential. This is not to suggest that the band and orchestra library should be composed exclusively of "great works," for every concert program needs material of a lighter nature, music which is here today and probably gone tomorrow. What *is* suggested, however, is that *the basic library be centered around a core curriculum of permanent works of musical stature*. Quality literature is fundamental to quality music education.

Another consideration in selecting musical works for performance is the technical demands inherent in the music itself. New scores should be thoroughly examined to determine whether or not the parts are in keeping with the abilities of the performers and if they can be achieved with reasonable practice and rehearsal. Thought must be given also to the requirements of the instrumentation as to whether or not all vital parts can be covered with the players currently available and, if not, whether cross-cueing is provided. Quality music fare, including both transcriptions and original works from all periods of music history, can be found for every level of musical development and maturation, from elementary through high school and beyond.

Very special considerations must be given to the selection of music for beginning level ensemble performance, for in this area the director is working with students of extremely limited range, reading ability, endurance, playing technique and musical experience. At this plateau of music making, the prime factor in choosing program material is playability. To be considered also at this level of performance capability is the fact that the ensemble instrumentation may be incomplete and far from balanced. There are many series of numbers currently available for elementary and junior high bands and orchestras in which such limitations of ability and instrumentation have been taken into account by the writers. Directors can choose from among them, selecting those which best conform to the needs and limitations of their groups and, of equal importance, deciding which contain the most potential for stimulating positive student response, teaching basic musicianship, achieving ensemble sonority and providing aesthetic musical satisfaction.

MUSIC LIBRARY STORED IN FILE CABINETS
(Photo courtesy of The Instrumetalist Co.)

It is essential that the instrumental music director, whether a novice or veteran, keep abreast of new publications. When one considers the hundreds of new numbers issued each year, the task seems not only terribly time consuming, but mind boggling as well. How *can* one keep up with such a seemingly insurmountable job? There are many sources of information concerning new music available, the handiest perhaps being through the services of one's local music dealer. Publishers customarily supply their retail outlets and distributors with sample scores, brochures and promotional recordings for free dissemination to area music teachers.

Another on-going source of information concerning new publications is to be found in professional music journals, all of which carry publishing advertisements and many of which run regular critical revue columns of the latest in concert and training materials. Publishers are eager to attract your attention to their latest offerings through both magazine and direct mail advertising, and are glad to send you samples and information in response to your request.

Attendance at state and national professional meetings provides a splendid opportunity to view new publications at first-hand, to pick up sample scores of all sorts of program materials and to hear excellent performances of both old and new works. The rows of publisher exhibits offer a marvelous overview of the latest in educational music publications. There are many well-established professional conferences held annually throughout the country at which publishers display their materials. The most venerable is the Mid-West National Band and Orchestra Clinic which by tradition convenes in Chicago each December. Other similar meetings include the Mid-East Instrumental Music Conference in Pittsburgh, the Tri-State Music Festival in Enid, OK, and the All-Eastern Band and Instrumental Clinic in Norfolk, VA. In addition to such conferences as these, there are of course the meetings of the MENC. Every instrumental director owes it to himself to attend such a conference, at least occasionally, in order to see and hear the latest program materials.

In addition, new music reading clinics, sponsored by music dealers, colleges and state associations offer the director a first-rate opportunity to see and hear the newest in published band and orchestra music. Very often at such sessions the local directors themselves form the performing ensemble and take turns conducting. Music dealers and publishers are generally very cooperative in loaning materials, and sometimes furnishing clinicians, for such sessions.

There are many lists of concert works available also, the type most familiar to band and orchestra directors being the state contest listings. Such graded numbers as ascertained by state committees are a good barometer as to what publications are most popular and deemed most worthy for concert and/or contest preparation.

In addition to state contest listings, there are several graded lists available to band and orchestra directors. Among these are the various Selective Music Lists published from time to time and available from the Music Educators National Conference, 1902 Association Road, Reston, VA 22091. Another set of highly select listings, the results of a survey of outstanding college and university directors and encompassing concert music at all levels of difficulty, can be found in the July, 1979 issue of The Instrumentalist magazine under the title THE INSTRUMENTALIST'S BASIC LIBRARY.

CHAPTER VIII

THE PRODUCTIVE CONCERT REHEARSAL

This chapter has to do with rehearsal procedures and techniques, and with those personal-musical attributes of the conductor which are vital for productive rehearsals and teaching. Although the emphasis of the text is directed to the rehearsing of major ensembles, the same principles apply equally to rehearsals of all groups. There is no valid reason or excuse for musically short-changing the members of ensembles which may be of lesser musical calibre than the so-called "top" band, orchestra, or wind ensemble. Beginning ensembles, "second" bands and other apprentice groups deserve rehearsals of seriousness of purpose and dedication to musical standards equal to those of the more advanced groups. While it is perhaps natural for conductors to take more care and pride with their best performing groups, when one considers that the major concern is the individual child—whatever his personal aptitude or musical maturity—the picture of the director's teaching responsibility comes more clearly into focus.

The band or orchestra rehearsal should amount to much more than a perfunctory practice session, a running through, a rehashing of yesterday's musical fare. In addition to offering each student the challenge of performance, every rehearsal should provide an adventure in music learning and listening, an opportunity for a better understanding of music as well as development of aural discrimination and sensitivity. For many children the band or orchestra experience may well be the one and only chance of a lifetime for whetting their musical tastes and expanding their musical horizons. There are five basic guide rules for rehearsing which will help bring about better student attentiveness and, as a result, a higher degree of musical accomplishment.

165

A productive rehearsal:

1 — Begins with a thrust into the music.

> The impetus of a direct musical beginning sets the tone for the entire rehearsal to follow. Administrative affairs such as collecting money, discussing trips or taking attendance, if necessary at all, should be reserved for the end of the rehearsal.

2 — Maintains its momentum.

> The rehearsal, once under way, must be kept in motion at a businesslike pace. Dull or boring time lags resulting from the conductor's dalliance or unpreparedness are at the root of most student inattentiveness.

3 — Concerns itself only with music and music making.

> The sole intent of the rehearsal should be music making. That purpose alone should totally absorb the interests of both the performers and the conductor. Any interruptions of the rehearsal flow due to nonmusical intrusions should be minimal.

4 — Has order, variety and change of pace.

> All rehearsals should be structured to include warm-up exercises and sight-reading along with the current concert fare. Just as any program should be a musical menu of contrasting moods and styles, so too should the rehearsal itself.

5 — Totally involves the students in playing and/or listening at all times.

> It is only when we lose a student's attention that his thoughts, and sometimes his actions, come to cross-purposes with our own. The student who is totally involved musically, either in performance or in listening, will seldom be a discipline problem. It is the teacher's responsibility to keep the lines of communication taut, to hold the students' attention, and to keep the rehearsal moving at all times.

THE REHEARSAL ENVIRONMENT

The rehearsal environment, both physical and acoustical, has a great bearing on the amount of accomplishment which a director may expect during a rehearsal. A well-arranged, well-lighted and acoustically treated rehearsal room, free of extraneous sounds, is essential to teaching efficiency. The acoustical havoc created by competitive school sounds such as droning air-conditioners (what pitch?) or bounding basketballs (what rhythm?) can, even through the subconscious, complicate or destroy the intensity of communication needed between a conductor and his performers. For psychological as well as physical reasons the room should be attractive and orderly in appearance, with assigned space for storage of instrument cases, equipment and music. The few minutes of time immediately prior to the actual rehearsal are extremely important for setting an atmosphere conducive to serious rehearsing. Rules of procedure and conduct must be formulated and followed which will ensure that, when the downbeat is given, everyone will be ready, willing, and able to give their best physical and mental efforts.

The instrumental director himself is, in a sense, an integral aspect of the students' rehearsal environment. He is the focal point, and it is his personal attitudes and aptitudes which will account for the ultimate success or failure of the rehearsal. The conductor's seriousness of musical intent, whether expressed or implied, is critical to rehearsal accomplishment. Scores should be studied before rehearsal, not only to ensure better musical preparation but, also, to signify in the student's mind that the teacher cares enough to have done his own homework. The numbers to be rehearsed should be listed on the chalk board prior to rehearsal, not only for the increased efficiency of the rehearsal, but also because it is an indication that the teacher has given forethought to the goals of the rehearsal.

THE IMPORTANCE OF LISTENING

Successful instrumental directors must condition themselves for intense objective listening if they are to really hear both the sum and the parts of their ensembles. Under the aural barrage of amateur sounds to which most instrumental directors are subjected in the course of an average school day, it is easy to seek refuge in casual listening . . . to listen but not to hear. Perhaps it is nature's own system of protection by which we become enured of, or block out, undesirable sounds! There is a tendency also to read into the ensemble sound that which we would *like* to hear; the cold reality of a tape recording, unenhanced by acoustical reverberation or our own imagination, will quickly uncover those matters of intonation, balance and musical accuracy which slip past our ears unless we listen with critical attention. The development of such an aural attention span of intense listening is essential to productive rehearsing. The demand of such unflagging mental concentration is one of the most exhausting aspects of the conductor's art.

Sometimes, especially with large bands, the room acoustics may tend to blur the musical lines and camouflage the harmonic components to a degree that the sound is opaque and thus difficult for the ear to assimilate. For purposes of rehearsing under such conditions it may be expedient to subdivide the large ensemble into smaller ensembles, each with a more or less complete instrumentation. A 90-piece organization, for example, can be split into three 30-piece or two 45-piece groups. With such a subdivision within the total organization itself, each smaller ensemble will in turn sound with greater clarity, making it easier for the director and the performers to pinpoint problems of intonation and technique. For instance, in rehearsing a particularly ambiguous sounding passage, the conductor can call on the "red band" to perform, then the "blue band," then the "green band" and, finally, all three groups together. Such a separation will also provide a critical listening experience for the students who are *not* involved in playing at the moment.

GROUP CONTROL

The lines of communication between the director and his students must be kept taut if the rehearsal is to be productive. To maintain the total interest and attention of the students at all times—and thus preclude discipline problems—the director must spark and sustain great intensity of communication. This can be accomplished by (1) a total involvement in the music, (2) a sense of momentum stemming from a brisk, controlled rehearsal pace, and (3) a sincere spirit of enthusiasm on the part of the conductor for the task at hand. The school conductor must at all times be alert and aware of the rehearsal environment, sensitive to the constant, albeit usually unspoken, feedback from his or her students. He or she must also act with authority based on competence, for in matters of musicianship and personality children are quick to distinguish between the secure and insecure teacher. Group control is directly related to the image of authority, confidence and sincerity projected from the podium.

DIAGNOSTIC TEACHING

The ability to diagnose musical performance, whether in a class lesson or in a large ensemble rehearsal, is of extreme importance to rehearsal efficiency. It is unfortunate that, in most music teacher training institutions, more opportunity isn't provided for the development of these kinds of skills. Just as no physician can possibly prescribe a remedy without first diagnosing the ailment, so also no instrumental director can hope to improve the musical effectiveness of his students without first diagnosing the sound, then providing a constructive prescription for improvement. Such diagnostic teaching requires constant critical listening and enough playing familiarity with each of the various instruments that demonstrations and/or recommendations can be given for corrective procedures. This process of diagnostic teaching is fundamental to all music pedagogy; without it musical improvement is left to the vagaries of blind repetition.

CONDUCTING

The communicative skill most obviously essential to productive rehearsing is conducting. Yet, here again, it is a course of study frequently given short shrift in music school curricula. As a consequence many instrumental music teachers acquire most of their conducting skills on the job in the course of their first years of teaching. The consideration here is not that the basic beat patterns haven't been mastered or that the ensemble can't be started or stopped on cue, but rather that the conductor himself may take a complacent attitude concerning the quality of his own skills. It is not uncommon to find instrumental directors who, of necessity, count off complete measures before the ensemble's entrance, who utilize the same style of beat regardless of the style of music, or who habitually stare at the score while giving scarcely a glance to the performers. These habits, subversive to productive rehearsing, are reinforced by many instrumental directors day after school day to a point of oblivion. Conducting is no less a skill than instrumental performance, and requires constant critical self-analysis and practice if it is to be improved.

Instrumental directors, particularly since they are working with student performers, need clear-cut definitions of beat patterns, precise downbeats and cutoffs. Yet for many inexperienced conductors such emphasis on precision sometimes leads to a sameness of style. Although some choral conductors may be accused of vagueness of beat, instrumental conductors more often can be indicted for unemotional and unimaginative conducting; conducting experience in both fields is a great asset to a conductor specializing in either field. Visual communication with all members of the ensemble also is essential to productive rehearsing. Freeing one's self from the nose-in-score syndrome in order to communicate with the eyes necessitates a development of confidence in, and reliance on, the inner ear. All matters of communication from the podium, whether they are matters of conducting technique or visual rapport, can be improved if the instrumental director is aware of *himself*, for the best means to rehearsal improvement is through *self*-improvement.*

A successful conductor:

1 — studies the score before rehearsal and knows the sound and interpretation needed.

2 — anticipates the performance problems and formulates solutions.

3 — accepts only the best of deportment and musicianship from his students in keeping with their maturity and experience.

4 — conducts with sensitivity, precision and authority.

5 — teaches not only "the notes" but comprehensive musicianship as well, using the score as a curriculum

---

*A more detailed study of conducting as a part of instrumental teaching education may be found in the author's *The Teacher on the Podium*, Alfred Publishing Co., Inc., 1975.

TONE AND INTONATION

The twin factors of tone and intonation are basic to all music making, regardless of the size and maturity of the ensemble or the technical prowess of its performers. Of the so-called "Four T's"—good *Tone*, in*T*onation, *T*echnique and *T*aste—the first two are inseparably linked and of utmost importance from a child's very first lesson and continuing throughout his entire years of performing. By the same token the instrumental teacher, always vicariously responsible for the tone and intonation of his players, must himself be acutely aware of the tonal and pitch qualities of his students. He must never let himself be lulled (or benumbed) into complacency by the seemingly insurmountable odds with which he is faced in daily confrontations with amateur sounds. When rehearsing, especially with younger groups, it is easy to become caught up in the problems of ensemble technique to the exclusion of more fundamental considerations. The most inexperienced band or orchestra can, with proper attention to matters of tone and intonation, sound musical; the most experienced performing group, without proper attention to these basics, can sound equally unmusical. If the instrumental director takes a callous or careless *attitude* about these matters, he can expect the same attitude from his students. Only by consistently showing that he cares about tone and intonation can the teacher expect his or her performers to take these fundamentals with equal seriousness.

Good tone quality per se is dependent on several factors including, for the woodwind and brass player, a correct embouchure, an open throat, a supported air column and a lip or reed free to vibrate. For string players a correct left hand position with firm finger pressure coupled with a positive bowing technique are necessary for a full, vibrant tone. Among rank beginners, before appropriate muscles and reflexes have been established, tone quality is usually a matter of being either acceptable or unacceptable and likewise, for the same reasons, is intonation. Consistent in-tune playing is impossible until the student is able to blow or bow a steady stream of sound and is capable of centering his tone. This fact is no excuse, however, for neglecting to have the student initially tune his instrument to a standard pitch. This necessity is obvious to string teachers but, among wind teachers, is sometimes disregarded. All wind instruments are built to be sharp when the tuning mechanism is in its shortest position, and it is invariably necessary to extend tuning slides and barrel joints in order to accommodate a standard tuning frequency.

Many mechanical tuning devices are available to teachers who feel the need for more consistency than might be expected from a student-given tuning pitch. Some are stroboscopic or electronic visual tuners, others are electronic audio devices. Despite the experience and ease of tuning afforded by visual tuners, *there is no substitute for the process of tuning by ear.* Such aural training is basic to a child's music education, and is a fundamental skill which must be persistently practiced if a student is to develop as a musician. Instrumental students should be given frequent opportunities to make subjective judgments in matters of pitch, for personal discrimination is mostly a matter of honing inborn facilities to their keenest edge. Perceptivity and sensitivity can only be developed by constant awareness of tone and intonation, and that sort of development is a major responsibility of the teacher to his students.

Fine tuning is a very personal process and requires more occasion for concentration than is usually available in the average school rehearsal room. The student must have the opportunity to match his pitch with a given pitch, to discern the beat differential between the two, and to adjust up or down accordingly. Each ensemble member should be encouraged to participate in the listening process as their peers go about tuning individuality; it is a splendid ear training opportunity. Granted that such tuning procedures are time consuming and can pre-empt a disproportionate amount of rehearsal time, nonetheless, in the long run of the school year, the time spent will have been well justified; there can be no music without good intonation. The director who daily subjects his students to uncorrected bad sounds, destroying their God-given sensitivities, is committing a crime of serious consequence.

For students beyond the beginning stage, a good intonation becomes more than simply a matter of "tuning up." Every instrument has its own idiosyncracies of scale, and each player must learn to adjust accordingly. Generally speaking, woodwinds tend to sharpen when the *shortest* length of pipe is used, e.g. the flute C# (roll the head-joint slightly inward) and the clarinet throat-tones (cover lowest right hand holes). Brasses tend to sharpen when the *longest* length of tubing is used, e.g. the 1–3 and 1–2–3 combinations on all three-valve instruments (extend the third valve slide). Brass instruments also suffer intonation-wise on many of the upper partials. Especially noticeable is the flatness of cornets and trumpets on third-space C# and chromatically upwards to open E (substitute fingerings on sustained tones, as for instance 1–2 for open E). Although it is true that high quality wind instruments have better overall intonation than others of lesser quality, even with the most expensive of professional models the problems remain.

Some directors make use of tuning "from the bottom up," correct in the theory that the higher sounding instruments should take their pitch from the overtones generated from the lowest instruments.

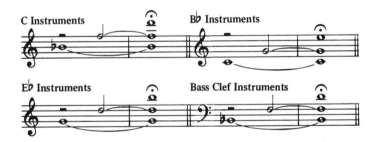

For a thorough tuning procedure, these triad-building exercises should be raised and lowered in half-steps according to the musical maturity of the students.

In matters of instrument intonation the most musical approach, and often the most effective, is through the *singing* of parts. This practice is best accomplished by use of music of a chorale-like nature, and is a procedure which can be used with beginning as well as with more advanced ensembles. Hymns which have frequent fermatas serve well for this type of hearing-singing-playing practice. When the end-of-phrase chords are played out of tune, the band or orchestra should be cut off and the chord sung. Then the chord should be replayed, each performer adjusting his pitch to match the singing pitch.*

Leonard Smith's *Treasury of Scales* is a classic collection of its kind, and is excellent reading material for scale and chordal tuning.**

By using a system of preassigned triads, a quick spot check of intonation can be made at the beginning of class lessons or rehearsals. Each stand of C instruments is assigned

and each stand of B♭ instruments is assigned

and each of bass clef or E♭ instruments

With but one player on each line of such a triadic progression, intonation discrepancies are easy to discern from stand to stand, trio to trio. It is important, however, that *all* students be involved in the listening process, forming their own individual critical opinions.

Another system, unison chromatic tuning, is shown on the next page. Play slowly and hold on each fermata until all instruments are brought into tune. Arrows indicate the most common trouble spots.

*For a demonstration of this and other tuning techniques, refer to Walter Beeler's recorded *Band Development Series,* Golden Crest CRG 1000, produced by and available from Crest Records, 220 Broadway, Huntington Station, NY.

**Smith, Leonard, *Treasury of Scales.* Melville, NY, Belwin-Mills, Inc., 1952. (Available for either band or orchestra)

Following is a simple tuning chorale, especially designed for young bands. The entire piece is centered around a constant B♭ concert sound, generated by an electronic tuner. A sustained pitch from a soloist or section may be substituted for the tuner.

TUNING CHORALE AND RHYTHMIC VARIATION
(Band with optional B♭ tuner and metronome)

Duration 3:00
CONDUCTOR

CHORALE

JOHN KINYON

* A sustained tone from an electronic tuner is recommended. If a tuning bar is used, strike quarter notes with a soft mallet throughout the chorale. If no tuning device is used, start at ③.

RHYTHM, PHRASING AND STYLE

From the very first weeks of practice the beginning student is involved in learning to sense rhythms (count), to phrase (breathe or bow), and to play in style (usually legato). These three basic considerations can never be overemphasized if the student is to develop as a thoroughly musical performer. Such concepts neglected early on in a child's musical development will be doubly difficult to instill once playing habits have become firmly established. In the primary matter of tone duration, the teacher must be adamant in his insistence on full tonal value for every note, unless otherwise indicated. Most of the problems of rushed tempos stem from the fact that students habitually tend to slight note (or rest) values. Such considerations, neglected in the early years of training, will return years later to haunt the instrumental director as he works with the same students in more advanced groups. The problems of carelessness in single note duration are compounded when notes are strung together in rhythmic fashion. Such a simple phrase as the opening bars of *America -*

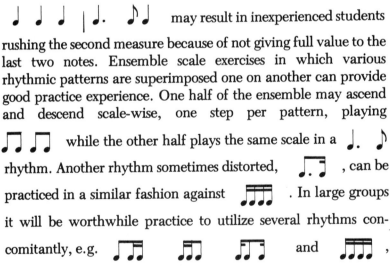

may result in inexperienced students rushing the second measure because of not giving full value to the last two notes. Ensemble scale exercises in which various rhythmic patterns are superimposed one on another can provide good practice experience. One half of the ensemble may ascend and descend scale-wise, one step per pattern, playing

while the other half plays the same scale in a

rhythm. Another rhythm sometimes distorted,   , can be

practiced in a similar fashion against   . In large groups it will be worthwhile practice to utilize several rhythms concomitantly, e.g.   and   ,

rotating the patterns among various sections of the ensemble. The number and variety of rhythmic practice exercises of this sort are limited only by the teacher's needs and imagination.

The concept of phrasing should be instilled in the student from the very first lessons, for breathing and bowing must always accommodate the musical phrase rather than the other way around. Whether at the beginning stage or at a more advanced level of ensemble performance, however, the musical *reason* for a particular phrasing should be understood by the performers. While it is easy for the conductor to suggest "breathe here" or "down-bow there," if the rehearsal is to be an educational experience the students should take part in the decision making. In matters of correct phrasing, musical logic and sensitivity will always provide the correct answers; the students, guided by the teacher, should be allowed to exercise their own musical instincts.

The conductor has a responsibility not only for teaching phrasing, but also for expressing that phrasing through his conducting beat. Many inexperienced instrumental directors tend to be merely "time beaters" and indicate through their beat patterns very little feeling for the musical phrase. Experienced conductors, on the other hand, are able to communicate a great deal to their performers concerning phrase continuity by "conducting the phrase." Such silent expression can convey more eloquently than words the feeling and flow of the musical line.

Stylistic performance is closely tied to the factor of tempo, and with student performers, tempo in turn is frequently governed by the degree of technical control possible. A "correct" tempo is one which allows the students to play in correct style, for style should never be sacrificed for the sake of tempo. This rule of musical accommodation applies to both extremes of the possible range of tempos, slow and fast, and should be applied in keeping with the technical proficiencies of the performers. School instrumental directors should resist becoming locked in, through force of habit, to the slow-medium-fast syndrome of conducting. A wide range of tempos is necessary in order to select the exact one which will, in a given musical movement, make possible both clean articulation and appropriate style. Such a tempo will be a three-fold consideration concerning (1) the composer's stylistic intentions, (2) the technical abilities of the performers, and (3) the acoustical characteristics of the rehearsal or concert hall. Choosing tempos which permit correct musical style is the direct responsibility of the conductor.

It must be stressed that the *sound* of the score must be in the inner ear of the conductor *before* the rehearsal begins. This is to say that the score must have been studied in its every aspect of form, style, tonality, timbre, melody and harmony, and *heard in the mind* of the conductor. His ultimate commitment is to match the actual sound of the ensemble with that of his own preconceived musical concept, rather than to merely accept a first rendition as being faithful to the musical intentions of either the composer or himself.

ADDITIONAL REFERENCES

Benner, Charles H., *Teaching Performing Groups.* Reston, VA: Music Educators National Conference, 1972.

Colwell, Richard J., *The Teaching of Instrumental Music.* New York, NY: Appleton-Century-Crofts, 1959.

Heisinger, Brent, *Comprehensive Musicianship Through Band Performance* (2 Vols. - Junior and Senior High). Menlo Park, CA: Addison-Wesley Publishing Co., 1972.

Hovey, Nilo, *Efficient Rehearsal Procedures for School Bands.* Elkhart, IN: The Selmer Co., Inc., 1976.

Labuta, Joseph A., *Teaching Musicianship in the High School Band.* West Nyack, NY: Parker Publishing Co., Inc., 1972.

Lacy, Gene M., *Organizing and Developing the High School Orchestra.* West Nyack, NY: Parker Publishing Co., Inc., 1971.

Robinson, William C. and Middleton, James A., *The Complete School Band Program.* West Nyack, NY: Parker Publishing Co., Inc., 1975.

Rothrock, Carson, *Training the High School Orchestra.* West Nyack, NY: Parker Publishing Co., Inc., 1971.

Weerts, Richard, *Developing Individual Skills for the High School Band.* West Nyack, NY: Parker Publishing Co., Inc., 1969.

Kohut, Daniel L. *Instrumental Music Pedagogy.* Englewood Cliffs, NJ: Prentice-Hall, Inc., 1973.

CHAPTER IX

THE JAZZ ENSEMBLE

Not unlike the marching band, the jazz ensemble serves purposes of public relations, functional services and musical experiences not possible with the more classically oriented school concert ensembles. Today's instrumental directors, not only cognizant of such practical advantages but also aware of the student enthusiasm which can be generated by a well-disciplined jazz program, have accepted and promoted the jazz band concept. Music educators generally agree that jazz, an original American art form, fused with the more commercial sounds of the modern studio orchestra, is truly a part of the musical heritage of today's children and, as such, deserves serious educational consideration. John T. Roberts, past president of the National Association of Jazz Educators, has said:

> Popular music and jazz are integral parts of American culture and can be used to advantage by wise music teachers at all grade levels. If presented in a wise relationship to the total music education program, popular music and jazz can lead to a better and deeper understanding of all music.*

The school "dance band" of earlier years, once considered an extra-curricular activity, has now come of age as a legitimate facet of school music programs throughout the country. As with

*Excerpted from *Jazz Education in the 70's, A High School Teacher's Guide*, published by Selmer, Inc.

the traditional concert band and orchestra, comprehensive musicianship as well as performance should constitute the core of the jazz band curriculum. A broad approach which investigates jazz history, styles and theory along with solo and ensemble performance techniques, can ensure the program being a truly educational experience.

The challenges inherent in teaching jazz performance can be divided into two areas, ensemble playing and solo improvisation. Both of these performance skills require a high degree of musical discipline on the part of the performer and presuppose a solid foundation in playing fundamentals. All those musical qualities of classical performance—tone, intonation, dynamics and phrasing—apply equally to jazz performance, both solo and ensemble. For this reason the best school jazz musicians are usually recruited from the ranks of the best school classical musicians. Membership in a jazz band also requires a high degree of personal responsibility, for with only one player on each part, each member of the ensemble is solely liable for his or her own contribution, and subsequently responsible for the entire solo or ensemble sound. In matters of recruitment, personal attitude must be considered as important as musicianship. The jazz ensemble should not become a haven for those students lacking listening sensitivity, who are too lazy to learn to read music or for whom jazz means promiscuous playing or sloppy performance.

As in the traditional marching or concert band, the background and experience of the director is of critical importance to the success of the program. This is especially true in working with jazz ensembles. Many, if not most, school instrumental directors have had professional experience in the field of pop and jazz, and they are able to organize and run a jazz program with authority and confidence. As with any art form, however, jazz education cannot be absorbed merely by reading books *about* jazz, and the teacher lacking personal playing experience in this field must seek out every possible opportunity to play or listen to jazz. Membership in the National Association of Jazz Educators* is highly recommended for those teachers in-

---

*Membership inquiries should be directed to Matt Betton, Editor, P.O. Box 724, Manhattan, KS 66502.

volved in jazz education; their official publication, the *NAJE Educator*, is indispensable for information concerning new ideas and publications in this fast-paced field.

Jazz groups run the gamut in size and instrumentation, from small combos to the standard ensemble which ordinarily consists of five saxes (2 altos, 2 tenors and 1 baritone), eight brasses (4 trumpets and 4 trombones) and four rhythm components (piano, bass, guitar and drums which may consist of a single trap set or multiple percussion including vibes and Latin instruments). Arrangements ("charts") should be selected with care, taking into consideration such factors as ranges, endurance and technical requirements. Young, inexperienced brass players shouldn't be forced into the extreme high register until their embouchures and breathing muscles are reasonably well developed. Saxophonists should be encouraged to blow with a full, sonorous tone. Intonation is of critical importance in all sections. Instrumental directors accustomed to working with wind instruments will find that with reasonable musical rehearsal and discipline, a clean, tight ensemble sound can be developed in the woodwind and brass sections.

For most jazz instructors it is the rhythm section which is the enigma. Clem DeRosa, one of the founders and past president of the National Association of Jazz Educators has written:

> The rhythm section is the heart of the Jazz Ensemble, and like its counterpart in our body, cannot be abused. Many jazz ensemble directors spend hours rehearsing the brass and reeds, but treat the rhythm section as an addendum which is glued on later.*

One reason for this state of affairs is that the rhythm section is comprised of four entirely different instruments, each with its own jazz techniques, which together must be molded into one functioning unit. Seldom will the average instrumental director have had experience with even one of these instruments, let alone all four. To further complicate the problem is the fact that im-

---

*Excerpted from *Jazz Education in the 70's, A High School Teacher's Guide*, published by Selmer, Inc.

provisation is at the basis of rhythm instrument effectiveness, the printed part for each serving mainly as a guide sheet for the arrangement at hand. The following are general suggestions concerning each of the four components of the rhythm section. For further and more specific techniques for each instrument, *The Jazz Rock Ensemble* by Ferguson and Feldstein, published by the Alfred Publishing Co., is highly recommended.

PIANO

In the early years of jazz the piano was essential in providing both the harmonic background and the rhythmic pulse of the music. In today's jazz ensembles, however, the fundamental beat and bass line are carried by the bass, thus freeing the pianist to improvise chordal rhythmic patterns (known as "comping") and to provide "fills" where appropriate. The modern jazz pianist must be thoroughly versed in harmony and harmonic progressions, be able to read both by note and from guitar notation, and have an innate sense of improvisation.

Helpful Books for Jazz Pianists-

Jazz-Rock Voicings for the Contemporary Keyboard Player, Haerle/ Jamie Aebersold
Functional Piano for the Improvisor - LaPorta/Kendor
Jazz Patterns Made Easier - Schwartz/Hansen
How to Play Blues Piano - Mance/Hansen
The Contemporary Jazz Pianist (Vol. I & II) - Dobbins/GAMT Music Press
Jazz Rock Chord Progressions - Farber/Alfred
Instant Improvisation - Ferguson/Alfred
Jazz Piano - Edison/Alfred
Piano Hand Guide - Manus/Alfred

GUITAR

The guitar, whether acoustic or electric, is capable of adding a pleasant and functional dimension to the stage band when played with good taste and in sensible amplified volume in balance with the ensemble. Big band guitar playing is far more subtle than the small rock group guitar playing which most young students are accustomed to hearing. The jazz band guitarist must have complete control of his fingerboard, including the ability to play melodic lines as well as to negotiate altered chords of harmonic complexity.

Helpful Books for Jazz Guitarists -

Jazz Guitar - Lee/Hansen
Melodic Rhythms for Guitar - Leavitt/Berklee Press
The Johnny Smith Approach to Guitar - Leavitt/Mel Bay Publishing
Guitar Chord Progressions - Rector/Mel Bay Publishing
The New Guitar Course - Manus/Alfred
The New Electric Guitar Course - Manus/Alfred
Jazz Guitar (Rhythm) - Edison/Alfred
Jazz Guitar (Lead) - Edison/Alfred
Guitar Chord Dictionary - Manus/Alfred

BASS

The bass, whether acoustic or electric (each has its own unique characteristics and functions), provides the basic pulse and the harmonic foundation for the entire musical overlay. Rhythmically and harmonically it is the single most important instrument in the band. For most jazz arrangements a straight two-beat or "walking" four-beat is adequate; rock arrangements tend to require a more agile technique. Bass players need a singing pizzicato tone, a good sense of time and an in-depth understanding of chordal structure and progression.

Helpful Books for Jazz Bassists -

Rhythmic Figures for Bassists - DeWitt/Hanson
Basic Impulse Bass Guitar - Bredice/Hanson
How To Play Electric Bass - Kaye/Gwyn Publishing
Electric Bass Lines - Kaye/Gwyn Publishing Co.
The Book on Bass Harmonics - Vees/Alfred
The Evolving Bass - Reid/Aebersold
Evolving Upward - Reid/Aebersold

No Nonsense Electric Bass - Cacibauda/Aebersold
Walking On Chords for String Bass - Davis/Aebersold
Bass Blues Bag - Menke/Mel Bay

DRUMS

The basic functions are to lay down a steady beat pattern in keeping with the style of the arrangement, to reinforce ensemble or section rhythmic figures, and to provide "fills" as needed. The bass drum should reinforce the bass, never nullify or obliterate it. The drummer must read (follow) his part, keeping his eye out for special rhythmic effects and his ear attuned to the ensemble in general. Many inexperienced jazz drummers put too much emphasis on technical exhibitionism rather than trying to subordinate their skills for the musical productiveness of the group.

Helpful Books for Jazz Drummers

A Manual for the Modern Drummer - Dawson & DeMichael/
  Berklee Press
Begin to Play Jazz & Rock - Feldstein/Alfred
Club Date Dictionary - Feldstein/Alfred
Drum Set Artistry (Book & Record) - Burns/Alfred
Drum Set Reading - Fink/Alfred
It's Time - Lewis and DeRosa/Kendor
Student's Guide to Dance and Stage Band Drumming -
  Morey & Collins/Kendor

Along with the teaching of jazz ensemble performance (and of equal importance if the term jazz is to be interpreted in its primary sense) is the teaching of improvisation. The greatest musicians of history, from Bach to Basie and beyond, have been gifted improvisors, for improvisation is a highly specialized form of musical expression requiring not only complete control of one's instrument but also acute aural perceptivenes and uninhibited musical imagination. Until recent years this was a performance skill given little attention, most teachers either not believing improvisation could be taught or not knowing quite how to go about it. Today in jazz study much emphasis is placed on skills of ad libbing, and young musicians are proving equal to the challenges.

Students of "improv" should initially pursue a style of playing within their own technical capabilities. Too many young players try to imitate the tremendous techniques of a Charlie Parker or Dizzy Gillespie and end up by merely wiggling their fingers in frenzied fashion and honking senseless sounds. There are currently available in published form several systems for teaching improvisation. Many of these methods are based on the study of major scales and certain other modes which, because of their inherent structure, emphasize what were in earlier days known as "blue notes."

The student must do a lot of listening and much experimentation on his own. Copying or imitating by ear the recorded solo work of great jazz artists is good practice. There are also available several recordings (see listing at end of chapter) which feature back-up rhythm sections and which are excellent for home experimentation in the art of solo improvisation. The basic 12-bar blues progression also provides an easy frame of reference for first efforts in jamming. The scale of the key should be analyzed and the sounds of the flatted third, fifth and seventh demonstrated. As the student gains confidence in improvised musical expression after the initial awkward experimentation, he must be guided to an awareness of the more refined aspects of the art. The uses of such musical devices as repetition and motivic development should be thoroughly investigated and practiced. Whatever the method or course of study used in teaching *about* improvisation, in the final analysis it is the student's ability to "connect his fingers to his ears" that will determine his improvisational ability.

ADDITIONAL REFERENCES

Coker, Jerry, *Improvising Jazz*. Englewood Cliffs: Prentice-Hall, Inc., 1964.

Coker, Jerry, *The Jazz Idiom*. Englewood Cliffs, NJ: Prentice-Hall, Inc., 1975.

Coker, Jerry, *Patterns For Jazz*. Lebanon, IN: Studio P/R, 1970.

Scianni, Joe and Feldstein, Sandy, *The Sound of Rock*. Sherman Oaks, CA: Alfred Publishing Co., Inc. 1972

Strommen, Carl and Feldstein, Sandy, *The Sound of Jazz*. Sherman Oaks, CA: Alfred Publishing Co., Inc. 1974.

Carubia, Mike, *The Sound of Improvisation*. Sherman Oaks, CA: Alfred Publishing Co., Inc. 1976.

Ferguson, Tom and Feldstein, Sandy, *The Jazz Rock Ensemble*. Sherman Oaks, CA: Alfred Publishing Co., 1976.

Wiskirchen, George, *Developmental Techniques For The School Dance Band Musician*. Boston: Berklee Press, 1961.

Lead sheets and recorded rhythm section backups designed for teaching improvisation can be found in the catalogs of:

Jamie Aebersold
1211 Aebersold Drive
New Albany, IN 47150

Music Minus One
46 West 61st Street
New York, NY 10023

Alfred Publishing Co., Inc.
15335 Morrison Street
Sherman Oaks, CA 91403

Music with instructional cassette tapes (mixed down from full ensemble to various sections with rhythm) helpful for full band and sectional rehearsal can be found in *The Director's Series* published by:

Webb Music Publishing Corporation
1543 N.E. 123 Street
Miami, FL 33161

THE MARCHING BAND

MARCHING BANDS, REPRESENTING LARGE AND SMALL COMMUNITIES ACROSS THE COUNTRY, ARE A PHENOMENON OF AMERICAN MUSIC EDUCATION. THIS COLLAGE OF CLIPPINGS, TAKEN FROM THE SYLVA, (N.CAR.) HERALD SHOWS THE POSITIVE PUBLIC RELATIONS WHICH CAN BE GENERATED BY A PROUD AND SPIRITED MARCHING ORGANIZATION. (Photo courtesy of Bob Buckner, director of the Sylva-Webster H.S. Golden Eagles Band)

One of the most controversial subjects within the realm of instrumental music education has always been that of the marching band. The major question has been, and remains, whether or not marching activity is a valid aspect of music education. It cannot be denied, as Richard Colwell has stated, that,

> Though the orchestra came into the public schools first, the marching band has been the vehicle through which the instrumental music program flourished, obtaining equipment, public attention, numbers, building space, and professionally trained teachers in a manner impossible for the concert band or orchestra. Music has a fairly secure place, not because it has caused a noticeable upgrading of musicianship in society or in the school, but because the marching band has publicized the school, attracted public attention, created excitement and spirit for competitive athletics, and made colorful holidays more colorful.*

Marching band proponents back their stand with historical facts concerning the band as the traditional purveyor of mobile music. Other advocates cite the benefits of physical activity and personal discipline so necessary for a well-presented halftime show. Administrators prize the marching band, often above the concert band, for its public relations potential. And of course the general public, the taxpayer, is enthralled with the marching band as a medium of entertainment.

Those who hold opposing views regarding the validity of the marching band in the music education curriculum suggest that such activities, often more physical than musical, belong more properly in the province of physical education. Other detractors are quick to point out the seeming exhorbitant amount of time spent in drilling which could be better put to purely musical endeavors. Further critical views are based on the extra expense of marching band equipment, the disproportionate use of pop music of poor quality, and the tendency toward the development of bad playing habits among young performers.

---

*Colwell, Richard J., *The Teaching of Instrumental Music*. New York, N.Y., Appleton-Century-Crofts, 1969.

Thus this two-sided coin can be flipped and *made* to come up heads or tails, depending on the instrumental director's own philosophical bent. But all arguments as to the marching band's educational validity, pro or con, are purely academic at this point in music education history. We have perpetuated the tradition to serve our own interests; despite the prevailing dichotomy in educational philosophy, the marching band is an essential adjunct to most instrumental music programs.

Not all instrumental music departments are required to field a marching and maneuvering band. Some schools need marching units only for infrequent parades and ceremonies. By contrast, the great majority of high schools across the country (and occasionally junior high schools) have a tradition of marching bands, well-disciplined and colorful organizations which serve as musical ambassadors not only for their respective schools, but often to represent their entire town, community or state as well. As Frederick Fennell has so aptly described the situation,

> The public appearances of school and college marching bands are the services by which the general public best knows and judges the value of institutional music. It is not surprising, therefore, that the first "requirement" for the training of a college or high school band director in the eyes of the public and those who administrate its schools is his proficiency in the art of the marching band.*

No attempt can be made within the confines of this chapter to investigate the technical intricacies of the marching show band. Ideally the director himself will have had the experience of participation as a marching band member, either in high school or college. There are many authoritative and graphically illustrated books available on the subject, the most popular of which are listed in this chapter's bibliography.

The instrumental director who is expected to teach marching band must accept the challenge with wholehearted dedication and enthusiasm. Any hint of disparagement will soon be

---

*Fennell, Frederick, *Time and the Winds*. G. Leblanc Corp., Kenosha, WI, 1954.

reflected in the attitudes of the students. The key ingredients needed for developing a successful marching band are *preparation, organization* and *discipline,* all of which are the direct responsibilities of the director. As Robert Foster has so pointedly stated,

> We frequently hear marching bands criticized. We are told that they take too much time, or that they are "not relevant". This criticism is misdirected! Marching bands are not necessarily irrelevant, and do not necessarily take too much time. It is not the marching band that is bad, but too frequently the marching band *teaching* that is bad.*

Once the marching band program has been developed to a point of efficient productivity and has struck a proper balance in relation to the entire instrumental music program, the benefits to the students, the director and the school community will become obvious. Like all positive music programs, the marching band will regenerate itself year to year, carried along on its own momentum—fueled by its own success. Hundreds of people, who might not ordinarily attend a school concert, will become aware that the music department is functionally active. Public relations with the community will improve, increasing the possibility of increased budget considerations. Most important, however, a pride of accomplishment will permeate the entire music department, providing added prestige and credibility to the total instrumental program.

---

*Foster, Robert E., *Multiple-Option Marching Band Techniques*. Alfred Publishing Co., Inc., Sherman Oaks, CA, 1977.

ADDITIONAL REFERENCES

Binion, W. T., Jr., *The High School Marching Band*. West Nyack, NY: Parker Publishing Co., Inc., 1973.

Casavant, A. R., *The Exhibition Marching Series*. Chattanooga, TN: ARC Products Co., 1977.

Foster, Robert E., *Multiple-Option Marching Band Techniques*. Sherman Oaks, CA: Alfred Publishing Co., 1975.

Foster, Wanamaker, Duffer, Cowles, *Championship Auxiliary Units*. Sherman Oaks, CA: Alfred Publishing Co., Inc., 1979.

Hopper, Dale F., *Corps Style Marching*. Oskaloosa, IA: C. L. Barnhouse, Co., 1977.

Lee, Jack, *Modern Marching Band Techniques*. Winona, MN: Hal Leonard, 1958.

Wright, Al, *Marching Band Fundamentals*. New York, NY: Carl Fischer, Inc., 1963.

Wells, James R., *The Marching Band In Contemporary Education*. Bryn Mawr, PA: Theodore Presser Co., 1976.

Student Musicians at Athletic Events: Half-time Education? Reston, VA: Music Educators National Conference, Vol. 65 No. 4 (December 1978).

The VC Journal of Exhibition Marching. Write P.O. Box 1124, Chattanooga, TN 37401 (published twice each year).

CHAPTER XI

PURCHASING MUSIC, INSTRUMENTS AND EQUIPMENT

Purchasing music, instruments and equipment is one of the major responsibilities of the instrumental director. Since most purchases involve school budget monies, it is important that all such ordering be done according to the prescribed procedures instituted by the school system. Teachers new to their teaching situation should check with the school's purchasing official to ascertain the proper steps to be followed. In the course of a school year, music teachers require the products and services of literally dozens of different publishers and manufacturers. Ordinarily such needs are directed to the local music dealer who acts as an expediter, consolidating orders and billings, and serving as resident representative for the entire music industry.

Some retail stores specialize in sheet music, some in instruments and some are equipped to handle both. The more progressive dealers offer various extra services including repair work, browsing libraries, private teaching studios, field services and occasional clinics. Music stores which offer service by efficient and knowledgeable representatives deserve the support of the local music teachers. By comparison with out-of-town discount houses, local merchants have a personal as well as a vested interest in your music program and are in a position to give personal service when needed. Also offering significant sheet music service to instrumental directors, especially to those not fortunate enough to have satisfactory local service, are the music distributors. These large and well-organized music houses, specializing in mail orders, offer complete stocks of music of all publishers, on-approval and charge account services, browsing facilities and sample packets as well as quick mail delivery.

In the constant search for new (and old) music and teaching materials, teachers will benefit by placing themselves on the mailing lists of publishers who cater to their area of specialization. This can be accomplished either by personally registering at the music industry exhibits at state, division or national conferences, or by writing directly to the publishers themselves. Sample music received should be filed by category for perusal and reference. All publishers and distributors offer free catalogs of their materials, and are glad to mail them to you providing you apprise them of your special fields of interest.

In ordering music, teachers will do well to patronize their local dealer or mail order house rather than to purchase directly from publishers. Most publishers are geared to wholesale marketing and rely on their dealers to service customers at the retail level. An added advantage of ordering through a local music agency is that the billings from various publishers can be consolidated into one account, a practical advantage when submitting either orders or bills to the school purchasing agent.

If instrument purchases are to be made by parents through local music stores, the dealers should be made aware of your own recommendations regarding brands and models. If the orders are for school instruments or equipment, all specifications should be included in the order. This is especially important if, as is usually the case, the order is to be put up for bid among several competing companies. It goes without saying that any under-the-counter collusion between the director and his dealer would not only be highly unprofessional but, in most states, illegal. The teacher and his dealer have a moral obligation to see that both the school and the parents receive total and honest value for their investments.

A guide, published by the Music Industry Council of the MENC and reprinted with permission in the appendix, will serve not only as a source of ideas for use in correspondence and transactions with publishers, manufacturers and music dealers, but also as a splendid reference directory of the majority of publishers, manufacturers and distributors in the music industry.

CHAPTER XII

CONTESTS

Among those debatable philosophical questions of our profession, ranking in popularity with the everlasting controversy concerning the educational validity of marching bands, is the subject of music contests. Almost without exception in the years since the first such competitions of the mid-twenties, the contest movement has flourished. Today only a minor percentage of secondary school music departments are not involved in this annual rite of spring, the opportunity to perform for critical and constructive evaluation and the chance to earn that coveted superior rating.

On one side of this continuing debate are the directors who believe that rehearsal time sacrificed in "perfecting" contest numbers might better be spent on broader and more meaningful teaching endeavors, that the time, effort and expense of preparation for attendance at district or state competition is not justified by the end results. The extremists of this faction might be inclined to agree with Béla Bartók to whom is attributed the motto: COMPETITION IS FOR HORSES, NOT FOR ARTISTS. On the opposite side in the debate are those directors who believe that striving for musical perfection has its own rewards, that annual competitive exposure is of value to both students and conductor, and that the time, effort and expense of preparation for participation in contests *do* justify the educational results. The slogan for this group is often expressed as: LIFE ITSELF IS COMPETITION. The conscience and beliefs of most instrumental directors stand somewhere between these two poles of thought.

Whatever may be said concerning contests as befitting the arts, it is an undeniable fact that there is no greater unifying and motivating force than competition. That sort of team spirit aroused by competition in athletics is also generated in bands and orchestras competing in music contests. Nothing will prompt soloists and ensemble members to practice more arduously than an imminent contest where personal pride and school honor are at stake. Many successful directors regard contests as the major motivating force in their programs.

Of course the music contest, as with any other educational enterprise, is what we make it, both for our students and for ourselves, and a reasonable perspective must be taken in order to counterbalance the emotional fervor generated by contest ratings per se with their true educational implications. The insecure director who cannot accept criticism and who habitually blames his group's less-than-top rating on the system, on the adjudication or on politics has no business taking his students to contest. Of more serious consequence is the fact that his negative attitude will be directly reflected in the attitudes of his students. Although there is no denying that the contest rating itself is of great importance to all concerned in terms of personal pride, group morale and public relations, it is well to remember that the true educational worth lies in the *experience* of competition. This includes both social and musical experiences, and has to do with the students' personal growth in terms of attitude and behavior as well as musicianship. The director who thoroughly prepares the contest music for music's sake, who encourages his students to listen to and evaluate the performances of competing ensembles, who seriously shares with his students the adjudicators' constructive suggestions and who graciously accepts both praise and criticism will be helping his students derive the greatest possible educational benefit from competitions.

The concept of solo and concert contests has changed since the earliest days of national competitions when bands, orchestras and soloists merely were ranked in numerical order from top to bottom of the performance pile. Today contests are designed to make each contestant a "winner", if not in ranking at least in the sense that the soloist or ensemble will have been given a positive experience by which to grow musically. Although systems vary widely throughout the country, most contest ratings are based on a plateau scale of SUPERIOR (I or A), EXCELLENT (II or B),

FAIR (III or C) and POOR (IV or D). The contest music itself is categorized into grades of difficulty ranging from Grade I (very easy) through Grade VI (very difficult). Some state organizations in charge of competitions offer extensive cumulative lists from which to choose contest numbers; others require that music be chosen from more narrowly defined select lists. Many state band and orchestra associations require a separate sight-reading number to be performed in addition to the usual three prepared selections. In some concert contests the grade of difficulty of the music to be performed is left to the discretion of the director, in others it is based on the school enrollment of the competing ensemble.

Marching band contests sponsored by private organizations as well as those sponsored by state music educators associations are popular in many areas of the country. In some states such as Florida, high school bands entering concert competitions are generally required to also enter marching competition. The adjudication systems for marching contests are fairly well standardized, the contesting groups being judged in percentage points for inspection, musical performance, marching and maneuvering, and general effect.

Instrumental directors new to a school district and desirous of entering their groups into competition should check with their local and/or state music association well in advance to determine the proper procedures necessary for participation. The appropriate instrumental organization of the state music educators association will furnish both enrollment materials and requirement information.

ADJUDICATION FORMS

The following pages contain adjudication forms copyrighted by and available from the Music Educators National Conference. Although most state associations issue grading sheets in keeping with their own system of adjudication, the basic items considered in judging are similar to these.

Band

Order or time of appearance_____

Event No._____

Class_____

Date_____19___

RATING

Use no plus or minus signs in final rating

Name of Organization_____

School_____Number of Players_____

City_____State_____District_____School Enrollment_____

Selections _____

Adjudicator will grade principal items, A, B, C, D, or E, or numerals, in the respective squares. Comments must deal with fundamental principles and be constructive. Minor details may be marked on music furnished to adjudicator.

TONE (beauty, blend, control)_____ ☐

INTONATION (chords, melodic line, tutti)_____ ☐

TECHNIQUE (articulation, facility, precision, rhythm)_____ ☐

BALANCE (ensemble, sectional)_____ ☐

INTERPRETATION (expression, phrasing, style, tempo)_____ ☐

MUSICAL EFFECT (artistry, fluency)_____ ☐

OTHER FACTORS (choice of music, instrumentation, discipline, appearance)_____ ☐

*May be continued on other side.

Signature of Adjudicator_____

Orchestra or String Orchestra

RATING

Use as plus or minus signs in final rating

Order or time
of appearance_____

Event
No._____

Class_____

Date_____ _____19___

Name of Organization_____

School_____Number of Players_____

City_____State_____District_____School Enrollment_____

Selections _____

Adjudicator will grade principal items, A, B, C, D, or E, or numerals, in the respective squares. Comments must deal with fundamental principles and be constructive. Minor details may be marked on music furnished to adjudicator.

TONE (beauty, blend, control)_____ ☐

INTONATION (chords, melodic line, tutti)_____ ☐

TECHNIQUE (articulation-bowing, facility, precision, rhythm)_____ ☐

BALANCE (ensemble, sectional)_____ ☐

INTERPRETATION (expression, phrasing, style, tempo)_____ ☐

MUSICAL EFFECT (artistry, fluency)_____ ☐

OTHER FACTORS (choice of music, instrumentation, discipline, appearance)_____ ☐

*May be continued
on other side.

Signature of Adjudicator_____

Sight Reading—Band or Orchestra

RATING

Use no plus or minus signs in final rating

Order or time
of appearance_____ Event No. _____ Class _____ Date _____ 19___

Name of Organization _____

School _____ Number of Players_____

City _____ State _____ District _____ School Enrollment _____

Selections _____

Adjudicator will grade principal items, A, B, C, D, or E, or numerals, in the respective squares. Comments must deal with fundamental principles and be constructive. Minor details may be marked on music furnished to adjudicator.

TECHNICAL ACCURACY (articulation-bowing, correct notes, note values, rhythm figures, signature)_____ ☐

FLEXIBILITY (balance, precision, response to director)_____ ☐

INTERPRETATION (expression, phrasing, style, tempo)_____ ☐

MUSICAL EFFECT (confidence, fluency, intonation, tone)_____ ☐

GENERAL COMMENTS_____ ☐

*May be continued on other side.

Signature of Adjudicator_____

Instrumental Ensemble—Wind

RATING

Use no plus or minus signs in final rating

Order or time of appearance_____ Event No._____ Class_____ Date_____ 19___

Name of Ensemble_____

School_____City_____State_____District_____

Selection_____

Instrumentation_____

Performers Names_____

Adjudicator will grade principal items, A, B, C, D, or E, or numerals, in the respective squares. Comments must deal with fundamental principles and be constructive. Minor details may be marked on music furnished to adjudicator.

TONE (beauty, blend, control)_____ ☐

INTONATION (harmonic parts, melodic line)_____ ☐

TECHNIQUE (articulation, embouchure, facility, precision, rhythm)___ ☐

BALANCE_____ ☐

INTERPRETATION (expression, phrasing, style, tempo)_____ ☐

MUSICAL EFFECT (artistry. fluency)_____ ☐

OTHER FACTORS (choice of music, stage presence and appearance)___ ☐

*May be continued on other side.

Signature of Adjudicator_____

Instrumental Ensemble—String

RATING

Use no plus or minus signs in final rating

Order or time of appearance_____ Event No._____ Class _____ Date_____ _____19___

Name of Ensemble_____

School_____City_____State_____District_____

Selection_____

Instrumentation_____

Performers Names_____

Adjudicator will grade principal items, A, B, C, D, or E, or numerals, in the respective squares. Comments must deal with fundamental principles and be constructive. Minor details may be marked on music furnished to adjudicator.

TONE (beauty, blend, control)_____ ☐

INTONATION (harmonic parts, melodic line, tuning)_____ ☐

TECHNIQUE (bowing—choice and execution, fingering, precision, rhythm)_____ ☐

BALANCE_____ ☐

INTERPRETATION (expression, phrasing, style, tempo)_____ ☐

MUSICAL EFFECT (artistry, fluency)_____ ☐

OTHER FACTORS (choice of music, stage presence and appearance)_____ ☐

*May be continued on other side.

Signature of Adjudicator_____

Wind Instrument Solo

RATING

Use no plus or minus
signs in final rating

Order or time
of appearance_____

Event
No._____ Class_____ Date_____ ___19___

Name_____

School_____

City_____State_____ District_____

Selection_____

Instrument_____

Adjudicator will grade principal items, A, B, C, D, or E, or numerals, in the respective squares. Comments must deal with fundamental principles and be constructive. Minor details may be marked on music furnished to adjudicator.

TONE (beauty, characteristic timbre, control)_____ ☐

INTONATION_____ ☐

TECHNIQUE (articulation, auxiliary fingerings, breathing, embouchure, facility, rhythm)_____ ☐

INTERPRETATION (expression, phrasing, style, tempo)_____ ☐

MUSICAL EFFECT (artistry, fluency)_____ ☐

OTHER FACTORS (choice of music, stage presence and appearance)_____ ☐

MEMORIZING (when required)_____ ☐

*May be continued
on other side.   Signature of Adjudicator_____

String Instrument Solo

RATING

Order or time
of appearance_____

Event
No._____ Class_____ Date_____19___

Use as plus or minus
signs in final rating

Name_____

School_____

City_____State_____District_____

Selection_____

Instrument_____

Adjudicator will grade principal items, A, B, C, D, or E, or numerals, in the respective squares. Comments must deal with fundamental principles and be constructive. Minor details may be marked on music furnished to adjudicator.

TONE (beauty, control)_____ ☐

INTONATION_____ ☐

TECHNIQUE (bowing, facility, fingering, rhythm)_____ ☐

INTERPRETATION (expression, phrasing, style, tempo)_____ ☐

MUSICAL EFFECT (artistry. fluency)_____ ☐

OTHER FACTORS (choice of music, stage presence and appearance)_____ ☐

MEMORIZING (when required)_____ ☐

May be continued
on other side.

Signature of Adjudicator_____

Percussion Solo and Ensemble

RATING

Use no plus or minus signs in final rating

Order or time of appearance_____	Event No._____	Class_____	Date_____ 19___

Name of Ensemble_____

Kind of Solo or Ensemble_____

School_____City_____State_____District_____

Selection_____

Performers Names_____

Adjudicator will grade principal items, A, B, C, D, or E, or numerals, in the respective squares. Comments must deal with fundamental principles and be constructive. Minor details may be marked on music furnished to adjudicator.

TONE_____ □

RUDIMENTS — TECHNIQUE _____ □

POSITION (body, hand, instrument)_____ □

INTERPRETATION (balance, dynamics, expression, phrasing, rhythm, tempo)_____ □

SIGHT READING (accuracy, dynamics, tempo)_____ □

MUSICAL AND GENERAL EFFECT (artistry, stage presence and appearance)_____ □

MEMORIZING (when required)_____ □

*May be continued on other side.

Signature of Adjudicator_____

Jazz Performance

RATING

Use no plus or minus signs in final rating

Event _____ Order of Appearance _____ Class _____ Date _____ 19_____

Name of Organization _____ No. of Players _____

School _____ Director _____

City _____ State _____ District _____ School Enrollment _____

Adjudicator will grade items, 1-2-3-4-5-6-7-8, in the respective squares. Comments must deal with fundamental principles and be constructive.

LEGEND

SELECTIONS

Ensemble	Points	Solos	
Fair	1	Fair	1
Below Average	2	Good	2
Average	3	Excellent	3
Above Average	4		
Good	5		
Very Good	6		
Excellent	7		
Superior	8		

1. _____
2. _____
3. _____
4. _____
5. _____
6. _____

SELECTION

	1	2	3	4	5	6
BALANCE — BLEND						
INTONATION						
PHRASING						
DYNAMICS						
TIME						
INTERPRETATION						
PRECISION						
JAZZ EXCITEMENT						
FRESH IDEAS						
COLORS — TEXTURE						
PROGRAMING						
STAGE PRESENCE						
CHOICE OF MATERIALS						
COMMUNICATION						

COMMENTS

SOLOS

TOTALS

SELECTION
1 ☐
2 ☐
3 ☐
4 ☐
5 ☐
6 ☐

☐ Final Total

Signature of Adjudicator _____

Marching Band

Order or time
of appearance _____

Event
No. _____   Class _____   Date _____ 19 ___

RATING

Use no plus or minus signs in final rating

Name of Organization _____ —

School ___ _____ Number of Players_____

City_____ State_____ District_____ School Enrollment _____

Selections _____
_____
_____

Adjudicator will grade principal items, A, B, C, D, or E, or numerals, in the respective squares. Comments must deal with fundamental principles and be constructive. Minor details may be marked on music furnished to adjudicator.

REQUIRED MOVEMENTS   _____ ☐

(1) Forward March — while playing and while not playing.
(2) Halt — while playing (continue to play after the halt) and while not playing.
(3) Column Right — while playing.
(4) Column Left — while playing.
(5) Countermarch — while playing.
(6) Diminish Front — while playing.
(7) Increase Front — while playing.
(8) Choice of Right Oblique, Left Oblique, Column Half Right, or Column Half Left — while playing.
(9) Start Playing and Cease Playing — while marching.
[Movements 3, 4, 5, and 8 are to be executed with an interval of not less than two paces (60 inches), measured from center of one position to center of next.]

PLAYING (balance, intonation, rhythm, selection, sonority, style)_____ ☐

MARCHING FUNDAMENTALS (alignment, cadence, carriage, discipline, precision)_____ ☐

SPECIAL ROUTINES (originality, suitability, taste, variety)_____ ☐

GENERAL EFFECT (artistry, continuity, showmanship)_____ ☐

INSPECTION SCORE—See Form MBIS-17 (when required)_____ ☐

*May be continued on other side.

Signature of Adjudicator_____

Marching Band Inspection Sheet

RATING

Use no plus or minus signs in final rating

Order or time of appearance_____	Event No._____	Class_____	Date_____ 19___

Name of Organization _____

School_____ Number of Players_____

City_____ State _____ District_____ School Enrollment_____

Adjudicator will grade principal items, A, B, C, D, or E, or numerals, in the respective squares. Comments must deal with fundamental principles and be constructive. Minor details may be marked on music furnished to adjudicator.

POSTURE (military bearing, response to commands)_____ ☐

UNIFORMS (clean, pressed, shoes, socks, accessories)_____ ☐

INSTRUMENTS (clean, playing condition, mouthpiece)_____ ☐

PERSONAL APPEARANCE (haircuts, fingernails, jewelry)_____ ☐

GENERAL APPEARANCE (discipline, orderliness, regularity of ranks and files)_____ ☐

Note: Judge will note location of individual deficiencies on the back of this sheet.   Signature of Adjudicator_____

Twirling—Solo or Ensemble

		RATING
Order or time of appearance_____	Event No._____ Class_____ Date_____19___	

Name_____

School_____

City_____State_____District_____

Adjudicator will grade principal items, A, B, C, D, or E, or numerals, in the respective squares. Comments must deal with fundamental principles and be constructive. Minor details may be marked on music furnished to adjudicator.

SINGLE HAND FUNDAMENTALS—Check List_____ ☐

LEFT   RIGHT
- ☐ Vertical wrist twirl ☐
- ☐ Horizontal wrist twirl ☐
- ☐ Vertical Figure 8 ☐
- ☐ Horizontal Figure 8 ☐
- ☐ Finger twirl ☐
- ☐ Time toss-with catch ☐
- ☐ Forward whip ☐
- ☐ Reverse whip ☐

ADDITIONAL FUNDAMENTALS—Check List_____ ☐
- ☐ Forward cartwheel
- ☐ Reverse cartwheel
- ☐ Two-hand twirl—right to left, left to right
- ☐ Pass around back—right to left
- ☐ Pass around back—left to right
- ☐ Low aerial
- ☐ High aerial
- ☐ Salute

ROUTINE—TECHNICAL MASTERY (ambidexterity, continuity, retention of baton, revolution, smoothness, speed)___ ☐

ROUTINE—SHOWMANSHIP (originality, rhythm, stage personality, variety)_____ ☐

GENERAL COMMENTS (confidence, facial expression, posture)
(Ensembles only: Uniform style and ability)_____ ☐

*May be continued on other side.

Signature of Adjudicator_____

CHAPTER XIII

TESTING AND GRADING

Testing students is an important responsibility and a necessary function of the instrumental director, for test results serve many purposes essential to the efficient operation of an instrumental music department. Tests which measure a child's musical *aptitude*, natural talents, can be helpful when used as part of the criteria for the selection of beginners. Tests which measure musical *achievement*, the acquisition of skills and knowledge, are necessary in determining teaching effectiveness, musical improvement, ranking within sections and report card grades.

MUSIC APTITUDE TESTS

An array of aptitude tests is available for helping teachers ascertain, within certain limits of reliability, the natural musical sensitivities of their students. Many, if not most, directors routinely administer such tests in the selection process for determining potential instrumental music talent. One of the most sophisticated of its kind is the venerable Seashore Measures of Musical Talent, a recorded test which measures aptitude in the areas of pitch, rhythm, loudness, timbre, duration and tonal memory.* Other recorded tests of a similar nature include:

Gordon Musical Aptitude Profile
- tonal imagery (memory and harmony), rhythm imagery (tempo and meter), musical sensitivity (phrasing, style and balance).

Kwalwasser Music Talent Test
  pitch, time, rhythm, loudness.

*Available from Psychological Corporation, 304 East 45th Street, New York, NY 10017.

Drake Musical Aptitude Test
- musical memory, rhythm.

Bentley Measures of Musical Abilities
- pitch, tonal memory, chord analysis, rhythmic memory.

Other less sophisticated and less reliable aptitude tests are published by and available from musical instrument manufacturers such as:

Chicago Musical Instrument Co.
7373 N. Cicero Avenue
Lincolnwood, IL 60646

Gretsch Manufacturing Co.
1801 Gilbert Avenue
Cincinnati, OH 45202

G. B. Conn, Ltd.
616 Enterprise Drive
Oak Brook, IL 60521

Scherl and Roth, Inc.
616 Enterprise Drive
Oak Brook, IL 60521

Frank Holton Co.
320 North Church Street
Elkhorn, WI 53121

Selmer, Inc.
Box 310
Elkhart, IN 4655

G. Lebanc Corporation
7019 30th Avenue
Kenosha, WI 53141

One of the most comprehensive and reliable of current methods for predetermining the student's chance for success in instrumental music study is a battery of three tests devised by Dr. James Froseth. The three areas are 1) *music aptitude* as determined by the Gordon Music Profile.* 2) *academic achievement* as indicated by a standardized academic achievement battery (e.g. Iowa Test of Basic Skills), and 3) *music interest* as shown by How I Feel About Music,** a music interest inventory. All three scores are converted to student profiles by means of percentile rankings. The entire testing process along with recommended procedures for recruiting are set forth in the NABIM Recruiting

*Available from Houghton-Mifflin Co. 110 Tremont Street, Boston, MA 02107.

**By James Froseth, available from Music Learning Research Division of G.I.A. Publications, Inc., 7014 S. Mason Ave., Chicago, IL 60638.

Manual available free of charge from either local instrument dealers or the National Association of Band Instrument Manufacturers, Inc.

Many directors prefer to compose their own tests which usually consist of simple matching exercises of pairs of pitches and rhythms. Whether the test is simple or sophisticated, it is well to keep in mind that the results should be taken with a grain of salt, for no musical aptitude test is of absolute validity or foolproof in its results. If a child scores high, chances are that he or she should do well in the study of a musical instrument. A child scoring low, however, may possibly have been overly excited or confused when the test was administered. Certainly no talent test should be used as the *sole* basis for admittance to the instrumental study program. In the final analysis, factors such as personal interest and determination very often carry more weight in determining success in instrumental music study than does the "talent" as indicated through aptitude test results.

Another method of testing for talent is by means of the preinstrumental exploration program by which candidates for orchestra or band training can be screened by means of their participation in tonette, flutophone or recorder classes. Such courses, usually held the semester prior to the start of regular instrumental study, will not only provide the teacher first-hand insights into the child's natural musical abilities but will also serve as an informal indicator of the student's work habits and personal maturation, factors which are equally important as talent during the beginning stages of instrumental study. Such classes will not ordinarily need to extend beyond a ten- or fifteen-week period, depending on the age of the children and the frequency of the classes. The course of study will serve to teach the reading of simple notation and, of particular advantage to future woodwind students, the concepts of breath control, tongueing and basic fingerings.

MUSIC ACHIEVEMENT TESTS

It is often necessary to give performance achievement ratings to individual students for purposes of grading, ranking within a section or for making periodic checks of progress. The standard test for this is the Watkins-Farnum Performance Scale, a series of graded sight-reading exercises available in two sets (Forms A and B) for all band and orchestra instruments.* The following sample score sheet, reprinted by permission, illustrates the design and plan of this popular testing device.

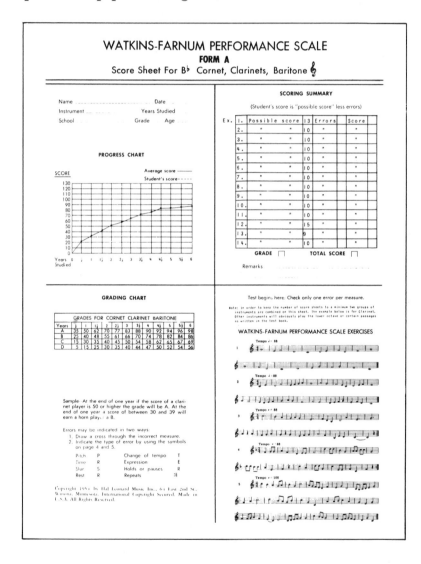

*Available from Hal Leonard Music, Inc., 64 East 2nd Street, Winona, MN.

Tests for achievement in musical understanding are equally important as those for achievement in musical performance. Such exams can be formulated by the teacher, based on music which the band or orchestra is currently studying and performing. The following test is drawn from the band number on page 222. The collective results of such a test will indicate to the director not only the degree of learning that has taken place, but also the effectiveness of the teaching.

TRIUMPHANT FESTIVAL
from *MUSIC FOR THE ROYAL FIREWORKS*

1st B♭ Cornet

GEORGE FRIDERIC HANDEL
Arr. by John Kinyon

GORHAM JUNIOR HIGH BAND
MUSICAL COMPREHENSION EXAM

For grading period : 3/19   Composition: *Triumphant Festival*

History   Circle correct answer:

1. Handel lived in the same era as:
   a — George Washington
   b — Abraham Lincoln
   c — Woodrow Wilson

2. Although Handel spent much time in both Italy and England, his native country was:
   a — Germany
   b — Norway
   c — America

3. Although the music from which this band arrangement is taken was originally written for wind instruments to be played in outdoor performance, for indoor concerts the composer later added: .
   a — full percussion
   b — clarinets
   c — strings

4. Handel wrote another piece of music for an outdoor celebration known as the:
   a — Water Music
   b — Symphony for Band
   c — Outdoor Rock

5. The style of the music is called:
   a — romantic
   b — contemporary
   c — baroque

Theory

6. This band arrangement represents only one movement of Handel's original:
   a — suite
   b — symphony
   c — concerto

7. The abbreviation "mf" in measure 25 means:
   a — medium loud
   b — medium soft
   c — medium fast

8. The abbreviation "cresc." in measure 31 means:
   a — gradually softer
   b — gradually louder
   c — gradually slower

9. The *concert* key of this arrangement is:
   a — Eb major
   b — C minor
   c — F major

10. In keeping with the general style of this number, the eighth notes should be played:
   a — legato
   b — staccato
   c — fortissimo

An excellent series of tests of comprehensive musical understanding is The Selmer Band Manual Quizzes, seven separate tests based on the text of The Selmer Band Manual by Nilo Hovey. Manuals and sets of quizzes are available from Selmer, Inc., Box 310, Elkhart, IN 46515. Below is a sample from the series.

Name ....   Quiz score   ....

THE SELMER BAND MANUAL
QUIZ 3

Circle "T" if the statement is true; circle "F" if false:

I. The composer always indicates the style to be used in his composition.   T   F

II. Explosive use of the tongue results in an effective marcato style.   T   F

III. Proper use of dynamic contrast adds to the effectiveness of a musical performance.   T   F

IV. A good director will emphasize CONTROL of the tone at any and all volume levels.   T   F

V. All notes marked *staccato* should be played as short as possible.   T   F

Circle the letter which answers the question or completes the statement most accurately:

VI. What are the two English words which best describe *legato* playing? (a) heavy, detached, (b) light, separated, (c) smooth, connected?   a b c

VII. What clue that a composition should be played *legato* is provided by the director? (a) a flowing beat, (b) short jerky motions, (c) quick preparatory beat?   a b c

VIII. What fault causes so many school bands to play *marcato* in a harsh and unmusical manner? (a) not watching the director, (b) playing too softly, (c) tonguing too heavily?   a b c

IX. What single word might be added to the definition of *staccato* with good effect? (a) loud, (b) light, (c) long?   a b c

After each *number* put the *letter* which identifies the best definition of the given term:

X.
1. da capo (DC)	a. loud	1............
2. dal segno (DS)	b. very loud	2............
3. diminuendo (dim)	c. with fire, energy	3............
4. dolce	d. grand or noble style	4............
5. energico	e. forcefully accented	5............
6. forte (f)	f. from the beginning	6............
7. fortissimo (ff)	g. furiously	7............
8. forzando (fz)	h. joyfully	8............
9. con fuoco	i. from the sign	9............
10. furioso	j. energetically	10............
11. giocoso	k. gradually softer	11............
12. grandioso	l. sweetly	12............

GRADING

Many directors view the giving of grades as a bothersome administrative necessity, a time-consuming and arbitrary exercise of compliance with school policy. This need not be the case, however, for the giving of grades, equitably based, can serve the director as a strong force in the motivation of student members of his ensembles. Students will take music grades just as lightly or as seriously as they are given, and the director who assigns grades perfunctorily or capriciously cannot expect to derive positive results from the system. Good grades should be coveted, and marks should be awarded on the basis of earned merit rather than solely according to attendance, seating rank or personal charm.

There are many composite methods of grading, some of which are based on elaborate point systems. These work well as long as the points are fairly assigned and as long as the point-keeping chores are not overwhelming in terms of time and paperwork. Whatever the system of grading decided upon, the essential considerations should be *achievement in musical performance and comprehension.* Other factors to be considered may include everything from attendance and attitude to more mundane matters such as instrument and uniform inspections.

NORTHPORT HIGH SCHOOL
INSTRUMENTAL MUSIC POINT SYSTEM

Name _____ Semester _____

TOTAL POINTS FOR PERIOD

	1	2	3	4

Points

5 each — parade or field participation
        — assembly or special program "back-up" ensemble
        — small ensemble "entertainer" assignment in community

10 each — formal concert participation
         — solo performed in public
         — pass written comprehensive musicianship test

15 each — all county band or orchestra membership
         — home practice (minimum: 3 hrs. per week)
         — all-state ensemble competition (superior rating only)

20 each — all-state band or orchestra membership
         — all-state solo competition (superior rating only)

         60 points per grading period = A   Total
         50 points per grading period = B   points
         40 points per grading period = C
         30 points per grading period = D   Grades

ADDITIONAL REFERENCES

Bessons, Malcolm E., Tatarunis, Alphonse M. and Forcucci, Samuel L., *Teaching Music in Today's Secondary Schools.* New York, NY: Holt, Rinehart and Winston, Inc., 1974.

Colwell, Richard J., *Music Achievement Tests*, Chicago, IL: Follett Educational Corp., 1968.

Colwell, Richard, *The Evaluation of Music Teaching and Learning.* Englewood Cliffs, NJ: Prentice-Hall, Inc. 1970.

Colwell, Richard, *The Teaching of Instrumental Music.* New York, NY: Appleton-Century-Crofts, 1969.

Holz, Emil A. and Jacobi, Roger, *Teaching Band Instruments to Beginners*, Englewood Cliffs, NJ: Prentice-Hall, Inc. 1966.

Lehman, Paul R., *Tests and Measurements in Music*, Englewood Cliffs, NJ: Prentice-Hall, Inc., 1968.

Leonhard, Charles and House, Robert W., *Foundations and Principles of Music Education*, New York, NY: McGraw-Hill Book Co., Inc., 1959.

Whybrew, William E., *Measurement and Evaluation in Music.* Dubuque, IA: Wm. C. Brown Co., 1971.

CHAPTER XIV

MOTIVATION

Teaching effectiveness is closely related to the degree of student motivation. Successful teachers, well aware of this relationship, are ever sensitive to the level of motivation among their students and constantly strive to provide a learning environment which includes positive incentives. Motivating devices run a wide range of both intrinsic and extrinsic factors, from the most subtle of teacher-student interactions to the most obvious of carrot-on-the-stick games. Even the casual taken-for-granted aspects and activities of the classroom can serve as motivation . . . a successful rendition of an exercise, an attractive bulletin board, a teacher's smile . . . or even a scowl. Students, and especially young students, are more highly sensitive to such everyday subtleties than many teachers realize. So inseparably linked is motivation with musical achievement that teachers owe it to themselves and to their students to constantly evaluate their modus operandi with an eye to examining why some students sustain interest in their music studies while others do not. As Charles Benner has so aptly pointed out,

> The student continues to do those things in which he can have a feeling of success, and those things that satisfy his own psychological and functional characteristics. The effective teacher will be sensitive to fluctuations in interest of individuals and of the group. The teacher's assumption that students *ought to be interested* often evades responsibility for analyzing *why they are not interested*.*

The following are but a few of the many motivational devices usually considered in the operation of a successful music program:

*Benner, Charles H., *Teaching Performing Groups*, Reston, VA, Music Educators National Conference, 1972.

Membership qualifications - Standards for admittance to any organization serve to enhance the desirability of membership. This is true at the adult level regarding selective membership in civic and fraternal groups. The same axiom holds true with school organizations, where candidates for the varsity teams, the honor society or major musical ensembles are highly motivated by the feeling of prestige that acceptance will bring. Qualifications for membership in instrumental ensembles need not be formidably high, yet unless certain basic standards are required, membership in the band or orchestra will be much less coveted. All candidates should be required to meet standards of proficiency and musicianship commensurate with their age and experience before being accepted into an ensemble.

Tradition of excellence - Instrumental music departments which over the years have established a tradition of excellence will seldom have problems of maintaining esprit de corps. The motivational momentum inherent in the prestige and creditability of proven musical achievement runs deep and strong. Framed pictures of former students and ensembles on the music room walls, an official scrapbook of programs and activities, or a trophy case of awards won all testify to past achievements and help perpetuate tradition. Students develop loyalties to those organizations of which they are proud.

Competitive seating plans - Competitive seating plans, based on a system of challenges, are a proven medium of motivation and one widely used by many instrumental directors. The prestige of playing first chair is undeniable and, for many students, irresistible. The validity of the system rests with the method of the challenges; stringent rules must be established by the director and the members of the ensemble which will give everyone a fair opportunity for advancement but which, at the same time, will not promote personal grievances or jealous repercussions within the section.

Quality music - Those directors who program a preponderance of music of an entertainment nature in an effort to win over their students are defeating their own purposes. That genre of music which can be had so readily at the turn of the dial of a transistor radio holds no long term fascination or challenge for most students. There is no substitute for the study of quality musical literature, in its every aspect, as a factor of motivation. This does not necessarily imply music of great difficulty but, rather it infers music of substance. In the long run the challenge of the meticulous performance of great music is one of the strongest factors of motivation for student performers.

Creative tension - Creative tension is a valid force of performer motivation when used judiciously and with proper intent. Such rehearsal tension is generated by the dynamic nature of the conductor, and stems from the conductor's personality and propensity toward *demanding* nothing less than the best from his or her performers. Some conductors, stern and serious by natural disposition, easily provoke feelings of challenge through subtle (and sometimes not so subtle!) intimidation which can quickly charge the ensemble to perform at a higher-than-ordinary level of artistic or technical ability. All such tension generated by conductors must be substantiated by their own musical authority and proficiency, however, for the demanding teachers who are musically shallow cannot bluff their way among children. For those conductors of more casual and *undemanding* persuasion, some thought should be given to the possibility of greater group motivation through creative tension brought about by an intensification of personal dynamics.

Clinicians - The appearance of guest soloists, conductors and composers can have great motivational influence on student musicians. Professional artists, especially those who are educationally oriented, have both artistry and inspiration to offer young instrumentalists. Well-known conductors of stature can often bring fresh rehearsal techniques and constructive criticisms to bands and orchestras grown complacent about the methods of their own teacher. Composers, conducting or discussing their own works, can provide meaningful insights into the techniques of their craft. Many publishers and most instrument manufacturers maintain rosters of active clinicians and often, in conjunction with their retail dealers, are willing to help underwrite the expenses of their clinic appearances.

Concerts - Home concerts are the natural high spots of the school music year, bringing to artistic fruition the hours of practice and preparation. There is no greater motivational experience than participation in a musically exciting and satisfying concert. If the students feel they have done well, the applause of the audience is but an additional layer of frosting on the cake of self-esteem. It is that feeling of pride of accomplishment that propels the members of the ensemble (*and* their conductor!) on toward the *next* concert. Exchange concerts can be even more stimulating, challenging the students outside the security of their home auditorium and provoking them to give the best of their musical efforts. Concerts should not be limited to a perfunctory one or two a year but, rather, should be scheduled as often as feasible in order to provide continuing new objectives and to maintain the momentum of motivation which public performance affords.

Awards - Awards for musical proficiency, improvement or services rendered are an effective motivational device. Such recognition may come in the form of contest medals, plaques, uniform service stripes,* chenille letters, certificates of merit and scholarships. Local merchants, civic groups and Parent-Teacher Associations can often be prevailed upon to sponsor such awards, thereby adding community prestige to the presentation. Popular awards among instrumental directors are the John Philip Sousa Senior High Band Award given "in recognition of outstanding achievement and interest in instrumental music," the Louis Armstrong Jazz Award given "to the outstanding instrumentalist in the field of jazz, as demonstrated through superior musicianship, character, and individual creativity," the Director's Award for Junior High Band students, and the National School Orchestra Award "in recognition of singular merit and outstanding contributions to the success of the school orchestra." Plaques and related items for this series of awards are available from The Instrumentalist Co., 1418 Lake Street, Evanston, IL 60204.

Solos and small ensembles - Although music teachers are prone to think of slow students as needing the most motivation, this is not necessarily true. Motivation is of equal importance to the talented child who may become bored and disinterested when

---

*For information concerning The Bandribbon Plan write: Bandribbons, P.O. Box 145, Monmouth, OR 97361.

confined to the "average" musical mold. The opportunity for solo and small ensemble performance will serve to motivate such students by providing more challenging musical experiences coupled with additional personal responsibilities.

Grades - The giving of report card grades, although an administrative chore, can be turned to an advantage when the grades are used for motivational purposes. It is essential that the students be apprised of the grading system and that the grades be commensurate with the effort expended by the students. The awarding of grades solely on the basis of attendance is a poor system which, in the long run, will be self-defeating. Factors which can be used in determining grades are attendance at rehearsals and/or public appearances, written exams based on either rehearsal discussions or outside assignments, solo and small ensemble performances, self-improvement as a performer based on assigned lessons, amount of home practice (see Home Practice Reports), and outside of school projects such as home listening and attendance at professional concerts. Many directors formulate these factors into a competitive point system by which grades can be determined objectively.

Home practice reports - A proven motivational device, especially for elementary-age children, has always been the home practice report. Such practice records can be purchased in quantity lots or can be devised and printed by the teacher. The card or paper should be stapled directly to the student's lesson book. Since the system requires the signature of the parent each week, it serves not only as motivation for the student to practice but also as a reminder to the parent that practice *is* necessary and expected.

STUDENT'S NAME _____

Symbols used for director's rating
E - Excellent
S - Satisfactory
N - Insufficient Practice Time

This practice report will prove helpful in keeping an accurate record of your practice time and will serve as a check on your weekly progress. Record the amount of time practiced each day and present this card to your director each week for his rating and comments.

WK	MT	T	W	TH	FR	SA	SU	DIRECTOR'S RATING	PARENT'S INITIAL
1									
2									
3									
4									
5									
6									
7									
8									
9									
10									
11									
12									
13									
14									
15									
16									
17									
18									

PRACTICE SPELLS P - E - R - F - E - C - T - I - O - N

--FOLD HERE--

WK	MT	T	W	TH	FR	SA	SU	DIRECTOR'S RATING	PARENT'S INITIAL
19									
20									
21									
22									
23									
24									
25									
26									
27									
28									
29									
30									
31									
32									
33									
34									
35									
36									

F1067   IMPROVE YOUR PLAYING WITH A KING

SAMPLE STUDENT PRACTICE REPORT
(Courtesy King Musical Instruments, Inc.)

Contests and Festivals - Competing for acceptance in all-county and all-state festival ensembles is an intense form of motivation, as are solo and ensemble competitions of all kinds. For many directors and their students, the participation in such competitive events is the strongest motivational device of all (see chapter on *Contests*).

Teacher Motivation - The other side of the coin from student motivation, one less often examined, is the matter of *teacher* motivation. This factor in and of itself has a direct bearing on student motivation, for surely no student can be inspired by an uninspiring teacher, no student challenged by an unchallenging teacher. Instrumental directors are able to maintain their own motivational momentum through a personal sense of professional pride, an urge to teach well and a desire for their students to achieve. Additional motivational impetus, a boosting of spirit and charging of the ego-battery, come from emotional crests such as a successful concert, a well-executed halftime show or a superior contest rating. In the course of day-to-day teaching however, when faced with a myriad of teaching and administrative responsibilities common to all instrumental directors, there may be a tendency to lose one's elan. That vitality of spirit generated at the school year's beginning may tend to ebb as the semester settles in. Indeed, among some few teachers secure in tenure and habituated to routines, the motivational spark may flicker but weakly. Every instrumental director should take stock of himself occasionally, as objectively as possible, to ascertain his own motivational level. Teachers cannot hope to motivate students to their best efforts if they themselves reflect less than genuine enthusiasm for and interest in both their music and their students.

Many instrument manufacturers provide motivational materials. A letter to any or all of them, addresses contained in M.I.C. appendix, should be well worth your while.

CHAPTER XV

PROFESSIONAL ORGANIZATIONS AND PERIODICALS

Today's instrumental music educator has many opportunities available for membership in professional groups within his or her particular field of interest. The major organization is, of course, the *Music Educators National Conference*, the national association which serves all music educators in giving direction, stability and unification to the common causes of our profession.* From this parent organization stems every state's *Music Educators Association*, each with its own system of component groups representing various specialized fields of music teaching. It is both professional and practical for every music educator to belong to MENC and to his state's music educators' association. The modest dues for national and state membership provide each member with subscription to the prestigious Music Educators Journal as well as to his own state's music educator's magazine. An active membership card also entitles the member to attend all national, divisional and state music educators' conferences and to share in the organization's program of commissions, workshops and special projects.

---

* For further information or application write: Music Educators National Conference, 1902 Association Drive, Reston, VA 22091. (All graduating music education majors who hold student MENC memberships are eligible for a reduced dues rate in their first year of professional teaching.)

MUSIC EDUCATORS NATIONAL CONFERENCE

EASTERN DIVISION

Connecticut
Delaware
District of Columbia
Maine
Maryland
Massachusetts
New Hampshire
New Jersey
New York
Pennsylvania
Rhode Island
Vermont

NORTH CENTRAL DIVISION

Illinois
Indiana
Iowa
Michigan
Minnesota
Nebraska
North Dakota
Ohio
South Dakota
Wisconsin

NORTHWEST DIVISION

Alaska
Idaho
Montana
Oregon
Washington
Wyoming

SOUTHERN DIVISION

Alabama
Florida
Georgia
Kentucky
Louisiana
Mississippi
North Carolina
South Carolina
Tennessee
Virginia
West Virginia

SOUTHWESTERN DIVISION

Arkansas
Colorado
Kansas
Missouri
New Mexico
Oklahoma
Texas

WESTERN DIVISION

Arizona
California
Guam
Hawaii
Nevada
Utah

Organizations which are associated with the Music Educators National Conference and which are of special interest to instrumental directors include:

American String Teachers Association (ASTA)
  Publication: American String Teacher Magazine

College Band Directors National Association (CBDNA)

National Association of College Wind & Percussion Instructors (NACWP)
  Publication: NACWPI Journal

National Association of Jazz Educators (NAJE)
  Publication: NAJE Educator

National Band Association (NBA)
  Publication: Journal of Band Research
       NBA Journal

National School Orchestra Association (NSOA)
  Publication: NSOA Bulletin

Other national organizations which are of particular interest to instrumental directors, some of which have varying restrictive qualifications for membership include:

Women Band Directors National Association (WBDNA)
Publication: Women of the Podium
Official Organ: The School Musician

National Catholic Bandmasters' Association (NCBA)
Publications: Newsletter and magazine
Official Organ: The School Musician

American School Band Directors Association (ASBDA)
Official Organ: The School Musician
Membership: By Invitation

American Bandmasters Association (ABA)
Publication: Journal of Band Research
Membership: By Invitation

Association of Concert Bands of America, Inc. (ACBA)
Official Organ: Woodwind - Brass & Percussion

Percussive Arts Society (PAS)
Publication: Percussionist, Percussive Notes

In addition to the official periodicals published by the state and national associations, there are also available to instrumental directors professional magazines, each designed to apprise the teacher of the latest trends and developments in the field and each maintaining regular columns on teaching techniques, music reviews, advertisements for new instructional materials and products, and articles of particular interest to the readership. The following are among the most relevant for school instrumental directors:

The Instrumentalist - (12 issues annually - 1 yr. $14.50, 2 yrs. $27.00, 3 yrs. $39.00)

The Instrumentalist Company
1418 Lake Street
Evanston, IL 60204

The School Musician - Director & Teacher - (10 issues annually - 1 yr. $12.00, 2 yrs. $20.00, 3 yrs. $25.00)

The School Musician - Director & Teacher
4049 West Peterson
Chicago, IL 60646

Woodwind, Brass & Percussion - (8 issues annually - 1 yr. $9.00 2 yrs. $17.00, 3 yrs. $24.00)

Evans Publications
25 Court Street
Deposit, NY 13754

A SELF-EVALUATION CHART FOR FUTURE INSTRUMENTAL MUSIC DIRECTORS

Music teaching effectiveness is governed not only by a teacher's acquired professional skills but also, to a large extent, by his or her personal characteristics. Each music education major, early in the course of college training, should become intimately aware of not only his or her own teaching skill potential but also of his or her own self as a human being, for the two sides of the mirror are mutually reflective and have great bearing on one's success or failure as a professional educator.

Below is a chart by which to rate yourself in both areas either prior to, or during the course of, your student teaching experience. Give yourself a candid appraisal on each of the ten listed items of evaluation, scoring *4* for OUTSTANDING, *3* for GOOD, *2* for ACCEPTABLE, *1* for POOR and *0* for INADEQUATE. If your average is *3* or above, consider yourself to be an excellent teaching candidate in instrumental music education!

PERSONAL TRAITS

1. LEADERSHIP:____
Do you project an image of authority through demeanor, verbal skills and body language?

2. DEPENDABILITY:____
Are you punctual, reliable and loyal?

3. EMOTIONAL MATURITY:____
Do you maintain your composure under the stress of everyday school problems? Do you gracefully accept constructive criticism?

4. SOCIAL SENSITIVITY:____
Are you friendly, tactful and gracious in your relations with other people?

5. ENTHUSIASM:____
Are you inspiring, positive and convincing enough to motivate your students?

PROFESSIONAL SKILLS

6. PERFORMANCE SKILLS:____
Can you accompany, conduct and demonstrate instrumental techniques as necessary?

7. PREPARATION SKILLS:____
Do you formulate plans and objectives in advance of the class? Do you know and select music series, methods and literature appropriate for the class? Do you know the score or lesson material well enough to maintain eye contact with the students?

8. TEACHING SKILLS:____
Do you get to the point and follow through? Do you maintain a reasonable pace? Are you insistent in your standards and goals? Do you diagnose and prescribe? Are you sensitive to individual and ensemble sights and sounds, and do you react to them in a constructive way?

9. BEHAVIOR CONTROL SKILLS:____

   Are you consistent in your behavior expectations? Do you have psychological control of the class through total communication and personal command?

10. COMMUNICATION SKILLS:____

   Are your explanations clear and thorough? Do you use language appropriate to the student's level? Do you speak with sufficient volume and do you enunciate clearly? Are your thoughts organized and expressed in logical order? Do you avoid monotonous speech by means of change of pace and voice modulation?

There is as much need for capable music teachers today as there ever has been in the eight decades of instrumental music education's existence in the schools of this country. Despite the generally inadequate funding, scheduling and staffing which plague most music programs and which tend to have a debilitating influence on our profession, there are thousands of dedicated instrumental directors, men and women of highest personal and musical qualifications, who continue to believe in the unique value of instrumental participation in the development of children. They give to their students knowledge, skills and, above all, an awakened sensitivity to the sounds of music. They also give of themselves. Perhaps *that* is what teaching is all about.

THE MUSIC INDUSTRY COUNCIL

GUIDE FOR MUSIC EDUCATORS

FOREWORD

For more than forty-five years, the Music Industry Council (formerly the Music Education Exhibitors Association) has served as a liaison between the music educators of the United States and the manufacturing and publishing firms that supply the materials and equipment used in music education. Throughout these years, there has existed a very fruitful and satisfying relationship between music educators and the members of the Music Industry Council.

This is as it should be, because public music education in the United States was founded in large part through the activities of the businessmen of music. Lowell Mason, whose vision resulted in the first public school program of music instruction, was essentially a businessman rather than a teacher. A little later, the textbook companies provided materials for public school music and summer training courses for the education of teachers.

Our great program of instrumental music was initially promoted and substantially supported by the manufacturers and distributors of band and orchestra instruments and other equipment. The pioneering salesmen of instruments awoke students and their parents to the benefits of bands and orchestras in our schools. Similarly, recording companies have cooperated both by supplying materials and by developing with the teachers the listening programs that have become such a valuable part of today's music education. Recently, fund-raising companies have joined the Music Industry Council, offering aids to music educators in raising funds for special programs and equipment.

When these early programs of public music education proved successful, the great possibilities of a wider application were recognized by the colleges and universities, and these institutions assumed their rightful responsibilities for providing the necessary teaching potential.

Growing concurrently with the Music Educators National Conference, the Music Industry Council has been of great help to the Conference in handling the considerable detail of the exhibits at the national and divisional conferences. The fees paid for these exhibits by MIC members have been an important source of financial support for the many useful activities of MENC.

The Music Industry Council continues, as a nonprofit service organization, to provide information on and understanding of the many business problems that confront the music educator.

THE MUSIC INDUSTRY COUNCIL
Headquarters: 1902 Association Drive
Reston, Virginia 22091
Telephone 703-860-4000

Introduction to the business guide

ITS SERVICE TO YOU

The selection, purchase, and maintenance of the physical materials of music education involve a mutual responsibility between you, the user, and ourselves, the manufacturers and distributors. In these pages, you will find specific suggestions for your guidance in the business contacts that are an essential part of your teaching program. Many may seem rather obvious and, perhaps, unnecessarily detailed, but they are the outgrowth of many years of experience in education-purveyor relationships and, despite their simplicity, are important.

Whether you are in need of half a dozen replacement copies of a choral piece or are faced with a major investment in instruments, electronic equipment, or band uniforms, there are accepted procedures that help to ensure that you get what you want when you want it, and that it is of the utmost quality permitted by your budget. This guide provides a ready reference to these procedures. It also outlines many of the minor pitfalls that may lead to major disappointments, delays, and misunderstandings and, in addition, includes a useful directory of the firms with which you will be dealing.

ITS SERVICE TO US

The Music Industry Council, insofar as the basic materials and services of music education are concerned, *is* the music industry. Its membership is composed of those firms that actively support the work and policies of the Music Educators National Conference and act as its Permanent Committee on Exhibits for national and division conferences. The activities of the Music Industry Council are financed entirely by the dues of member firms. Any other income handled by the Council, such as proceeds from the sale of exhibit space, is returned to the MENC treasury.

Some years ago, the Council conceived, as a basic and needed function, the improvement of the music industry's communication with its educator-patrons and the creation of a more complete understanding of mutual business problems. While such an effort would undoubtedly tend to benefit the educator's service, the decision was not entirely altruistic. Misunderstandings, delays, errors, or incomplete information on orders are not only annoying to you, but they are equally unwelcome, costly, and embarrassing to the firm with which you are dealing. It is for these reasons that this guide is published.

HOW TO USE YOUR GUIDE

Since the suggestions made in the following pages have grown out of repetitive incidents that interfere with the service to which you are entitled, we recommend that you familiarize yourself with their general nature. By reading through the material, you will recognize the various areas of your particular business activities in which misunderstandings are most likely to occur. Then, when you have occasion to correspond with MIC member firms, a quick reference to the proper section of your guide will ensure that your inquiry or order will reach them, will be referred to the proper department, and will be promptly and efficiently handled.

YOUR OWN SUGGESTIONS WILL BE WELCOMED

Many of the music industry's methods of working with the music educator have been developed from constructive criticism and helpful suggestions from teachers like yourself. Actually they have accounted for many recommendations included here. Because we are constantly trying to better our service, streamline our business procedures, effect savings of time and money for both our customers and ourselves, and, perhaps most importantly, develop improved products and services, your own suggestions will be welcomed. Your business problems inevitably become ours – and ours yours. Because the suggestions in this guide are based on collective industry-educator experience, we believe that if you will study and follow them, you will find our service more efficient and your work more effective.

PROSPECTIVE MUSIC EDUCATORS

Teacher's agencies and college and university placement bureaus can be helpful in establishing contacts for you. Here are some general suggestions on how you can make the best use of their service.

How to register

(1) Secure the agency's enrollment blank.
(2) Supply *carefully and in detail* the information requested by the blank.
(3) Make certain that your application photograph is a good one. (Do not, for your own sake, depend on a poor one.)
(4) Give correct names and addresses of your references.
(5) Let the agency know, in a letter what you want and what kind of position you are ready for.
(6) Write a follow-up letter to the agency from time to time.

Making applications

(1) Follow instructions, routine or special, as to the proper person to whom applications should be made.
(2) Make applications promptly upon receipt of notices.
(3) Inform the agency immediately as to whether you intend to apply for any vacancy about which you have received notice.

FIRST CONTACTS WITH THE MUSIC INDUSTRY

Many of the readers of the guide will be coming into the field for the first time. Others will be accepting new positions and fresh responsibilities, which require contact with many of our member firms. In either case, it is not only vital for you to know who they are and what they provide – information accurately listed here – but equally important that they know who *you* are, what you do, and something about your interests and needs – information listed nowhere until you, yourself, see that it is.

In order to assure yourself of receiving the basic tools of buying – the catalogues, price lists, information about new materials, and music – your first step should, by all means, be to make your name and work known to each of the firms, listed with whom you are likely to do business or whose mailings would be of interest to you. A simple, inexpensive, and efficient way to accomplish this is to prepare a mimeographed letter such as the one reproduced here. The materials and equipment are usually near at hand, and it can be stenciled, run off, and in the mail within a couple of hours. Each should be addressed separately and directly to each firm.

September 20, 19____

The Specific Music Company
100 Main Street
City and State, Zip

Gentlemen and Ladies:
    Please place my name on your mailing list.

Name: Dorothy C. Webster
Position: Supervisor of Music
Address: Bottstown High School
            320 Edgewood Drive
            Bottstown, PA 35303
Home Address: 622 Laurel Street
            Bottstown, PA 35303

*Formerly located at: Williamsport, New Jersey

Successor in Bottstown to: Florence Potter

Interested particularly in: High school choral music, band instruction books, band instruments, junior high school general music class materials.

                    Very truly yours,
                    Dorothy C. Webster

(*If you did not have a personal charge account at your former address and wish to open one, include your request.)

PERSONAL CONTACT AS WELL

In addition to being included among those who automatically receive the business news of music education, it is most useful—and, on occasion, particularly helpful—to know someone personally from the firms with which you deal. Our representatives attend national and division conferences and many other educational meetings not only to extend our acquaintance, but also to learn about your needs and problems firsthand and to offer every cooperation possible.

It will prove well worthwhile for you to set aside a definite time in your personal convention schedule to meet and identify yourself to those representatives—most of them whom are qualified to deal expertly with every aspect of their fields. Ask them about their products in relation to your work. Tell them of your needs for new materials that should be developed and placed on the market. The experienced music educator realizes and makes efficient use of the fact that the most important, and by far the largest, responsibility of sales and educational representatives is service.

Your business correspondence

Fortunately (or perhaps, unfortunately), in discussing such matters as writing a letter, we reflect the experience of our entire membership: Letters that are legible, concise, and well-organized receive immediate attention. Letters requiring deciphering or further correspondence with the writer must be set aside, thereby creating a service delay of as much as several days.

We make every effort to handle our mail promptly and efficiently. The following suggestions will help speed your business correspondence.

TYPE WHEN YOU CAN

Typewritten letters offer far less opportunity for error in reading. In handwritten correspondence, it is wise to print titles, proper names, and street addresses. Special care should be given to the legibility of numbers to prevent mistakes in identifying the quantity of merchandise.

YOUR OWN PROFESSIONAL LETTERHEAD

Many established music educators have found that a printed letterhead giving their name, position, and address is most useful in business and professional correspondence. Its combined virtues of dignity and accuracy are well worth its moderate cost. However, whether you use an individual letterhead or not, here are three important but easily overlooked suggestions for your business letters.

(1) Your full address (street name, town, state, and zip code) should appear at the top of your letter.

(2) Sign your full name and initials plainly. If your signature is one of those with more personality than legibility, be sure to type or print your name beneath it. Always use the same signature form; not "May Hewitt Joyce" at one time and "Mrs. J. P. Joyce" another.

(3) State your official position in every letter.

AVOID THE MULTIPURPOSE LETTER

We often receive letters in which several unrelated items of business are included in a single communication; a rush order, for instance, a payment on account, and a request for information about other materials. This single sheet must travel through three different departments, waiting in each until the matter is completed.

Three brief memorandums in one envelope, each addressed to the proper department ("Order Department," "Cashier," and "Correspondence"), would ensure that all three transactions were completed in less than one third the time.

Some general suggestions on ordering

To get exactly what you want and to get it when you want it requires some care on your part as well as on the part of the well-trained staffs who receive and fill your order. Unclear orders invite delay and error. Here are some of the ways to avoid them.

YOUR CATALOGUE IS YOUR BEST BUYING GUIDE

As we recommended earlier, you should have at hand the *current* catalogues of the firms handling the materials and services in which you are interested. Any of our member firms will send one on request. If you refer to your catalogue, your ordering will be greatly simplified and the possibility of error sharply reduced.

WHAT ABOUT PRICE?

Please remember that the lowest price does not always pay off. Service, an important factor to you, the user (though not always to your Purchasing Department), may be sacrificed by the lowest price. Good and adequate service should be required and included in your purchasing procedures and specifications.

Also keep in mind that the musical instruments and materials are not immune to price changes. It is wise to obtain the latest price information before issuing purchase orders, bids, and so on. Try to anticipate future price changes when submitting budget proposals to your administration.

CHECK AND LIST TITLES AND NAMES CAREFULLY

Whatever you order should be positively identified by complete name, description, and, where one is given, stock number used by supplier. A few minutes spent in checking such details will assure you of prompt shipment of the correct item.

IF YOU HAVE A PURCHASING DEPARTMENT

If your school or school system has a purchasing department – or specifically requires administrative approval of orders – our member firms usually will have been notified to that effect. You will understand that we *must* observe such purchasing procedures as have been established. If you observe them as well, it may avoid delay and embarrassment.

Another source of confusion occurs when adequate detail about purchases is not supplied to your own administrative departments. Where there is a central purchasing agency – such as the clerk of a Board of Education or a college business manager – it is important that complete and accurate information be provided. Bear in mind that these people may not be specialists in the jargon of your field.

BE SPECIFIC IN SHIPPING INSTRUCTIONS

Errors in shipping instructions provide some of the more spectacular frustrations for both buyer and seller. It may seem difficult to believe, but many of our otherwise careful customers neglect to state clearly to whom the shipment is to be sent! Even more frequently, they fail to inform us to whom it is to be charged and how they wish it to be sent (parcel post, UPS, and so on). It is important to be sure your directions are explicit.

CHARGE ACCOUNTS CAN BE CONFUSED
AND CONFUSING

The widespread interests and activities of music educators frequently involve them in the purchase of materials for more than one organization and, as a result, in the establishment of more than one account. Often, a person may have a personal account in addition to that of the school. These accounts are welcome, of course, and they require no more than the usual business references furnished for your gasoline or other credit cards and take no longer to establish. If you have not already set up your personal account through the recommended mimeographed letter (see page 5), it should be done at least a week or two in advance of your first order.

MIX-UPS ARE EMBARRASSING
TO EVERYBODY CONCERNED

Please help to prevent transactions on your personal accounts from becoming entangled with accounts of an organization or institution with which you are affiliated. School officials and purchasing agents are annoyed by receiving statements for materials that should have been charged to personal accounts. Instructors are annoyed by finding that their personal accounts have been charged for items that belong on the accounts of their organizations, and we, unhappily, are often in the middle. Transactions involving separate accounts should be kept separate. This is the best way to maintain your personal credit standing, as well as your professional relationships with your administrative superiors.

HOW TO HANDLE "ON APPROVAL" ORDERS

To order materials to be sent "on approval" requires the same definite and concise treatment as your purchase orders—with additional responsibility if the materials are to be returned. Such orders receive exactly the same expert and thoughtful attention as outright purchases from our member firms, and in turn, the "on approval" privilege, we feel, should be safeguarded by those to whom it is of service.

Order carefully. The fact that you order materials "on approval" rather than buying them outright automatically implies that they *may* not be exactly what you need. The more our specially trained staffs know about your interests and needs, the better opportunity we have to help you.

Make your decision as soon as possible. Materials sent you for inspection remain "on approval" for only a specified time. It has been our experience that, too often, misunderstandings arise because instructors – either through carelessness or the belief that "nobody will mind" if they keep the materials beyond the stipulated period – delay completing the transaction.

Materials "on approval" are charged to your account. This is obviously our only way of keeping track of them. Materials returned within the specified period are promptly credited and not billed.

After the approval period, they become outright purchases. In every instance, you will find that the manufacturer or distributor has allowed reasonable time for inspection and decision. In unusual circumstances, a written request will often permit an extension of the period. But at the end of that time, it is only reasonable that we take for granted that you wish to keep the materials and that they may legitimately and justly be charged to your account.

Unlike printed materials, a used recording cannot be resold commercially. If it is returned, it can only be scrapped. It is, therefore, improper to *presume* that the manufacturers or dealers can provide an "on approval" recording service. Some can, some can't. Ask first!

TO RETURN SUCH ORDERS FOR CREDIT

If you receive "on approval" packages from several sources at the same time, the materials should carefully be kept separate. It is not unusual for one of our firms to receive items that had been sent by another.

To assure that you receive full credit for material returned, always enclose a copy of the billing – or, at least, some indication of the invoice number.

If merchandise was originally shipped to one address but billed to another (for example, to a central purchasing authority), that information is also necessary for credit to be issued correctly.

Don't enclose an order with returned materials. To do so not only is against postal regulations, but also will delay the filling of your order. Send your order separately in a letter.

Your appreciation of the "on approval" privilege can be best expressed by ordering from the firm extending it.

SOME GENERAL SUGGESTIONS ON SHIPPING

When a package of music, instruments, uniforms, or equipment is returned, there are several points at which confusion sometimes occurs. While many of the following suggestions may seem obvious, they refer to errors and oversights that recur persistently.

(1) Check with supplier or manufacturer as to procedures, authorizations, requirements, special instructions, and so on that are necessary to return merchandise. Pack well so the material may reach its destination without damage or loss.

(2) Address plainly and accurately. Be sure to note a *return address* on the package so the receiver will know *exactly* from whom and where the shipment has been made.

(3) If the material has been charged to an account, make certain the account is plainly identified on the package so proper reference and adjustment can be made.

(4) When you send the package, write a letter telling the receiver (a) what the package contains, (b) why it is being sent, (c) what you want done about it, (d) the date on which it was sent, and (e) the method by which you sent it (parcel post, UPS, and so on).

(5) Do not enclose any written material in any parcel post package. This is contrary to strictly enforced postal regulations. Enclosing written communication of any kind automatically requires the full first-class rate for the entire package. The following three suggestions refer, in one application or another, to this rule.

(6) Printed and manuscript music, phonograph recordings, tapes, and books may be mailed at special rates, if the package is clearly marked "Educational Material" and contains no correspondence.

(7) A simple way to have your letter accompany the package to which it refers, is to address, seal, and stamp it exactly as you would for a separate first-class mailing, then paste or cement it firmly to the outside of the package. The stamp must, of course, represent first-class postage for the letter alone, the package carrying its own lower-rate stamps.

(8) Enclose the original invoice, or a copy, in the return package. You may also send a copy by first-class mail with any written information that is important to the transaction.

(9) Insurance on parcel post packages and adequate valuation of UPS and freight shipments are recommended as a worthwhile safeguard.

When you are ordering music

CHORAL

Many choral compositions are published in several arrangements, and confusion can occur unless the form and voicing desired is made completely clear. Most publishers use different catalogue numbers for various voice arrangements of the same title.

Be sure to specify the arrangement you want by voice (SSA, SAB SATB, and so on) and by catalogue number where one is given.

When solo voice selections appear in high, medium, and low keys, be careful to note which you want.

When ordering from a source where the publications of more than one publisher are carried, do not order by number only. Give the title, composer, voice arrangement, arranger, number, and publisher. Choral music is usually filed by title, and very often, the same octavo number is issued by several publishers.

Often, large choral works require accompaniments by orchestra or other instrumental groups. Most publishers indicate in their piano-vocal scores whether the instrumental score and parts for that work are available on outright purchase or rental. Generally, the instrumental materials for an extended choral work are on a rental basis only. The conductor should plan well in advance in obtaining the necessary materials from the publisher. All fees and permissions must be negotiated directly with the publisher.

INSTRUMENTAL

Instrumental music, by its multiple and varying nature, presents multiple opportunities for misunderstanding and error in ordering. In preparing an order for band or orchestra music, particular attention should be paid to the instrumentation desired.

The publisher's or dealer's catalogue will indicate to you whether a composition is available for small orchestra, full orchestra, symphonic orchestra, full band, symphonic band, or other instrumental group. If you need extra parts, you may find it more economical – after checking the number of additional parts you need – to order two complete instrumentations rather than buying the parts separately.

If you do buy parts separately, however, list them carefully, and for better accuracy in both making and filling your order, we recommend that you list them in the same sequence (see page 17) as that used by professional librarians.

Contests, festivals, and clinics usually require a great many copies of music – very often on short notice. When the selections are made, the publishers concerned should be notified immediately so they will have enough copies printed to take care of your needs.

Extended works – the larger forms, especially in the orchestral and operatic fields – usually demand early and careful attention. Many are not printed and sold but are rented by publishers in manuscript or photostat editions. Fees for use vary, and in some cases, performances are restricted. A conductor planning to use such a work should notify the publisher as far in advance as possible to see that the music is available when needed and that permissions and fees are understood.

COPYRIGHT

Under the U.S. Copyright Law, copyright owners have the exclusive right to print, publish, copy, and sell their protected works. The copyright owners of the books and music you purchase are indicated on those publications. It is illegal for you to copy a publication in any way without the written permission of the copyright owner. Copyright owners have every right to prosecute offenders under the U.S. Copyright Law. Most of them would prefer to rely on you to recognize the rights of composers, arrangers, authors, and their publishers by not making or using unauthorized copies.

Certain uses of copyrighted music may require prior clearance. To assist you in comprehending the situation concerning copyright and to facilitate clearance where necessary, the music publishers' associations have available, at no cost, the pamphlet "Clearance of Rights in Musical Compositions, A Guide and Directory." This may be secured from either National Music Publishers' Association, Inc., 110 East 59th Street, New York 10022, or Music Publishers' Association of the United States, Inc., 130 West 57th Street, New York 10019.

Guidelines

These GUIDELINES are a brief introduction to the new Copyright Law. We recommend that you refer to MUSIC EDUCATORS JOURNAL of May, 1978 for more complete information.

Guidelines for the educational uses of music, developed by representatives of the Music Publishers' Association of the United States, the National Music Publishers' Association, Inc., the Music Teachers National Association, the Music Educators National Conference, the National Association of Schools of Music, and the Ad Hoc Committee on Copyright Law Revision, and printed in the House Judiciary Committee Report (H.R. Report 94-1476), pp. 70-71.

GUIDELINES FOR EDUCATIONAL
USES OF MUSIC

The purpose of the following guidelines is to state the minimum and not the maximum standards for educational fair use under Section 107 of HR 2223. The parties agree that the conditions determining the extent of permissible copying for educational purposes may change in the future; that certain types of copying permitted under these guidelines may not be permissible in the future, and conversely that in the future other types of copying not permitted under these guidelines may be permissible under revised guidelines.

Moreover, the following statement of guidelines is not intended to limit the types of copying permitted under the standards of fair use under judicial decision and which are stated in Section 107 of the Copyright Revision Bill. There may be instances in which copying which does not fall within the guidelines stated below may nonetheless be permitted under the criteria of fair use.

A. PERMISSIBLE USES
    1. Emergency copying to replace purchased copies which for any reason are not available for an imminent performance provided purchased replacement copies shall be substituted in due course.
    2. (a) For academic purposes other than performance, multiple copies of excerpts of works may be made, provided that the excerpts do not comprise a part of the whole which would constitute a performable unit such as a section, movement or aria, but in no case more than 10% of the whole work. The number of copies shall not exceed one copy per pupil.

(b) For academic purposes other than performance, a single copy of an entire performable unit (section, movement, aria, etc.) that is (1) confirmed by the copyright proprietor to be out of print or (2) unavailable except in a larger work, may be made by or for a teacher solely for the purpose of his or her scholarly research or in preparation to teach a class.

3. Printed copies which have been purchased may be edited or simplified provided that the fundamental character of the work is not distorted or the lyrics, if any, altered or lyrics added if none exist.

4. A single copy of recordings of performances by students may be made for evaluation or rehearsal purposes and may be retained by the educational institution or individual teacher.

5. A single copy of a sound recording (such as a tape, disc, or cassette) of copyrighted music may be made from sound recordings owned by an educational institution or an individual teacher for the purpose of constructing aural exercises or examinations and may be retained by the educational institution or individual teacher. (This pertains only to the copyright of the music itself and not to any copyright which may exist in the sound recording.)

B. PROHIBITIONS

1. Copying to create or replace or substitute for anthologies, compilations or collective works.

2. Copying of or from works intended to be "consumable" in the course of study or of teaching, such as workbooks, exercises, standardized tests and answer sheets and like material.

3. Copying for the purpose of performance, except as in A(1) above.

4. Copying for the purposes of substituting for the purchase of music, except as in A(1) and A(2) above.

5. Copying without inclusion of the copyright notice which appears on the printed copy.

Penalties for infringement

The remedies provided by the law to a copyright owner could mean that a music educator found making illegal copies, or otherwise infringing, could face:

1. Payment of from $250 to $10,000 (statutory damages) and if the court finds willfullness, up to $50,000; and
2. If willfull infringement for commercial advantage and private financial gain is proved, fines of up to $50,000 and/or two years' imprisonment, or both.

OUT-OF-PRINT MUSIC

Sometimes, music may be erroneously reported to be out-of-print. If you are in doubt and the music is vital, try writing directly to the publisher.

AN ORDER FORM FOR INSTRUMENTAL MUSIC

Many experienced music educators have devised forms and procedures of their own to ensure a clear understanding of their orders. One of the most useful of these has to do with instrumental music, and we reproduce it here because it can be adapted easily to your own needs and instrumentation. This simple mimeographed form has the additional advantage of being listed in the universally accepted order. We believe you will find that the time you take in preparing it will be repaid many times, and we commend it for your use.

Board of Education   *703 Peach St.*   *Dowville, MI 49050*

Date _____

To (Supplier): _____

Charge to: _____

Street _____

City _____ State _____ Zip _____

Ship To: _____

Street _____

City _____ State _____ Zip _____

☐ Definite Order—
  Purchase Order No. _____

☐ Definite Order—
  A Purchase Order Will Follow

☐ Definite Order—
  No Further Authorization Required

ORCHESTRA

Title: _____

Composer: _____

Copies

_____ Full Score	_____ 3rd B♭ Trumpet
_____ Piano Conductor	_____ 1st Trombone
_____ Piccolo	_____ 2nd Trombone
_____ 1st Flute	_____ 3rd (Bass) Trombone
_____ 2nd Flute	_____ Tuba
_____ 1st Oboe	_____ Timpani
_____ 2nd Oboe	_____ Percussion
_____ English Horn	_____ Harp
_____ 1st B♭ Clarinet	_____ Celesta
_____ 2nd B♭ Clarinet	_____ Piano
_____ Bass Clarinet	_____ Advanced Violin
_____ 1st Bassoon	_____ 1st Violin
_____ 2nd Bassoon	_____ 2nd Violin
_____ Contra Bassoon	_____ 3rd Violin
_____ 1st F Horn	_____ Viola
_____ 2nd F Horn	_____ Cello
_____ 3rd F Horn	_____ Double Bass
_____ 4th F Horn	Other instruments not listed:
_____ 1st B♭ Trumpet	_____ _____
_____ 2nd B♭ Trumpet	_____ _____

Band

Title: _____

Composer: _____

Copies

_____ Full Score	_____ 1st F (or E♭) Horn
_____ Condensed Score	_____ 2nd F (or E♭) Horn
_____ Piccolo	_____ 3rd F (or E♭) Horn
_____ 1st Flute	_____ 4th F (or E♭) Horn
_____ 2nd Flute	_____ 1st B♭ Cornet
_____ 1st Oboe	_____ 2nd B♭ Cornet
_____ 2nd Oboe	_____ 3rd B♭ Cornet
_____ English Horn	_____ 1st B♭ Trumpet
_____ 1st Bassoon	_____ 2nd B♭ Trumpet
_____ 2nd Bassoon	_____ 1st Trombone
_____ Contra Bassoon	_____ 2nd Trombone
_____ E♭ Clarinet	_____ 3rd (Bass) Trombone
_____ 1st B♭ Clarinet	_____ Baritone (Treble Clef)
_____ 2nd B♭Clarinet	_____ Euphonium
_____ 3rd B♭ Clarinet	(Baritone-Bass Clef)
_____ E♭ Alto Clarinet	_____ Tubas
_____ B♭ Bass Clarinet	_____ String Bass
_____ Contrabass Clarinet	_____ Timpani
(E♭or B♭)	_____ Percussion
_____ 1st E♭Alto Saxophone	Other instruments not listed:
_____ 2nd E♭Alto	
Saxophone	_____ _____
_____ B♭ Tenor Saxophone	_____ _____
_____ E♭ Baritone	_____ _____
Saxophone	_____ _____

Ordered by _____

Position _____

~ 18 ~

Uniform manufacturers and agents

It is important to differentiate between firms that manufacture uniforms and those that act only as sales agents. Local retailers often serve as agents for manufacturers in obtaining local business. The quality of service in such instances depends on the experience of that dealer. It is recommended that purchasers check carefully the reputation and reliability of both manufacturer and agent.

INFORMATION

You should feel free to call on the manufacturer for full information concerning uniforms and accessories. The manufacturer who has specialized in making band uniforms or choir robes is familiar with their requirements and specifications and has available specially prepared catalogues and literature.

SERVICE AND QUALITY

You should make certain that the firm you choose will be willing to continue service after the first big order. Some firms are not interested in "fill-in" orders.

If you are in doubt at any time concerning the relative quality of materials and workmanship in uniforms, consult an established reputable tailor in your community and request his unbiased evaluation.

PRICES

Because uniform manufacturing is a very specialized business with fluctuating costs, most manufacturers price their uniforms from their home office. Purchasers should write out detailed specifications that will allow several manufacturers to bid on the same uniform. Purchasers should request a stock sample that is as close to their specifications a possible and that they can examine for quality of construction and best possible price. After a decision is made, they can ask the manufacturer of their choice to submit a special sample to their exact specifications. The order can then be placed, contingent upon the purchaser's approval and acceptance of the sample.

TIMING

The band uniform business is essentially seasonal in nature. You can benefit yourself by placing orders during the slack season. Most purchasers allow too little time for delivery. Except for minor accessories, uniforms are made to order. You should order two to three months ahead of time.

CONSUMERS' EDUCATION BOOKLET

"How to Buy Band Uniforms" is a booklet that is available, without charge, from the National Association of Uniform Manufacturers, 1156 Avenue of the Americas, New York City 10036. It discusses the following subjects: How to select a band uniform style . . . Consider the age group in your style selection . . . Sizes . . . Percentage relation of boys to girls in your band . . . Should girls wear skirts or trousers . . . Freak styles . . . How to write style specifications . . . Uniform fabrics— cottons, twills, gabardines, worsted fabrics, whipchord, serges . . . Synthetic and blended fabrics . . . Crease reaction and resistance . . . The Wool Labeling Act . . . Moth- and waterproofing . . . Cleaning methods . . . Color fastness . . . Life expectancy of a band uniform . . . How to write fabric specifications . . . Color selection . . . Popular neutral colors . . . Maintenance costs . . . Color or shade variations . . . Storage of uniforms . . . Deposit system, etc.

Guide to musical instrument buying

A lifetime of experience in manufacturing, sales, and appropriate use for educational purposes is, in brief, the success story of our member firms represented in the Music Industry Council.

Areas of our industry can advise you concerning instrumentation balance, how to build it, and how to acquire instruments of the correct size, for the different age levels of instruction (elementary, junior high school, and senior high school).

Plan your instrument purchases to include time for prompt delivery. We suggest the following guide:

Instruments needed in September should be delivered in June and early July, with August 15 as the latest delivery date for receiving them so they can be recorded properly for inventory purposes and assigned to individual schools and so student loan contracts can be prepared and affixed to the individual instruments. However, many instruments that may be needed for September could require as much as a year or more for delivery from the manufacturer. You should familiarize yourself well in advance with delivery schedules of the instruments required for your program. Obtaining this information from the manufacturer or dealer will help you avoid disappointments and inconvenience.

Nationally advertised band and orchestra instruments have proved over the years to give superior results, longer years of service, and superior learning results. Lower maintenance costs year to year and longer service years combine for the very best use of tax dollars and the best dollar value return on the investment. These instruments are available in convenient price ranges and represent the products of the most successful firms.

Many members of the Music Industry Council, including manufacturers and publishers, distribute their products through local retail dealers. These dealers can perform valuable and helpful services for you in recruiting beginners, repairing instruments, improving public relations, and, perhaps, obtaining the services of clinicians and consultants available from their suppliers. Learn to know these dealers—ask the MIC members which dealers represent them in your area so you can become acquainted with them and benefit from their services.

Helpful technical educational charts, and brochures are available from many MIC members. They contain the results of years of independent research and cooperation with schools planning for successful instructional results. Samples are usually sent on request.

OBTAINING QUOTATIONS AND ORDERING INSTRUMENTS

When you are preparing specifications for quotations, seeking competitive bids, and ordering instruments, you must provide certain specific information if you are to obtain the exact items you have planned to purchase:

(1) Model number, size, quantity, finish.
(2) Material—metal, wood, composition, fiber glass, plywood, hardwood, and so on.

(3) Complete outfits or partial outfits – if partial, name the items to be omitted.

(4) Color.

(5) Mouthpieces – if other than standard, as listed in the catalogue, be sure to state cup, facing, and so on.

(6) Accessories – specify the exact accessories to be included, especially when desired accessories are in addition to the standard equipment.

(7) Music stands – whether sheet music stands or instrument stands, type, and material.

STRINGED INSTRUMENT SPECIFICATIONS

COMPLETE VIOLIN OUTFITS

Violin: (1) in full, 3/4, 1/2, 1/4, 1/8, 1/10, or 1/16 sizes; (2) equipped with 1-, 2-, or 4-string adjusters (specify); (3) strings in place, bridge properly fitted, and ready to play.

Bow: (1) correct size for instrument; (2) equipped with silver wire winding soldered at both ends with Saffian leather bow grip.

Case: (1) hard shell; (2) correct size for instrument; (3) with compartments for two bows.

COMPLETE VIOLA OUTFITS

Viola: (1) in junior, intermediate, standard 15″, 15½″, 16″, or 16½″ sizes; (2) equipped with 1-, 2-, or 4-stringed adjusters (specify); (3) strings in place, bridge properly fitted, and ready to play.

Bow: (1) correct size for instrument; (2) equipped with silver wire winding soldered at both ends with Saffian leather bow grip.

Case: (1) hard shell; (2) correct size for instrument; (3) with compartments for two bows.

COMPLETE CELLO OUTFITS

Cello: (1) in full, 3/4, 1/2, or 1/4 sizes; (2) equipped with 1-, 2-, or 4-string adjusters (specify); (3) strings fitted to pegs, bridge properly fitted, and ready to play.

Bow: (1) correct size for instrument; (2) equipped with silver wire winding soldered at both ends with Saffian leather bow grip.

Case: (1) correct size for instrument; (2) with button or zipper closing (specify).

COMPLETE STRING BASS OUTFITS

String bass: (1) in full, 3/4, 1/2, or 1/4 sizes; (2) fiber glass, plywood, or hardwood (specify); (3) equipped with chrome steel strings; (4)

strings fitted to pegs, bridge properly fitted, and ready to play; (5) with telescopic adjustable endpin; (6) with D-string measurement.

Bow: (1) French or Butler model bow (specify); (2) correct size for instrument; (3) good and correct arch equipped with silver wire winding soldered at both ends with Saffian leather bow grip; (4) fully lined genuine ebony frog.

Cover: (1) correct size for instrument; (2) with button or zipper closing (specify).

IMPORTANT

When instruments are purchased without the case or cover, it is extremely important to specify this fact.

Scotch bass drums: (1) 10" by 28" diameter; (2) separate tension; (3) wood, metal, or synthetic shell; (4) plastic heads; (5) fiber cases.

Timpani: (1) available in 20", 23", 26", 29", and 30" diameters; (2) 23" and 26" diameters recommended as standard sizes, (3) fiber glass kettles; (4) leg rest mounted; (5) tuning gauge mounted; (6) carrying sling and mallets; (7) retractable legs.

Cymbals: (1) mounted on straps; (2) medium weight; (3) 15" to 16" diameter.

CONCERT PERCUSSION

Timpani: (1) copper kettles; (2) pedal tuning; (3) in pairs, 25" and 28" diameters or 26" and 28" diameters; (4) third timpani should be 23" diameter; (5) fourth timpani should be 32" diameter; (6) fifth timpani should be 20" diameter to encompass two-octave range (7) alternate timpani could be fiber glass or plastic kettles.

Snare drums: (1) three snare drums recommended for each section for wide range of performance – 3" by 13", 5" by 14", and 6½" by 14" diameters; (2) wood, metal, or synthetic shell; (3) separate tension, extended snares where possible; (4) fourth drum can be added from the marching percussion section in form of a 12" by 15" parade drum.

Bass drum: (1) one bass drum, 14" by 32", 16" by 32", or 18" by 36", depending on the size of the organization; (2) wood, metal, or synthetic shell; (3) mounted on adjustable tilter stand.

Concert tom-tom: (1) set of four to perform percussion ensemble music where required; (2) 12", 10", 8", and 6" diameters (other sizes also available); (3) single head; (4) tunable tom-tom; (5) mounted on adjustable stands.

Timbales: (1) set of two timbales; (2) 6½" by 14" and 6½" by 13" diameters; (3) metal or synthetic shell; (4) mounted on adjustable stand.

Gongs or tam-tams: (1) one gong or tam-tam, 28″ to 34″ diameter.

Cymbals: (1) several pairs of cymbals, mounted on straps; (2) medium weight; (3) 18″ and 20″ diameter; (4) one suspended cymbal, 20″ diameter, medium weight.

Trap table: one trap table, with assortment of traps – including triangle, beater, tambourine, ratchet, wood block, siren – as called for by scores to be performed.

Temple blocks: one set of temple blocks, five to eight tuned blocks mounted on stand.

Orchestra bells: (1) mandatory (bell lyre may be used as a substitute, but quality and resonance not as good for indoor use); (2) full octave keyboard; (3) mounted in case; (4) bells made of steel.

Xylophone: (1) one xylophone; (2) full 3-octave keyboard; (3) rosewood, hardwood, or synthetic bars.

Marimba: (1) one marimba; (2) full 3½-octave keyboard; (3) rosewood, hardwood, or synthetic bars; (4) sturdy frame with brakes on wheels.

Chimes: (1) one set of chimes; (2) 20 notes; (3) extended 1½-octave range with adequate muffler.

Vibes: used in stage band and percussion ensemble.

NOTES

All instruments should be purchased with vulcanized fiber cases for maximum protection when not in use and overall protection when being transported from one place to another.

GUIDELINES FOR INSTITUTIONAL PURCHASE OF KEYBOARD INSTRUMENTS

In every case, the choice of a keyboard instrument must be determined by

(1) the exact function it must fulfill;

(2) monies available for its purchase;

and in that order. Inadequate equipment will never suffice no matter how low the expenditure.

Important in your purchase plans are

(1) payment schedules: lease, with or without purchase option; installment purchase (with interest charges separately disclosed).

(2) written minimum warranty with Underwriter's Laboratory approval on electrical items.

(3) installation, service, and maintenance facilities.

(4) cost and availability of local contractual service and maintenance.

(5) delivery schedule and total transportion and delivery charges.

(6) consultant services.

In the purchase of keyboard equipment such as conventional pianos and organs, your local dealer is of great importance. He will be your contact with the manufacturer, your source of service, and often a source of experienced advice. However, some special electronic equipment must be purchased directly from the manufacturer. It is important to know exactly who the supplier is to ensure proper response to your inquiries and bids.

When bids specify a group of proprietary features, they should always include the invitation for substitute bids for "equal" products. It is always wise to send a copy of your bid to the manufacturer or dealer whose product is specified.

Alternate bids submitted in this way can offer advantages not contemplated in early consideration.

Your most difficult task will be the determination of the functions you wish to serve. Consider ways to make equipment fulfill many requirements—that is, use in performance, use for instruction, and use for practice.

When you have decided on your instructional and performance requirements, consider for your specifications the essential features you need.

PIANO

Keyboard; full 88-note or shorter.

Pedals; 3, 2, or 1.

Sound-producing components.

Case dimensions and finish (in specifying grand pianos, the case length relates directly to the volume of sound—important in equipping rooms of different sizes).

Options (special casters or moving frames, and so on).

Bench inclusion design.

ORGAN

Number of keys per manual.

Number of manuals required.

Pedal requirements.

Case design and finish.

General stop specifications (voice, pitch-length couplers, accessories).

HARPSICHORD

Specifications are similar to those for organ.

Same specifications for piano, plus—
Requirements for communication.
Specific audio aids and other options.

Guide to ordering recordings

Last year's recording catalogue is obsolete! Use current catalogues only. If in doubt, write for new ones. Note: no one dealer's catalogue can be complete—or as up-to-date as the manufacturer's.

Prices are subject to change. Ask suppliers for formal quotations before ordering. Avoid delays and awkward correspondence.

Monaural or stereophonic? Today's recording methods and equipment make it practical to play stereo records on regular (mono, "hi-fi") phonographs. Monaural recordings should not be played on stereo phonograph unless it is equipped with an alternate monaural needle. It is possible that suppliers might make certain stereo-for-mono substitutions. (Mono-stereo prices are, generally, parallel.)

Suppliers should not be required to guess! Make orders specific and accurate. Use manufacturer's name and catalogue numbers. Include title and even performing artist for positive identification.

Plan ahead! No dealer maintains a stock of all recordings. He may have to "special-order" for you. Even the manufacturer may be temporarily out-of-stock. Judicious planning on your part is indispensable if you are to receive good servicing of your requirements.

General music equipment information

General music equipment includes all equipment built specifically for the music rehearsal room or performing area.

This category includes portable risers; acoustical shells; portable practice rooms; stands for music and instruments; conductor's podiums and stands; and storage for music, instruments, uniforms, and robes, risers, staging, and acoustical shells.

A list of manufacturers of general music equipment is found on page 67. This equipment is sold either directly from the manufacturer or by a distributor to schools and institutions only. A complete catalogue and detailed information can be obtained by writing directly to these firms. Normally, they will also furnish without charge or obligation cost estimates for budget purposes and bidding specifications.

These suggestions in regard to ordering apply to general music equipment. The following additional suggestions are furnished for the specific types of equipment.

GENERAL MUSIC EQUIPMENT SPECIFICATIONS

PORTABLE RISERS

Considerations: (1) weight; (2) stability; (3) quietness; (4) storage requirements; (5) separate parts; (6) portability; (7) indoor or outdoor use; (8) number of performers per unit.

Standing chorus: (1) materials—plywood, plywood and steel, plywood and aluminum, aluminum; (2) construction—folding, rollaway, modular, three-step, separate step; (3) style—semicircular, rectangular; (4) depth of step—13", 16", 18"; (5) elevations—8", 16", 24"; (6) covering—plastic, rubber or rubber-like tread, carpet, spray-on finish.

Seated chorus: (1) materials—aluminum, plywood, steel; (2) construction—folding, rollaway, modular; (3) style—semicircular, rectangular; (4) depth of step—32" to 36"; elevations—8", 16", 24".

Band and orchestra: (1) materials—aluminum, plywood, steel; (2) construction—folding, rollaway, modular, (3) style— semicircular, rectangular; (4) depth of step—48"; elevations—8", 16", 24".

MUSIC CABINETS AND RACKS

Considerations: (1) conservation of space; (2) systematic handling; (3) quick and easy transfer from permanent file to folio and back; (4) protection of music.

Specifications: (1) types – storage, sorting, handling; (2) materials – steel, wood; (3) construction – rollaway, stationary (but movable); (4) styles – shelf type (with separate compartments for each arrangement), regular steel file (letter or legal); (5) sizes – band and orchestra, chorus, marching band.

Considerations: (1) handling; (2) conservation of space; (3) prevention of loss and damage; (4) whether instruments must be removed from rehearsal room.

Specifications: (1) types – cabinets (for all instruments including percussion), chairstands, stands (for larger instruments such as sousaphone, tuba, string bass, cymbals, bell lyre, snare drum, and bass drum); (2) materials for cabinets – wood, steel; (3) materials for chairstands and stands – steel, steel and wood; (4) construction of cabinets – rollaway, stationary; (5) construction of chairstands and stands – permanent, folding.

Considerations: (1) whether uniforms or robes will be taken on trips; (2) whether they will be worn only for performance; (3) sturdiness; (4) weight; (5) mobility.

Specifications: (1) materials – wood, metal; (2) construction – rollaway, movable.

Considerations: (1) stability; (2) size; (3) adjustability; (4) quietness; (5) portability; (6) attractiveness.

Podium: (1) materials – wood with plastic or carpet tread; (2) construction – permanent (two-step), folding (for travel); (3) size – about 30" by 30" by 8" (folding), 36" by 36" by 16" (two-step).

Conductor's stand: (1) materials – steel, wood, aluminum, (2) construction – adjustable (height and tilt), mechanical or friction; (3) desk size – 14" by 21" to 19" by 31"; (4) variations – with or without shelves and light, combination conductor's stand and folio cabinet (rollaway).

Conductor's chair: (1) materials – steel and wood; (2) construction – adjustable (height, depth, back); (3) style – with or without built-in podium and foot ring; (4) upholstery – leatherette in colors, foam cushions.

MUSIC STANDS

Considerations: (1) sturdiness; (2) stability; (3) adjustability; (4) portability.

Specifications: (1) material – steel, aluminum, fiber board; (2) construction – permanent, folding; (3) styles – permanent, adjustable (height and tilt); mechanical or friction; (4) finish – plated, enameled, chrome; (5) color – charcoal, black, or other.

REHEARSAL CHAIRS

Consideration: (1) sturdiness; (2) stacking; (3) weight; (4) posture; (5) necessity for removal.

Specifications: (1) materials – steel, wood, steel and wood; (2) construction – permanent (nonfolding), folding (3) style – posture (folding or nonfolding), regular, low back for string players.

ACOUSTICAL SHELLS

Considerations: (1) acoustical effectiveness; (2) storage requirements; (3) portability; (4) adjustability; (5) ease of set-up and takedown; (6) attractiveness.

Specifications: (1) types – choral, instrumental, combination; (2) materials – wood, plastic, (3) construction – portable or rollaway, modular, adjustable (wings, canopy); (4) style – with or without overhead panels, with or without wings.

PORTABLE PRACTICE ROOMS

Considerations: (1) sound isolation; (2) acoustical environment; (3) self-contained; (4) relocatable; (5) ease of supervision; (6) ease of set-up.

Specifications: (1) materials – steel and glass, wood and glass, plastic and glass; (2) construction – modular and demountable; (3) size – approximately 30 square feet to 90 square feet; (4) lighting – flourescent fixtures, in excess of 70 foot candles; (5) ventilation – maintain ambient temperature within the module; (6) sound qualities – minimum noise reduction module to module, approximately 31 to 85 decibels over frequencies 125 to 2,000 Hz.

Members of the
Music Industry Council
Alphabetical listing

$\mathcal{A}$

Addison-Wesley Publishing Company, Sand Hill Road, Menlo Park, CA 94025; phone: 415-854-0300. Publishers of the Comprehensive Musicianship Program, a K-14 program developed at the University of Hawaii and centered on seven basic concepts of music: rhythm, melody, harmony, tone, texture, tonality, and form. Activities and arranging. Music of all cultures and all periods is used. Secondary programs includes courses in band, chorus, and orchestra. Leon Burton and William Thomson, general editors.

AGEI Publishing Inc., 923 Illinois St., Racine, WI 53405; phone: 414-632-9983. A comprehensive course in basic musicianship and reading music in five workbooks (teacher's edition, spirit masters, optional cassettes); Grades 2 through 6.

Alexandria House, Box 300, Alexandria, IN 46001; phone: 317-724-4439. Alexandria House serves as full selling agent for various publishers. Among which are Fred Bach Publications, Gather Music, Paragon Press and Hamblen Music as well as Joey Song Records and Dynamic Medallion Records.

Alfred Publishing Company Inc., 15335 Morrison Street, Sherman Oaks, CA 91403; phone: 213-995-8811. Publishers whose catalogue of educational publications includes Alfred's Basic Guitar Course, Masterwork Piano Library, D'Auberge and Creating Music at the Piano Courses, Alfred's Basic Piano Library, Alfred's New Band Method, Basic Band Method, Basic Training Course and John Kinyon's Mini-Score Series. Also, full catalogues of stage band, marching band, concert band, choral, orchestra and classroom music books.

American Book Company, 135 West 50th St., New York, NY 10020; phone: 212-265-8700. Publishers of New Dimensions in Music, a K-8 program that includes student books, records, teacher's annotated editions with guide materials and piano accompaniment, and The ABC Choral Art Series—four nongraded student texts accompanied by eight records and a choral director's handbook—to be used by mixed male and female choral organizations.

American Federation of Musicians, 1500 Broadway, New York, NY 10036; phone: 212-869-1330. The object of the American Federation of Musicians shall be to unite all local unions of musicians regardless of race, creed, or national origin, into one grand organization for the purpose of general protection, advancement of their interests, enforcing good faith and fair dealing; as well as consistency with union principles in all cases involving members and/or local unions or the Federation.

American Society of Composers, Authors and Publishers (ASCAP), 1 Lincoln Plaza, New York City 10023; phone: 212-595-3050. ASCAP is America's performing rights society, which includes more than 23,000 men and women who create our nation's music, and their publishers. ASCAP is a nonprofit, membership organization that licenses the right to perform its members' copyrighted musical compositions in public, for profit, and in nondramatic form.

W. T. Armstrong Company, Inc., 1000 Industrial Parkway, Elkhart, IN 46514; phone: 219-293-8602. Manufacturers of flutes and piccolos since 1932. Now manufacturing and distributing Armstrong saxophones on a worldwide basis.

ARP Instruments, Inc., 45 Hartwell Ave., Lexington, MA 02173; phone: 617-861-6000. Manufacturers of electronic music synthesizers. Has a specialized staff to train teachers in the use and applications of each synthesizer. Free clinics available in many areas of the country. Textbooks for all grade levels and educational software; programs for general music, performance groups, and specialized areas of education. Factory service department and nationwide service network.

Artley, Inc., 2520 Industrial Parkway, Elkhart, IN 46516; phone: 219-522-8696. Manufacturers of student and professional woodwind instruments, including flutes, piccolos, and clarinets.

Sam Ash Music Stores, 301 Peninsula Boulevard. Hempstead, NY 11550; phone: 516-485-2122. Family-operated firm established in 1924. Five large stores in and around New York City. All band and orchestral instruments, amplifiers, electronic keyboards and synthesizers, sound reinforcement, sheet music, repairs. Warehouse houses school department that handles bids, rentals, repairs. Promoters of new and featured lines.

Associated Music Publishers, Inc., 866 Third Avenue, New York City 10022; phone: 212-935-4241. Music for all levels and combinations, vocal and instrumental, solo and ensemble. Sales and rental catalogues. Agents for Boelke-Bomart, Bote & Bock, Breitkopf & Haertel-Wiesbaden, Bruzzichelli, Doblinger, Enoch, Eschig, Leuckart, Nagels, Schroeder & Gunther, Simrock, U. M. E., Waterloo. With G. Schirmer, exclusive agents in the Western Hemisphere for Soviet music.

Audio House On Location Recorders, P.O. Box 219, 307 East 9th Lawrence, KS 66044; phone: 913-843-4916. Has twenty-eight years experience in on-location recording. Offers a satisfaction guarantee. Audio House has disc-mastering facilities and DBX noise reduction. Plain, stock, and custom albums available from art department.

Augsburg Publishing House, 426 South 5th Street, Minneapolis, MN 55415; phone: 612-332-4561. Publishers and sellers of sacred music all types, including choral, organ, vocal, and instrumental. Music available on thirty-day approval. Catalogues and listings sent regularly to interested people.

ℬ

Baldwin Piano and Organ Company, 1801 Gilbert Avenue, Cincinnati, OH 45202; phone: 513-852-7000. Offers a complete line of pianos and electronic organs for school, church, studio, and home. The Baldwin Music Education Division markets Electrosystems for group instruction, including the Baldwin Electropiano Laboratory.

Bandribbons, P.O. Box 145, Monmouth, OR 97361; phone: 503-838-1752. Manufacturers of a planned system of military-style, self-identifying, ribbon award decorations. 175 different Bandribbons include Service, Class, Officers, Organizations, Instruments, Position, and Honors. Custom Bandribbons, made-to-order, can be obtained quickly at a modest price.

Barcus-Berry, 5381 Production Dr., Huntington Beach, CA 92649; phone: 714-898-9211. Manufacturer and distributor of transducer systems for sound reenforcement and professional recording applications, amplifiers and public address systems. Other items in the product line include audioplate speakers, preamplifiers, mixers and other related electronic accessories.

Barker-Lins, Inc. – Sheet Music Service of Portland, 34 NW 8th Avenue, Portland, OR 97209; phone: 503-222-9607. Retailers of choral, pipe organ, and instrumental music for schools and churches. No piano or vocal music.

Beatrice Foods Co., Two North LaSalle St., Chicago, IL 60602; phone: 312-782-3820. Sponsor of ten regional high school marching band competitions each year in the U.S. The proceeds are for local charities. Regional winners perform in the Orange Bowl Parade and compete in the Orange Bowl Competition of Bands.

Belwin-Mills Publishing Corporation, 25 Deshon Drive, Melville, NY 11747; phone: 516-293-3400. Publishers and distributors of music covering every facet of the educational and professional field – sales and rental. Divisions include Franco Colombo Publications, Henry Adler Publications, Halbe composer statuettes, J. Fischer & Bro., H. W. Gray, Kalmus, McAfee, Dale Zdenek Publ., Ron Centola Publ., Music Boutique. Exclusive representative for printed products of Marks Music Corporation and MCA/Mills Joint Venture. Distributors of music books of leading books publishers.

Berklee College of Music, 1140 Boylston Street, Boston, MA 02215; phone: 617-266-1400. Literature and materials illustrating instructional techniques at Berklee College of Music. Method books, arrangements, and audiovisual theory instructions.

The Big 3 Music Corporation, 729 Seventh Avenue, New York City 10019; phone: 212-575-4978. Publishers of all types of school music – band, stage band, orchestra and string orchestra, choral, instrumental solos and ensembles, methods, cantatas, and community songbooks.

Blossom Festival School of Kent State University and the Cleveland Orchestra, Kent State University, Kent, OH 44242; phone: 216-672-2613. Summer study in instrumental and vocal performance in close association with distinguished professional musicians. Areas of instruction include chamber music, orchestral studies, opera, choral music, and solo performance.

Blue Lake Fine Arts Camp, RR 2, Twin Lake, MI 49457; phone: 616-894-8325. Blue Lake Fine Arts Camp is a summer school of the arts with the following major areas of study: band, orchestra, ballet, art, jazz, theatre, choir, and piano.

Boosey and Hawkes,Inc., *Sales Office:* P.O. Box 130, Oceanside, NY 11572; phone: 516-678-2500. *Executive Office:* 24 West 57th Street, New York City 10019; phone: 212-757-3332. International publishers of contemporary music for symphonic, operatic, educational, and concert fields, presenting music by Argento, Bartók, Bernstein, Binkerd, Britten, Copland, Del Tredici, Druckman, Grundman, Kolb, Maxwell Davies, Rorem, Stravinsky, Tull, Washburn. Agents for Editio Musica Budapest; Edizioni Suvini Zerboni, Milan; Josef Weinberger Ltd., London. Instrument Division: Sovereign and Imperial brass and woodwind instruments; accessories (i.e., Denis Wick mouthpieces, mutes; Jack Brymer mouthpieces), Golden Strad Bows.

Boston Music Corporation, 116 Boylston St., Boston, MA 02116; phone: 617-426-5100. Publisher of sheet music; seller of sheet music, records, stereo equipment, and instruments.

Bourne Company, 1212 Avenue of the Americas, New York City 10036; phone: 212-575-1800. Publishers of educational music at all levels for chorus, band, orchestra, and miscellaneous instrumental ensembles. Large assortment of concert music at the professional level available on rental.

Bowmar/Noble Publishers, Inc., 4563 Colorado Blvd., Los Angeles, CA 90039; phone: 213-247-8995. Publishers of music materials for early education through college.

Michael Brent Publications, Inc., 70 Winding Wood Road S., Port Chester, NY 10573; phone: 914-939-7632. Publishers of elementary and junior high vocal materials for music and the related arts. Operettas, musical plays, pageants, cantatas, varied vocal literature plus reference recordings, filmstrips, and teachers' guides available.

Broadcast Music Inc., 40 W. 57th St., New York, NY 10019; phone: 212-586-2000. Performing right licensing organization. Acquires performing rights from writers and publishers and licenses the public performing rights to users of music, such as broadcasters, hotels, nightclubs, colleges and universities.

Brodt Music Company, P.O. Box 9345, Charlotte, NC 28299; phone: 704-332-2177. Retailers for music of all foreign and domestic publishers in all categories. The wholesale division includes the publications department with a catalogue of choral, piano, organ, band, and instrumental works. Agents for several foreign publishers, including Banks, Cramer, Henle, Leduc, and Leslie.

Broude Brothers Limited, 56 W. 45 St., New York, NY 10036; phone: 212-687-4735. Broude Brothers Limited is a publisher and dealer of serious music. Broude Performing Editions include music for chorus, for orchestra, for small ensemble, and for solo instrument. Broude Brothers also publishes texts, scholarly editions, and reference works for libraries. Early music is particularly well represented in the Broude catalog.

Alexander Broude, Inc., 225 West 57th Street, New York City 10019; phone: 212-586-1674. Publisher and sole agent for Breitkopf & Hartel-Leipzig, Deutscher Verlag Fur Musik-Leipzig, Hofmeister Verlag-Leipzig, J. & W. Chester Ltd. Choral Catalogue, Israeli Music, Wilhelm Hansen Electronic Music. Distributor of music of all publishers.

Ted Brown Music Company, 1121 Broadway Plaza, Tacoma, WA 98402; phone: 206-272-3211. A retail music organization specializing in school music service. Extensive educational music department, band instrument rentals and sales, allied accessories, and a complete repair facility. Represents most publishing and top-quality instrument lines through the Northwest states.

Buffet Crampon International Inc., 55 Marcus Drive, Melville, NY 11746; phone: 516-420-1400. "The world's famous manufacturer of fine woodwind instruments," the Buffet soprano, alto, bass and contra-alto clarinets. Exclusive distributor of Buffet clarinets, saxophones, and oboes, as well as Schreiber bassoons and recorders, Evette and Schaeffer clarinets, and Evette clarinets. These products distributed exclusively in the United States and Canada.

C

Cambiata Press, P.O. Box 1151, Conway, AR 72032; phone: 501-329-6982. Publishers of choral music specifically designed for singing groups containing boys' changing voices.

Capitol Music Company, Inc., 1530 – 3rd Ave., Seattle, WA 98101; phone: 206-622-4013. Supplier of printed music representing all publishers.

CBS Musical Instruments, 100 Wimot Rd., Deerfield, IL 60015; phone: 312-948-5800. Sellers of musical instruments, including Fender guitars and amplifiers, Rogers drums and organs, Rhodes and Steinway pianos, Squier strings and accessories, and Gemeinhardt flutes.

Chappell Music Company, 810 Seventh Avenue, New York City 10019; phone: 212-977-7200. Publishers of popular sheet music, popular folios, educational textbooks, and materials for band, orchestra, and chorus.

Clarus Music Limited, 340 Bellevue Ave., Yonkers, NY 10703; phone: 914-375-0864. "Words and music for young people." Music publisher and record company. Producer of original LP recordings, cassettes, music books and teacher aids. Music plays. Materials for classroom and stage. Relates to basic curriculum. "Children Are People Series." Distributor of select recordings and multi-media kits. Request free catalog.

Clef House, Inc., P.O. Box 13248, Portland, OR 97213. Designers and creators of T-shirts, buttons, stationery, etc. with musical motifs, distributed by Belwin-Mills.

Coast Wholesale Music Company of Los Angeles, P.O. Box 5686, Compton, CA 90220; phone: 213-537-1712. Western distributor of Ludwig, Musser, Kitching, and Currier pianos; Ovation, Takamine, Ventura, and Aria guitars; Iida banjos; Becker, Schuster, and Suzuki string instruments; and Artist band and orchestra instruments.

College Conservatory of Music, University of Cincinnati, Cincinnati, OH 45221; phone: 513-475-2883. The following programs are available: Bachelor of Music in performance, education, composition, and theory; Bachelor of Fine Arts in musical theater, dance, broadcasting, and theater production; Master of Arts in performance, an opera certificate, and a D.M.A.

The College Music Society, Inc., Regent Box 44, The University of Colorado, Boulder, CO 80309; phone: 303-492-5049. The society is incorporated for the philosophy and practice of music in higher education and serves 5,000 persons in all areas of music at the college level. Publications include the monthly music faculty vacancy list, the Directory of Music Faculties in the U.S. and Canada, and College

Music Symposium. A mailing labels service is offered with 100 different lists for a total of 22,000 college music teachers. Annual meetings are held in the fall of each year.

Collegiate Cap and Gown Company, 1000 North Market Street, Champaign, IL 61820; phone: 217-356-9081. Manufacturers of choir robes and accessories for schools and churches. Complete catalogue with styles and fabric swatches available. Free sample service.

Computone, Inc., P.O. Box 488, Norwell, MA 02061; phone: 617-871-2660. Manufacturers and sells several varieties of Lyricon wind synthesizers.

C. G. Conn, Ltd., 2520 Industrial Parkway, Elkhart, IN 46516; phone: 219-522-3392. Established in 1875, C. G. Conn, Ltd., is the manufacturer of Conn brasses and exclusive international distributor for Artley woodwinds, Scherl & Roth stringed instruments, Conn guitars, and Conn organs. Conn is a substantial supplier of competitive brands of musical accessories through Continental Music Company.

Howard Core and Co., Inc., Route 1, The Cedars, Munford, AL 36268; phone: 205-263-1891. Wholesale distributors of bowed stringed instruments (violins, violas, cellos, and string basses) and related accessories.

Coyle Music, Inc., 2864 North High St., Columbus, OH 43202; phone: 614-263-1891. Sells full line of band and orchestral instruments; offers beginning music programs and a full-line service to schools, including repairs.

Creative Audio Visuals, 12000 Edgewater Drive, Cleveland, OH 44107. Specializes in sequential non-graded music materials for small groups, individuals, and large groups of all ages. Color filmstrips, cassette tapes, self-correcting Fun Sheets and books.

Creative Jazz Composers, Inc., P.O. Box T, Bowie, MD 20715; phone: 301-262-9099. A jazz oriented publishing record distributor and clinic services company, owned and operated by well-known jazz people. Catalog includes musical compositions by many highly respected "name" jazz composers, instrumental methods by Clark Terry and Urbie Green, and a list of 86 "name" jazz clinicians.

Crest Records, Inc., 220 Broadway, Huntington Station, NY 11746; phone: 516-423-7090. Custom recording pressings, and tape duplication from tapes supplied by schools and organizations. Producers of Golden Crest recordings featuring famous artists.

Custom Music Company, 1414 South Main Street, Royal Oak, MI 48067; phone: 313-546-4135 or toll-free: 800-521-6380. Custom Music offers a full line of professional and student musical instruments. Products offered include Cooper-Puchner and Kroner bassoons; Muramatsu flutes; Fredericks piccolos; R. Meinl, Sanders and Hirsbrunner tubas; Loree, Lucerne, Gordet, and Chauvet oboes and English horns; Alexander, Paxman, and Kroner horns; and Kori mallet percussion instruments.

𝒟

Dampp-Chaser Electronics, Inc., P.O. Box 1610, Hendersonville, NC 28739; phone: 704-692-8271. Manufacturer of device for maintaining stable relative humidity inside a piano keeping it in tune 3-4 times longer. The summer Dampp-Chaser prevents sticking keys, sluggish action, rust and out of tune pitch, and the winter humidifier eliminates dryness which may cause a cracked soundboard, flat pitch, and loose rattling action.

DeMoulin Brothers & Company, 1025 S. 4th St., Greenville, IL 62246; phone: 618-664-2000. In business since 1892, manufacturers of marching band uniforms and choir robes.

Dickson-Wheeler, Inc., 208 First Street, Scotia, NY 12302; phone: 518-374-1136. Publishers of the Let's Read Music series for elementary and junior music class or chorus. The Sol-Fa Book for improving sightsinging in secondary school or college chorus or choir; The Male Song Book, TTB arrangements specifically for middle or junior high school boys; and sacred and secular octavos.

Walt Disney Music Co., 350 So. Buena Vista St., Burbank, CA 91521; phone: 213-845-3141. Educational music for band, orchestra, chorus, and classroom music from the Disney song catalog, including exciting songbooks expressly designed for keyboard and guitar players, now available through the Hal Leonard Publishing Corporation. Disney youth musicals now available through the Silver Burdett Company.

Duquesne University, School of Music, Locust & Magee St., Pittsburgh, PA 15219; phone: 412-434-6080. The School offers the Bachelor of Music degree including all orchestra instruments, piano, and voice, also with emphasis on liturgical music and jazz. The Bachelor of Science in Music Education with the same instruments, and the Bachelor of Science in Music Education with Major in Music Therapy. The Master's degree in the Conservatory Program is offered in Music Theory and Composition and a Master's degree in Music Education.

E

Edition Musicus, P.O. Box 1341, Stamford, CT 06904; phone: 203-323-1401. Publishers of sheet music for educational recital purposes.

Editions Salabert, Inc., c/o G. Schirmer, Inc., 866 3rd Ave., New York City 10022; phone: 212-935-5100. Publishers of sheet music.

Educational Activities, Inc., 1937 Grand Ave., Baldwin, NY 11510; phone: 516-223-4666, or toll-free 800-645-3739. Carries audio-visual supplies for music education purposes; records and cassettes. Catalog available.

Elkan-Vogel, Inc., Presser Place, Bryn Mawr, PA 19010; phone: 215-525-3636. Publishers of sheet music and music books for the concert and educational markets, including vocal, instrumental, choral, band, orchestra, keyboard, and literature. Also, exclusive distributor for many French catalogues, including Durand, Lemoine, and Hamelle.

Engelhardt-Link, Inc., 185 King St., Elk Grove Village, IL 60007; phone: 312-593-5850. Manufacturer of quality lightweight laminated basses and cellos, built to conform to the standards of the String Committee of the MENC.

F

Forest R. Etling, Publisher, 1790 Joseph Court, Elgin, IL 60120; phone: 312-695-4884. Publications by nationally known composers and arrangers in the following categories: Concert Band, Full Orchestra, String Orchestra, String Class Methods, Solo Books, and Workbooks.

European American Music Distributors Corporation, 195 Allwood Rd., Clifton, NJ 07012; phone: 201-777-2680. Sole U.S. agents for Schott (Mainz, London), Universal Edition (Vienna, London), and Baerenreiter (partial catalog). Distributor for John Sheppard Press, Wollenweber, and several smaller European catalogs. Also major distributor of printed music material.

The Fechheimer Bros. Company, 4545 Malsbary Road, Cincinnati, OH 45242; phone: 513-793-5400. Manufacturers of band and orchestra uniforms, blazers, and accessories. Factory-trained sales representatives available to offer personalized service. Efficiency and attention to detail create fine-quality, individually designed uniforms.

Carl Fischer, Inc., 56-62 Cooper Square, New York City 10003; phone: 212-777-0900. Publishers of all types of music. Sole agent for Eastman School of Music publications, Fillmore, Paterson, Cundy Bettoney, R. D. Row Music Company, Ensemble Music Press, and others.

Carl Fischer of Chicago, Inc., 312 South Wabash Avenue, Chicago, Il 60604; phone: 312-427-6652. Offers one of the nation's largest inventories of music – music of all publishers in all categories. Carl Fischer specializes in educational music publications and has an extensive music approval service.

H. T. FitzSimons Company, Inc., 357 W. Erie St., Chicago, IL 60610; phone: 312-WH4-1841/2. Publishers of standard music for schools and churches; Aeolian and Canterbury Choral Series; Aeolian and FitzSimons editions for bands, orchestras, and ensembles; recreational materials, folk dances, and games; operettas; cantatas; sheet music; and books.

Harold Flammer, Inc., Delaware Water Gap, PA 18327; phone: 717-476-0550. Church music division of Shawnee Press, Inc. Specializes in church choral music, organ music, and handbell music.

Folkways Records, 43 West 61st Street, New York City 10023; phone: 212-586-7260. Folkways produces recordings and tapes in the fields of music education, music instruction, music for children, jazz. American folk music, and ethnic musics for more than 750 peoples around the world. Folkways keeps 1,500 albums in print at all times and has one of the largest collections in the world of folk and ethnic musics.

Formal Fashions and Accessories, 943 S. 48th St., Suite 110, Tempe, AZ 85281; phone: 602-966-4355. Fashion gowns, tuxedos, and accessories for orchestral and choral performances.

Mark Foster Music Co., Box 4012, Champaign, IL 61820; phone: 217-367-9932. Publisher specializing in choral music, and retailer of choral music of all publishers. Publishes books related to choral music and retailers of books related to choral music of all publishers. Distributor for Hamel batons, and sole selling agent for Helios Editions, Consort Press and Choral Aid Records.

Fox Products Corporation, South Whitley, IN 46787; phone: 219-723-4888. Manufacturers of Fox bassoons and contrabassoons, Renard oboes, and double reeds and accessories.

Sol Frank Uniforms, 702 South Santa Rosa, San Antonio, TX 78207; phone: 512-227-7361. Manufacturers of band uniforms, drum corps uniforms, and accessory items to complement the band.

Fruhauf Uniforms, Inc., 2938 So. Minneapolis, Wichita, KS 67216; phone: 316-522-1531. Manufacturer of concert and marching band uniforms.

G

Gamble Music Co., 312 S. Wabash Ave., Chicago, IL 60604; phone: 312-427-6652. Distributors of music and textbooks of various publishers. Worldwide mail-order service. Publishers of music.

Gates Music Inc., 1 Marine Midland Plaza, Suite 1635, Rochester, NY 14604; phone: 716-232-2490. Management firm for Chuck Mangione. Please write to Gates for all published and recorded music by C. Mangione and for any general information.

K. G. Gemeinhardt Company, Inc., P. O. Box 788, Elkhart, IN 46514; phone: 219-522-1339. Manufacturers of fine flutes and piccolos.

The Getzen Company, Inc., P.O. Box 161, Elkhorn, WI 53121; phone: 414-723-4221. Manufacturers of Getzen Eterna B , C, D, E , and Piccolo trumpets, cornets, fluegelhorns, trombones; Tone Choir, Capri, and "300" Series instruments; Meinl-Weston tubas; and Titleist bugles.

$\mathcal{H}$

Hallmark Music, Inc., 55 Marcus Drive, Melville, NY 11746; phone: 516-420-1400. Distributors of Mathias Thoma string instruments, Meinhart bassoons and recorders, Hallmark brass and woodwinds, M. Pierre oboes and English horns, and Hallmark guitars. Music of all publishers, and band, orchestra, and choral music.

Hansen House, 1860 West Ave., Miami Beach FL 33139; phone: 305-532-5461. Publishers of music for band, orchestra, and chorus; classroom music; and the Brimhall piano and Snyder guitar materials. Represents the catalogues of over forty major publishers, with worldwide production and distribution.

Frederick Harris Music Co. Limited, 529 Speers Rd., Oakville, Ontario, Canada L6K 2G4; phone: 416-845-3487. Educational music publishers, importer and distributor, in business over 60 years. Canada's largest publisher of educational music, specializing in educational and church choral publications. Publisher of the Royal Conservatory of Music of the University of Toronto. Mail order specialists. North American agents for Alfred Lengnick of England.

Henco, Inc., P.O. Box 547, Selmer, TN 38375; phone: 901-645-3255. Provider of fund-raising programs in 45 states. Groups can make more money in less time with fewer problems than with other programs. Students gain learning experience through selling high-quality products to customers.

High Fidelity Magazine, Warren B. Syer, The Publishing House, Great Barrington, MA 01230; phone: 413-528-1300. *High Fidelity* is edited for music listeners. CBS laboratory reports, supplemented by listening tests, news, and feature articles help readers choose the sound reproducing equipment best suited to their needs. Over a dozen specialists review the new tape and disc recordings – stereo and mono, classical, folk, jazz, and popular. Journalists from the USA and Europe take readers behind the scenes with music-makers to entertain and enlighten.

M. Hohner, Inc., Andrews Road, Hicksville, NY 11802; phone: 516-935-8500. Hohner lines feature harmonicas, Melodicas, accordions, electronic keyboards instruments, guitars, recorders, rhythm and percussion instruments, amplifiers, and musical accessories. Administrative, sales, warehouse, showroom, and service headquarters in Hicksville, New York.

Holt, Rinehart and Winston, Publishers, 383 Madison Avenue, New York City 10017; phone: 212-688-9100. Publishers of Exploring Music K-8 by Boardman, Landis, Andress (1975); texts, recordings, and TE's that develop skills and behaviors through performing, describing, and organizing. Ideas and topics skillfully developed and resolved. Individualized Music Program 1-3 (1975): cassettes, charts, duplication master worksheets. TG's based on Exploring Music may be used with any program.

Frank Holton Company, 320 North Church Street, Elkhorn, WI 53121; phone: 414-723-2220. Holton Band Instruments, the brasswind instrument division of the G. Leblanc Corporation, 7019 30th Avenue, Kenosha, WI 53140, offers a compete line ranging from models for students to those customed to the standards required by professional musicians. Models available are B trumpets, harmony trumpets, cornets, trombones, mellophones, horns, baritones, basses, and the new firebird and superbone. Call toll-free: 800-558-9421.

Hope Publishing Company, Division of Somerset Press, 380 S. Main Place, Carol Stream, IL 60187; phone: 312-665-3200. Publishers of school and church music for eighty-five years. Somerset Press, publishers of choral music, is the educational division of the company.

Byron Hoyt Sheet Music Service, 190 10th Street, San Francisco, CA 94103; phone: 415-431-8055. Retailers of band, orchestra, choral, vocal, piano, organ, and chamber music. Music of all publishers. Fast, dependable mail order service anywhere.

I

Indian River Quality Citrus, Inc., P. O. Box 3955, Fort Pierce, FL 33450; phone: 305-464-6622. Provider of various citrus fruits, depending on the season, to be used in fund-raising programs: ruby-red grapefruit, oranges, tangelos, etc.

Intelist Theatre, 2415 Mountainview Dr., Boise, ID 83706; phone: 208-342-4742. Audio-visual interpretations of masterworks, for use with introductory course in music and the humanities. Projection of themes, analysis & commentary (illustrations where applicable) during uninterrupted performance featured work. First series includes selections by Bach, Bartok, Beethoven, Dvorak, Hindemith, Respighi, Schumann, and Tschaikovsky. Slides, tapes, filmstrips, cassettes, text sheets, equipment.

Interlochen Arts Academy National Music Camp, Interlochen, MI 49643; phone: 616-276-9221. Interlochen Center for the Arts is an "umbrella name" for the nonprofit educational institutions of the National Music Camp, an eight-week session (July/August) offering arts instruction to students from eight-years old through college graduates, and the Interlochen Arts Academy, a coeducational, secondary boarding school offering college preparatory academics and intensive study of the arts.

Intermedia, Inc., 85 Carver Ave., Westwood, NJ 07675; phone: 800-631-1611. Supplier of marching band accessories specializing in parade boots and shoes, flags, rifles, sabres, and corps style uniforms. Intermedia sells direct to parade groups in all states. Call toll free at 800-631-1611 to request free 32-page full color catalog.

J

Jensen Publications, Inc., 2880 S. 171st St., New Berlin, WI 53151; phone: 414-784-4620. Publishers of performance materials: music for marching, concert and jazz bands and anthems and octavos for church and school choirs.

$\mathcal{K}$

Kendor Music Inc., Main and Grove Streets, Delevan, NY 14042; phone: 716-492-1254. Publishers of quality music for the elementary, junior high, high school, and college markets in categories of concert band, stage band, orchestra, solos, ensembles, chorus, and textbooks.

Kimbo Education, P. O. Box 477, Long Branch, NJ 07740; phone: 201-229-4949. Recorded teaching aids in music and movement. Using music to increase basic academic skills for preschool, elementary classrooms, special education, and music or dance theory. Albums and cassettes with teaching manuals by and for educators. Many dance, fitness and gymnastic recordings for all ages. Free catalog available.

King Musical Instruments, Inc., 33999 Curtis Boulevard, Eastlake, OH 44094; phone: 216-946-6100. Manufacturers of King, Tempo, and Cleveland instruments. The firm has been established for over eighty years, and its products have worldwide acceptance among professional and school musicians and educators. King is the exclusive distributor of the famed, custom-built Benge cornets and trumpets. DeFord flutes, and Manhasset stands.

Neil A. Kjos Music Co., 4382 Jutland Dr., San Diego, CA 92117; phone: 714-270-9800. Publishers of music for piano, guitar, band, orchestra, jazz groups, chorus.

KLM Royal Dutch Airlines, 2455 East Sunrise Boulevard, Suite 711, Fort Lauderdale, Fl 33304; phone: 305-563-8306. Experts in group travel. KLM specializes in carrying music groups to international festivals and on concert tours throughout the world. Instruments as well as passengers are given TLC on KLM's 747B and DC10-30 jets.

Krauth & Benninghofen, Inc., 3001 Symmes Road, Hamilton, OH 45012; phone: 513-874-4400. Manufacturers of Hamilton music stands, instrument stands, and accessory items. Sales are made through wholesalers of music merchandise.

$\mathcal{L}$

Lawson-Gould Music Publishers, Inc., 866 Third Avenue, New York City 10022; phone: 212-752-3920. Specialists in the choral field. Features series by such eminent arrangers and editors as Robert Shaw, Roger Wagner, Alice Parker, Robert de Cormier, Lloyd Pfautsch, Salli Terri, Abraham Kaplan, Donald Neuen, Howard Roberts, and Leonard de Paur.

G. Leblanc Corporation, 7019 30th Avenue, Kenosha, WI 53140; phone: 414-658-1644. Manufacturers of quality woodwind and brasswind instruments. Leblanc (Paris), Noblet, Normandy, Vito, Holton, Martin, Courtois, and Vandoren (reeds and mouthpieces) lines available. Models available include the complete clarinet family of soprano, alto, contra-alto, bass, contrabass, and octo-contra clariets; alto, tenor, and baritone saxophones; flutes; oboes; basset horns, English horns, piccolos, trumpets, and fluegelorns. Leblanc also offers a complete line of quality accessories. Call toll-free: 800-558-9421.

Editions Musicales Alphonse Leduc & Cie, 175, Rue St-Honore, 75040 Paris Cedex 01, France. Alphonse Leduc, founded in 1767 and still owned and managed by the Leduc family, is a world-renowned publisher of music for all instruments, voice, keyboards, band and orchestra as well as textbooks and theoretical subjects. Composers include Messaien, Ravel, Debussy, Bozza, Ibert and many others.

Hal Leonard Publishing Corporation, 8112 W. Bluemound Rd., Milwaukee, WI 53213; phone: 414-774-3630. Publisher of educational music in all categories. Catalogue consists of instructional and performance material for concert band, marching band, orchestra, choir, jazz ensemble, guitar, and keyboard (organ and piano). The company also specializes in recorded instructional aids in all instrumental and keyboard areas.

Lorenz Industries, 501 East Third Street, Dayton, OH 45401; phone: 513-228-6118. Publishers of a full line of educational materials for schools and churches. Three divisions: Lorenz Publishing Company, Sacred Music Press and Heritage Music Press. Lorenz Printing Company specializes in music printing for the entire industry.

Ludwig Industries, 1728 North Damen Avenue, Chicago, IL 60647; phone: 312-276-3360. Manufacturers of Ludwig drums and Musser mallet instruments, plus a complete line of percussion instruments and accessories for concert bands, stage bands, marching bands, and orchestra. Distributors of A. Zildjian cymbals.

Ludwig Music Publishing Company, 557-67 E. 140th St., Cleveland, OH 44110; phone: 216-851-1150. Established in 1921. Publishers of music covering every facet of educational, recreational, and professional fields and of works by well-known composers, including Paul W. Whear, Donald H. White, Ray Luke, Walter Watson, Albert O. David, Bin Kaneda, Walter Ehret, Theron Kirk, Clair McElfresh, Rex Mitchell, Robert Curnow, M. L. Daniels, and Francis Grant.

Lutton Music Personnel Service, Inc., State National Bank Plaza, Suite 405, 1603 Orrington Ave., Evanston, IL 60201; phone: 312-864-1005. Charles and Bert Lutton offer qualified music teachers in a nationwide opportunity for placement in public schools, colleges, universities, and conservatories of music.

Luyben Music, 4318 Main, Kansas City, MO 64111; phone: 816-753-7111. Supplier of very select sheet music and methods, and the finest instruments. Repair and service, as well as all types of instrumental accessories. Designer and manufacturer of special ligature for clarinet, and importer of special reeds.

Lyons Band, 530 Riverview Avenue, Elkhart, IN 46514; phone: 219-294-6602. One source for your teaching aids and materials. Educational recordings for most school publishers. Orff-Schulwerk and Kodály teaching programs and instruments. Tonettes, flutophones, recorders, Autoharps, and rhythm instruments. Marching band and music room equipment and band and orchestra method books.

M

Macie Publishing Company, Box 1207 Brookdale Station, Bloomfield, NJ 07003; phone: 201-748-0222. Publisher of the Ed Sueta Band Method, Books 1 and 2.

Magnamusic-Baton, Inc., 10370 Page Industrial Boulevard, St. Louis, MO 63132; phone: 314-427-5660. Specializes in materials for Orff-Schulwerk programs and in fine editions of music in all categories. Studio 49 Orff Instruments and Royal percussion; recorders by Moeck, Adler, Schott, Aura, Heinrich, and Aulos. Music: Hansen Group – Wilhelm Hansen, Chester, Norsk, Nordiska, Wilhelmiana; Henle, Barenreiter, Nagel, Hortus Musicus, Moseler, Consort, Magnamusic.

Majestic Color Studios, Inc., P. O. Box 845, Cleveland, TN 37311; phone: 615-476-7531. Provides fund-raising program: fifty per-cent profit to organization for selling $7.95 certificates to families for framed portraits, to be taken on pre-arranged dates.

Malmark, Inc., Bellcraftsmen, 21 Bell Lane, New Britain, PA 18901; phone: 215-345-9343. Designers and producers of English handbells. Malmark Handbells introduce new concepts in handbell design, tuning and performance. Beautifully toned, precision tuned English handbells for schools, colleges, churches, and institutions.

Markham Music Company, 1651 W. 26th, Erie, PA 16508; phone: 814-452-3340. Organized in 1927, Markham Music Co. is a supplier of brass, percussion, winds, and orchestral string instruments, as well as frets and electronics. Complete repair service and school music service for northwest Pennsylvania. School of Music facilities staffed by top professional teachers.

Edward B. Marks Music Corporation, 1790 Broadway, New York City 10019; phone: 212-247-7277. Since 1894, publishers of educational, concert, and popular music for chorus, band, orchestra, and ensembles. Publications by Dello Joio, Alfred Reed, Ernesto Lecuona, Leon*Block, Claudette Sorel, Ralph Hunter, and others. Representatives for the Chopin-Paderewski edition (PWM). Distributor for Marks: Belwin-Mills Publishing Corporation.

MCA Music, 445 Park Avenue, New York City 10022; phone: 212-759-7500. A division of MCA, Inc., MCA is a major music publisher and controls more than 30,000 compositions, including such standards as *Hawaiian Wedding Song, Orange Blossom Special, Strangers in the Night, The Girl from Ipanema,* and others. Subsidiaries around the world include leading companies in Australia, Canada, and Great Britain.

Medalist Stanbury Uniforms, Div. Medalist Industries, P. O. Box 100, Brookfield, MO 64628; phone: 816-258-2246. Custom manufacturer of band uniforms and blazers.

Mel Bay Publications, 107 W. Jefferson, Kirkwood, MO 63122; phone: 314-965-4818. Founded in 1927, a publisher of music for guitar, strings, recorder, piano, and band instruments. Features class methods for guitar, recorder, and strings; and children's instrumental band methods and solo books.

Mele Loke Publishing Co., Box 7142, Honolulu, HI 96821; phone: 808-734-8611. Publisher of collections of Hawaiian songs written by Carol Rose especially for children to perpetuate Hawaiian honor and tradition. Records, cassettes and hula instruction sheets are also available.

Melody Cradle, Inc., 1502 S. 12th St., Goshen, IN 46526; phone: 219-533-1085. Manufacturer of special piano cradle for use in moving piano easily, keeping the keyboard at the right height for playing.

Mirafone Corporation, 8484 San Fernando Rd., Sun Valley, CA 91352; phone: 213-767-2360. Distributor of Pearl flutes, and manufacturer and distributor of Mirafone tubas, euphoniums, trumpets, contrabass, trombones, French horns, oboes, English horns, and bassoons.

Mobile Music Man, Inc., 175 Rock Road, Glen Rock, NJ 07452; phone: 201-445-6060. Specializes in school services: rental and sales of music instruments and accessories; sales of educational materials; repair work.

Molzer Music Company, 1311 M Street, P.O. Box 81724, Lincoln, NE 68501; phone: 402-432-1011. School band and orchestra instruments, instrumental music, accessories, and repair service. Fulltime representatives working closely with schools. Rental trial plans. Sponsors clinics and workshops with local clinicians, and repair/maintenance clinics for schools. In business since 1926.

The Monroe Company, 353 Church Street, Colfax IA 50054; phone: 515-674-3511. Manufacturers and sellers of riser/stages for instrumental and choral groups. All sales by mail order. Literature and prices available direct from the factory.

E. R. Moore Co., 7230 Caldwell Ave., Niles, IL 60648; phone: 312-647-7950. Manufacturer of choir robes, as well as T-shirts, jackets, and warmup suits that can be imprinted with group identification for fund-raising purposes.

Mozart Music Corporation, 436 Granby St., P.O. Box 3, Norfolk, VA 23501; phone: 804-625-1673. Formed in 1939 by the former general manager of the Sternberg Piano Factory of Vienna and Sternberg Musical Instrument Company of Budapest (given title of Purveyor by the Royal Imperial Court of Austria), now a supplier of complete line of fine musical instruments, including keyboards, as well as a converter of keyboard instruments.

Multivox/Sopkin Music Co. Inc., 370 Motor Parkway, Hauppauge, NY 11787; phone: 516-231-7700. Manufacturers and distributors of fine musical instruments. Multivox electronic keyboards, sound modifying devices, Rhythm Aces, Premiere amplifiers, P.A. systems, guitar and piano labs, Hofner string instruments and accessories, Premiere Royce guitars, electric basses, mandolins, banjos, other fretted instruments and accessories, Revier flutes, trumpets and trombones.

Muramatsu Flutes-USA, 1414 S. Main St., Royal Oaks, MI 48067; phone: 313-546-4136 or tollfree: 800-521-6380. Muramatsu Flutes, a division of Custom Music Company, is the exclusive distributor for the U.S. and Canada of the handcrafted Muramatsu flutes and alto flutes and accessories, one of the world's outstanding three flutes. Available in solid sterling silver, gold bonded solid silver, and 14 K yellow, rose, and white gold.

Music Education Group, 1415 Waukegan Rd., Northbrook, IL 60062; phone: 312-498-3510. Suppliers of classroom-level instruments, accessories, and publications through an organization of educationally oriented music stores. A large proportion of M.E.G. instruments are engineered and manufactured by Oscar Schmidt-International, Inc., makers of the authentic Autoharp, and, more recently, of Orff percussion instruments.

Music Sales Corporation, 33 West 60th Street, New York City 10023; phone: 212-246-0325. Publisher of music books and books on music. Imprints include Oak Publications, Amsco Music Publishing (including Everybody's Favorite series), Consolidated Music Publishers (including Music for Millions series), Yorktown Music Press (The Joy Books), and Passantino Brands (music writing supplies).

Music Theatre International, 119 West 57th Street, New York City 10019; phone: 212-265-3600. Licensing agent for certain musical comedies and stage productions, including *Fiddler on the Roof; West Side Story; Music Man; Guys and Dolls; Jesus Christ, Superstar; The Fantasticks,* and *Jacques Brel Is Alive.*

Musical Encounters, Inc., P. O. Box 6567, Shawnee Mission, KS 66206; phone: 816-363-6737. Musical Encounters™ of the First, Second, and Third Kind™ are music teaching aids which feature the Kodaly concept for elementary students, utilizing linking blocks.

Musitronic Company, 555 Park Drive., Owatonna, MN 55060; phone: 507-451-7871. Manufacturers of Music Lab Equipment including a portable multikeyboard system, Intonation Trainer, Music Resource Center, and other functional music equipment for school music programs. A complete line of instructional materials for elementary, junior high school, and high school classes is also available.

Musser – Division of Ludwig Industries, 505 Shawmut Ave., La Grange, IL 60525; phone: 312-354-8383. A division of Ludwig Industries. Manufacturers of quality xylophones, marimba, vibes, orchestra bells, chimes, and Artist brand mallets.

N

National Educational Music Company, Ltd., 33135 Union Place, Summit, NJ 07901; phone: 201-277-3324. Staff, organization, facilities and experience devoted entirely to service and assistance to music education. Staff members are fully certified music educators with complete experience in music education.

National Music Publishers' Association, 110 East 59th Street, New York City 10022; phone: 212-PL1-1930. NMPA is the trade association of the popular music publishing business.

New England Conservatory of Music, 290 Huntington Avenue, Boston, MA 02115; phone: 617-262-1120. A private college offering undergraduate and graduate degrees in piano, voice, organ, harpsichord, guitar, orchestral instruments, composition, music education, jazz, third stream, and performance of early music. The master of music degree is also offered in theoretical studies, music literature, vocal accompaniment, and music education in Kodály.

Novello Publications, Inc., 145 Palisade St., Dobbs Ferry, NY 10522; phone: 914-693-5445. The North American subsidiary of one of the oldest and largest serious music publishers in the world.

O

Oxford University Press, 1600 Pollitt Drive, Fair Lawn, NJ 07410; phone: 201-796-8000; and 200 Madison Avenue, New York City 10016; phone: 212-679-7300. Publishers of music and books on music, with centers in Great Britain and the United States. Music for education, private study, and the concert hall; books for reference and for the study of history, theory, and biography. A full list of free catalogues.

P

Parrish Recorded Enterprises, Box 11270, West Trenton, NJ 08628.

Peabody Conservatory of Music, Peabody Institute of Johns Hopkins University, 1 E. Mt. Vernon Pl., Baltimore, MD 21202; phone: 301-837-0600. Offers degrees in Bachelor of Music (with emphasis either in performance or Music Education), Master of Music, Master of Music Education, and Doctor of Music Arts, in the following areas: piano, voice, organ, harpsichord, guitar, orchestral instruments, and composition. In addition graduate degrees are offered in Conducting, and Music History and Literature.

Pecknel Music Company, Inc., 1312 North Pleasantburg Drive, Greenville, SC 29607; phone: 803-244-7881. Rental music dealer supplying all school needs.

Peer-Southern Organization, 1740 Broadway, New York City 10019; phone: 212-265-3910. Publishers of outstanding contemporary music in all categories from all over the world.

Pennino Music Company, Inc., 6421 Industry Way, Westminster, CA 92638; phone: 714-897-2515. Wholesale distributors for Geitzen-Linton band instruments and Yamaha guitars and for Westminster guitars for the eleven western states.

J. W. Pepper and Son, Inc., P. O. Box 50, Valley Forge, PA 19482, phone: 215-66-9600. Retailers of educational sheet music of all publishers to schools and churches. Features Pepper Guides, selection services, and prompt delivery. Offices in Valley Forge, Pennsylvania; Atlanta; Detroit; and Tampa, Florida. Pepper also maintains a publishing division, Charter Publications, Inc.

Percussive Arts Society, Room 205, 110 South Race Street, Urbana, IL 61801; phone: 217-367-4098. To elevate the level of musicians' percussion performance and teaching, to expand understanding of the needs and responsibilities of the percussion students, teacher, and performer, and to promote a greater communication between all areas of percussion arts.

Performing Arts Abroad, Inc., 8013 Church Street, Richland, MI 49083; phone: 616-629-4979. Specializes in making arrangements for concert tours for nonprofessional music groups traveling both independently and in conjunction with music festivals.

The World of Peripole, P. O. Box 146, Lewiston Rd., Browns Mills, NJ 08015; phone: 609-893-9111. Designer, manufacturer, publisher and producer of materials for education and recreation-inclusion musican instruments, related publications, records and Sound Kits-Music Kits, for preschool through middle school. Exclusive distributor of Bergerault Orff-Schulwerk and professional mallet percussion instruments. Rhythm band instruments, band, tambourines, resonator and song bells, cymbals, recorders, Chromaharps, etc.

C. F. Peters Corporation, 373 Park Avenue South, New York City 10016; phone: 212-686-4147. Established in 1800. Publishers of fine contemporary American and European music. Catalogues available in the following categories: piano, organ, choral, vocal, orchestra, instrumental-chamber music, contemporary American music, band, Classical/Contemporary Highlights 1800-1975, and selected music of European publishers.

Peterson Electro-Musical Products, 11601 S. Mayfield Ave., Worth, IL 60482; phone: 312-388-3311. Manufacturer of electronic tuning devices for use by professional tuners, bands and orchestras, and gutarists.

Plymouth Music Company, Inc., 170 N.E. 33rd St., Fort Lauderdale, FL 33334; phone: 305-563-1844. Publishers and distributors of sacred and secular choral music by outstanding composers and arrangers. Distributors of the world-famous Music for Percussion catalogue.

Polisi Bassoon Corporation, 54-20 Kissena Boulevard, Flushing, NY 11355; phone: 212-463-2562. Manufacturers of standard, concert, and artist bassoon models. All bassoon accessories. Polisi bassoon chart. Recordings and Etudes for bassoon by Mel Solomon. Repairs, tuning, and servicing on all woodwinds.

B. Portnoy Clarinet Accessories, 115 Brooks Drive, Bloomington IN 47401; phone: 812-339-5820. Manufacturers of the Portnoy Clarinet Mouthpiece which is custom-made wih exclusively designed tooling and is individually tested for flexibility, response, and liquid quality throughout. Bore accurate with any modeled clarinet. Three facings: BPI close, BP2 personal, BP3 open. Also Portnoy Patented Clarinet Ligature with four points of contact, suspension over sides of reed, and controlled freedom of sound.

Morse M. Preeman Inc., 735 So. Spring St., Los Angeles, CA 90055; phone: 213-623-7211. Music of all publishers in all categories, including band, orchestra, choral, piano, vocal, instrumental, literature, etc.

Theodore Presser Company, Presser Place, Bryn Mawr, PA 19010; phone: 215-525-3636. Publisher of sheet music and music books in all vocal and instrumental categories. Sole selling agent for numerous domestic and foreign music publishers. Offers extensive rental catalogue of music from major domestic and foreign publishers.

R

Rabco, Inc., P.O. Box 610782, North Miami, FL 33161; phone: 305-947-4540. Manufacturer of "ReeDuAl," a patented single- and double-reed duplicator that works much like a key machine and uses your "Best" reed for a model. Thus, it accurately duplicates the dimensions and qualities of your best reed onto all unplayable reeds.

Professionals and students duplicate single and double reeds in seconds.

Radio-Matic of America, Inc., 760 Ramsey Avenue, Hillside, NJ 07205; phone: 201-687-0929. Manufacturers of mobile stereo consoles designed for music instruction, with complete recording and playback facilities from turntable, tape, and cassette recorders with public address intermix, multiple program stereo listening systems: rear projection carrels with synchronized cassette programming multimedia systems for programed sight and sound instruction.

Remo, Inc., 12804 Raymer Street, North Hollywood, CA 91605; phone: 213-764-7417. Manufacturers of Weather King, Controlled Sound, FiberSkyn, and Sound Master drum heads, tuneable practice pads and practice drum sets, new Roto Toms, and Mano hand drums.

Rhythm Band, Inc., P.O. Box 126, Fort Worth, TX 76101; phone: 817-335-2561. Manufacturers and distributors of elementary musical instruments, including Chromaharps, Pianicas, Kalumba drums, resonator bells, Orff instruments, and Artist Ltd. electronic pianos. Also, A New Introduction to Music, early childhood publications, and Bowmar Records.

Frank Richards' Music Center, 61 E. Mt. Pleasant Ave., Livingston, NJ 07039; phone: 201-994-0021 or 994-3730. Serves music educators throughout the country by supplying the music of all publishers. Also supplies all major brands of instruments and accessories.

Rico Corporation, P. O. Box 3266, North Hollywood, CA 91609; phone: 213-767-7030. One of the largest producers of reeds for clarinets and saxophones. Brand names: Rico Reeds, Rico Royal Reeds, Rico Plasticover Reeds, Rich Novapak Reeds and Dispenser, and the new Rico-Plex Reeds, the synthetic reeds that "play true longer." Also, Gregory Master Mouthpiece.

Rubank, Inc., 16215 NW 15th Avenue, Miami, FL 33169; phone: 305-625-5323. Publishers of instrumental music, including methods, studies collections, ensemble folios, band and orchestra folios, and band music, and sheet music.

❦ S

Salvi Harps/International Corporation, 1830 14th St., Santa Monica, CA 90404; phone: 213-451-4000. Sole U.S. distributors for Salvi Harps, Genoa, Italy, one of the world's largest manufacturers of harps recognized for their excellence of tone and workmanship. In addition to a variety of pedal harps. Salvi also produces two sizes of Irish harps, music stands, and piano stools.

Sampson-Ayers House of Music, West 915 First Ave., Spokane, WA 99204; phone: 509-624-3193. One of the nation's largest music stores, specializing in educational materials for orchestra, band, chorus, solos, and ensembles, in every classifications. Growing with the Northwest since 1929.

Scherl & Roth, Inc., c/o C. G. Conn Ltd., 2520 Industrial Parkway, Elkhart, IN 46516; phone: 219-522-3392. Producer of student and professional stringed instruments, including violins, violas, cellos, and basses.

Schilke Music Products, Inc., 529 South Wabash Avenue, Chicago, IL 60605; phone: 312-922-0570. Manufacturer of custom trumpets, cornets, fluegelhorns, horns, and piccolo trumpets. Superior repairs of brass instruments. Also, accessory items.

E. C. Schirmer Music Company, 112 South Street, Boston, MA 02111; phone: 617-426-3137. Music publishers. Catalogues of chordal, vocal, instrumental, orchestral and electronic music and books are available on request. Sole U.S. agents for Ione Press, Inc.; Foetisch Freres (Lausanne); Carpentier Music Manuscript Papers (Zurich); and Camera Music (London).

G. Schirmer, Inc., 866 Third Avenue, New York City 10022; phone: 212-935-5100. Publishers of music for all performing media in all musical styles, traditional to contemporary. Extensive sales and rental catalogues. Agents for Curwen and Faber Music, Ltd.; Amberson Enterprises; Lee Roberts and Lawson-Gould. With Associated, exclusive agents in the Western Hemisphere for Soviet music.

The School Musician, Director and Teacher, 4049 W. Peterson Avenue, Chicago, IL 60646. A music magazine published for the benefit of directors and teachers of school and college bands, orchestras, choruses, and jazz ensembles. Articles and special departments directed to all specialized interests. Official magazine of ASBDA, PBM, NCBA, WBDNA, and MMM. Exclusive departments for CBDNA, ABA, and ASTA. Founded in 1929.

School Specialties, P.O. Box 2394-R, 166 Ridgedale Ave., Morristown, NJ 07960; phone: 201-538-3004. Manufacturers of some of the finest in color guard equipment and form accessories, flags and banners, and awards (chenille, felt, pins, plaques). Servicing schools and colleges since 1945. Free, up-to-date catalogue on request.

Andrew Schroetter & Company, Inc., 55 Marcus Drive, Melville, NY 11746; phone: 516-420-1400. Exclusive manufacturer's representative of Academy guitars, Roderich Paesold guitars, Winter band instrument cases, and Schreiber recorders. Exclusive distributor of York band instruments, Series '76 band instruments, Live Wires guitars and guitar accessories, and York percussion. Also, Andrew Schroetter stringed instruments and bows, Lifton cases, Artur Teller and Wenzel Fuchs stringed instruments, and Richard Grunke artist bows.

Schulmerich Carillons, Inc., Carillon Hill, Sellersville, PA 18960; phone: 215-257-2771. Producers of American-made, precision-tuned, English-type handbells that are used for performing bell choirs and in music education. Manufacturers of carillons, bells, and chimes.

Scientific Music Industries, Inc., 525 N. Noble, Chicago, IL 60622; phone: 312-421-0836. Manufacturers and distributors of musical instruments for use in classroom settings. Tone educator bells, Swiss melode bells, Prelude xylophones, rhythm instruments, recorders, Autoharps, song bells, tuneable drums, guitars, ukuleles, Melodicas, metronomes, and others.

The Selmer Company, Box 310, Elkhart, IN 46515; phone: 219-264-4141. Manufacturer of band instruments, accessories, and collateral materials and amplifiers.

SESAC, Inc., 10 Columbus Cr., New York, NY 10019; phone: 212-586-3450. Music licensing organization representing performance, mechanical and synchronization rights in the copyrights of their affiliated writer and publishers. Operate on a national and international basis.

Shawnee Press, Delaware Water Gap, PA 18327; phone: 717-476-0550. Publishers of band, orchestra, choral, and keyboard music for educational use or professional performance, instrumental solos and ensembles. Publishers of the Fred Waring Choral Series and a vocal sight-reading method (Sight and Sound of Music). Sole selling agents for Harold Flammer, Inc.; Templeton Publishing Company, Inc.; and Malcome Music Ltd.

Silver Burdett Company, 250 James Street, Morristown, NJ 07960; phone: 201-538-0400. Publishers of basal programs for K-8: students' books, teachers' editions, recordings, cassettes, satellites, sound/color filmstrips, and supplementary materials for individualization and evaluation. Also, monthly subscription series using contemporary youth music; choral series; materials for using Orff and Kodály techniques; high school, college, and professional books; instrumental programs; enrichment books; and Time/Life recordings.

Slingerland–J. C. Deagan, 6633 North Milwaukee Avenue, Niles, IL 60648; phone: 312-647-0377. One of the world's leading manufacturers of precision percussion equipment, including the famous TDR-100 parade drum.

Smithsonian Institution, Collection of Recordings, 955 L'Enfant Plaza, Room 2100, Washington, D.C. 20560; phone: 202-287-3350. Produces and sells recordings: collections of jazz, classical, chamber works, and American theater music. The collection consists of reissues and recordings of live performances at the Smithsonian Institution.

Sound Preservers Co., 1915 N. Quince, Olympia, WA 98506; phone: 206-352-9097. Provides high-quality recording services, including recording production, album design, and individual mailing. Studio has room for full orchestras, large choirs, and symphonic bands and is among the finest in the world. Now in fourteeth year of service to music educators.

Southern Music Company, 1100 Broadway, San Antonio, TX 78215; phone: 512-226-8167. Distributors of music of all publishers. Worldwide mail order service. Publishers of music for band, orchestra, chorus, instrumental solos, and ensembles.

S.P.E.B.S.Q.S.A., Inc., P.O. Box 575, Kenosha, WI 53141; phone: 414-654-9111. Publishers of a complete line of music in the barbershop style of singing: books, single sheets, recordings, teaching recordings, and textbooks pertaining to barbershop harmony. Also, special sheet music and folios for the Young Men in Harmony program.

Steinway & Sons, Steinway Place, Long Island City, NY 11105; phone: 212-721-2600. For 125 years, Steinway & Sons have been a leader in the piano industry in the United States. The instruments of Steinway & Sons have won worldwide recognition from the most distinguished pianists and musical artists, and are used today in concerts throughout the country.

Stetson University, School of Music, DeLand, FL 32720; phone: 904-734-4121. Offers a Bachelor of Music, Bachelor of Music Education, and Bachelor of Arts with a major in music.

Summy-Birchard Music, Box CN 27, Princeton, NJ 08540; phone: 609-896-1411. Publishers whose catalogue includes piano, organ, choral, vocal, and instrumental music. Featured publications are The Frances Clark Library for Piano Students, the "Art of" series of instrumental methods, and Suzuki Method materials, for which Summy-Birchard is the sole selling agent outside Japan.

Super Sensitive Musical String Co., RR 4, Box 30-V, Porter Rd., Sarasota, FL 33583; phone: 813-371-0016. Family-owned business since the early '30's, manufacturer of metal strings for bowed instruments (violin, viola, cello and bass), including fractional sizes for the Suzuki Method, special strings for country music (Old Fiddle line), and Concertmaster strings with synthetic cores. Also suppliers of rosin and strings in bulk for restringing purposes.

T

Tams-Witmark Music Library, Inc., 757 Third Avenue, New York City 10017; phone: 212-688-2525. Has one of the world's finest and largest selections of quality Broadway musical shows for stage presentation by school and college groups. Everything needed is supplied on an economical rental basis.

Temple University College of Music, 13th and Norris Streets, Philadelphia, PA 19100; phone: 215-787-8301. Located in historical and cultural Philadelphia, Temple University's College of Music, and its nationally recognized artist faculty, offers Bachelor's through Doctoral degrees. Majors include Performance, Choral Conducting, Opera, Music Education, Music History, Theory and Composition. Temple, with 600 majors, has a long affiliation with the Philadelphia Orchestra in teaching, performance and recording.

Temporal Acuity Products, Inc., 1535 121st Ave. S.E., Bellevue, WA 98005; phone: 206-746-2790. Manufacturer and distributor of the TAP MASTER Rhythmic Sight Reading System, an individualized learning program with integrated hardware and software. This system by David L. Shrader stresses concept and skill development in reading rhythmic notation, elementary through advanced/professional levels.

Trophy Music Company, 1278 West 9th Street, Cleveland, OH 44113; phone: 216-696-1234. Manufacturers and distributors of Flutophones, Cambridge plastic and wood recorders, Alpine wood recorders, K-Lith and Crestline manuscript paper and books, Paganini violin and viola shoulder pads, mouthpiece puller, joint expander, brass instrument cleaners and brushes, batons, and Duplex percussion accessories. Publishers of Methods for Recorders and Flutophones.

$\mathcal{U}$

Unicord, 89 Frost St., Westburg, NY 11590; phone: 516-333-9100. Dealers of electronic instruments and amplifiers for guitar and bass.

Uniforms by Ostwald, P.O. Box 70, Staten Island, NY 10314. A total musicwear source offering band uniforms, frontline and color guard uniforms, band rainwear, I.D. jackets, stagewear, blazers, and uniform accessories. Also available: flags and banners.

$\mathcal{V}$

Vogt Quality Recordings, Box 302, Needham, MA 02192; phone: 617-444-8687. LP recording album engineering, design, and manufacturing. Specializes in four-channel, stereophonic, on-location recording. High-quality tapes also accepted from clients for complete, personalized LP albums. Well-designed album covers available from "stock" for economy productions. All albums carry unconditional VQR guarantee.

W

Wadsworth Publishing Co., 10 Davis Dr., Belmont, CA 94002; phone: 415-595-2350. Publishers of college textbooks. Some music texts are accompanied by tapes or records, workbooks, and study guides.

Walton Music Corporation, 501 E. 3rd St., Dayton, OH 45410. Specializes in choral music. Also, distinguished editions, adventuresome music of the twentieth century, and outstanding folk, rock, and pop arrangements. Publishers of Norman Luoff, Michael Hennagin, Frank Pooler, Brent Pierce, and Mason Martens. Also, Music from Scandinavia—editions and compositions from Scandinavia's foremost composers and editors.

Fred Waring Music Workshop, Delaware Water Gap, PA 18327; phone: 717-476-0510. Summer educational experience for music students, teachers, and choral directors, featuring a staff of working professionals in their field.

Warner Bros. Publications, Inc., 75 Rockefeller Plaza, New York City 10020; phone: 212-484-6215. Publications include Sesame Street, Blueprints, Living with Music, Gershwin-Bernstein, Kinyon, Neil Slater, Ada Richter, and Denes Agay.

Wenger Corporation, 555 Park Drive, Owatonna, MN 55060; phone: 507-451-3010. Manufacturers of innovative, problem-solving equipment for school music and the performing arts. Band, orchestra, and choral risers; portable stages; combination chair-stands for sousaphones, tubas, and other instruments; the Wenger Sound Module System (modular movable music practice rooms); acoustical shells; percussion cabinets; folio cabinets; and Mobile Center (shell, stage, and risers on wheels).

Western Music Sales Service, 6381 Hollywood Boulevard, Hollywood, CA 90028; phone: 213-465-2353. Established in 1956 by George Perl with main offices in Hollywood, California, and with associate Vic Melin in Seattle, Washington. Represents leading firms in all fields of music publishing and solicits music sellers, both wholesale and retail, in the Western states and British Columbia, Canada.

Westminster Choir College, Princeton, NJ 08540; phone for information: 609-921-7100. Inter-denominational, private, co-educational college emphasizing choral training. Students may obtain a Bachelor's or Master's degree in music.

Willis Music Company, 7380 Industrial Road, Florence, KY 41042; phone: 606-283-2050. Publisher of educational music for piano, including piano solos, ensemble pieces, and books Compositions of Edna Mae Burnham, John Thompson, William Gillock, and Frank Sanucci and available. Send for complete catalogue.

Wingert Jones Music, Inc., P.O. Box 1878, 2026 Broadway, Kansas City, MO 64141; phone: 816-221-6688. Retailer and publisher of educational materials for band, orchestra, and choral, and publisher of educational literature.

Word Music, Incorporated, P.O. Box 1790, Waco, TX 76703; phone: 817-772-7650. Publishers of sacred music of all types, including choral, vocal, and instrumental.

The Wurlitzer Company, 403 East Gurler Road, DeKalb, IL 60115; phone: 815-756-2771. A pioneer in keyboard teaching equipment. In addition to conventional school pianos and electronic organs. Wurlitzer Educational Products including Wurlitzer Music Laboratories, Mobile Music Learning Center, Classroom Console Electronic Piano, and the Key/Note Visualizer.

Y

Yamaha Musical Products, P.O. Box 7271, 3050 Breton Rd. SE, Grand Rapids, MI 49510; phone: 616-942-9223. Yamaha Music Products available in the U.S. include band instruments, combo products, guitars, organs, pianos, recorders, and accessories. Yamaha offers license agreement for Yamaha Music Schoo.

Z

Avedis Zildjian Company, P.O. Box 198, Accord, MA 02018; phone: 617-871-2200. Manufacturers of Avedis Zildjian cymbals and related accessory items.

Classified listing

W. T. Armstrong Company, Inc., 1000 Industrial Parkway, Elkhart, IN 46514; phone: 219-293-8602.

Artley, Inc., 2520 Industrial Parkway, Elkhart, IN 46516; phone: 219-522-8696.

Buffet Crampon International Inc., 55 Marcus Drive, Melville, NY 11746; phone: 516-420-1400

CBS Musical Instruments, 100 Wimot Rd., Deerfield, IL 60015; phone: 312-948-5800

C. G. Conn, Ltd., 2520 Industrial Parkway, Elkhart, IN 46516; phone: 219-522-3392.

Custom Music Company, 1414 South Main Street, Royal Oak, MI 48067; phone: 313-546-4135, or toll-free: 800-521-6380.

Engelhardt-Link, Inc.,185 King St., Elk Grove Village, IL 60007; phone: 312-593-5850.

K. G. Gemeinhardt Company, Inc., P.O. Box 788, Elkhart, IN 46514; phone: 219-522-1339.

The Getzen Company, Inc., P.O. Box 161, Elkhorn, WI 53121; phone: 414-723-4221.

Frank Holton Company, 320 North Church Street, Elkhorn, WI 53121; phone: 414-723-2220.

King Musical Instruments, Inc., 33999 Curtis Boulevard, Eastlake, OH 44094; phone: 216-946-6100.

Krauth & Benninghofen, Inc., 3001 Symmes Road, Hamilton, OH 45012; phone: 513-874-4400.

G. Leblanc Corporation, 7019 30th Avenue, Kenosha, WI 53140; phone: 414-658-1644.

Ludwig Industries, 1728 North Damen Avenue, Chicago, IL 60647; phone: 312-276-3360.

Magnamusic-Baton, Inc., 10370 Page Industrial Boulevard, St. Louis, MO 63132; phone: 314-427-5660.

Mirafone Corporation, 8484 San Fernando Rd., Sun Valley, CA 91352; phone: 213-767-2360.

Multivox/Sopkin Music Co. Inc., 370 Motor Parkway, Hauppague, NY 11787; phone: 516-231-7700.

Muramatsu Flutes – USA, 1414 S. Main St., Royal Oak, MI 48067; phone: 313-546-4136 or tollfree: 800-521-6380.

Musser – Division of Ludwig Industries, 505 Shawmut Ave., LaGrange, IL 60525; phone: 312-354-8383.

The World of Peripole, P.O. Box 146, Lewiston Rd., Browns Mills, NJ 08015; phone: 609-893-9111.

Polisi Bassoon Corporation, 54-20 Kissena Boulevard, Flushing, NY 11355; phone: 212-463-2562.

B. Portnoy Clarinet Accessories, 1115 Brooks Drive, Bloomington, IN 47401; phone: 812-339-5820.

Rabco, Inc., P.O. Box 610782, North Miami, FL 33161; phone: 305-947-4540.

Remo, Inc., 12804 Raymer Street, North Hollywood, CA 91605; phone: 213-764-7417.

Salvi Harps/International Harp Corporation, 1830 14th Street, Santa Monica, CA 90404; phone: 213-451-4000.

Scherl & Roth, Inc., c/o C. G. Conn, Ltd., 2520 Industrial Parkway, Elkhart, IN 46516; phone: 219-522-3392.

Schilke Music Products, Inc., 529 South Wabash Avenue, Chicago, IL 60605; phone: 312-922-0570.

Andrew Schroetter & Company, Inc., 55 Marcus Drive, Melville, NY 11746; phone: 516-420-1400.

The Selmer Company, Box 310, Elkhart, IN 46515; phone: 219-264-4141.

Slingerland–J. C. Deagan, 6633 North Milwaukee Avenue, Niles, IL 60648; phone: 312-647-0377.

Yamaha Musical Products, P.O. Box 7271, 3050 Breton Rd. SE, Grand Rapids, MI 49510; phone: 616-942-9223.

Avedis Zildjian Company, P.O. Box 198, Accord, MA 02018; phone: 617-871-2200.

BAND UNIFORM AND CHOIR GOWN MANUFACTURERS

Collegiate Cap and Gown Company, 1000 North Market Street, Champaign, IL 61820; phone: 217-356-9081.

DeMoulin Brothers & Company, 1025 S. 4th St., Greenville, IL 62246; phone: 618-664-2000.

The Fechheimer Brothers Company, 4545 Malsbary Road, Cincinnati, OH 45242; phone: 513-793-5400.

Formal Fashions and Accessories, 943 S. 48th St., Suite 110, Tempe, AZ 85281; phone: 602-966-4355.

Sol Frank Uniforms, 702 South Santa Rosa, San Antonio, TX 78207; phone: 512-227-7361.

Fruhauf Uniforms, Inc., 2938 So. Minneapolis, Wichita, KS 67216; phone: 316-522-1531.

Intermedia, Inc., 85 Carver Ave., Westwood, NJ 07675; phone: 800-631-1611.

Medalist Stanbury Uniforms, Div. Medalist Industries, P.O. Box 100, Brookfield, MO 64628; phone: 816-258-2246.

E. R. Moore Co., 7230 Caldwell Ave., Niles, IL 60648; phone: 312-647-7950.

School Specialties, P.O. Box 2394-R, 166 Ridgedale Ave., Morristown, NJ 07960; phone: 201-538-3004

Uniforms by Ostwald, P.O. Box 70, Staten Island, NY 10314.

MUSIC TEXTBOOK PUBLISHERS

Addison-Wesley Publishing Company, Sand Hill Road, Menlo Park, CA 94025; phone: 415-854-0300.

AGEI Publishing Inc., 923 Illinois St., Racine, WI 53405; phone: 414-632-9983.

Alfred Publishing Company, Inc., 15335 Morrison St., Sherman Oaks, CA 91403; phone: 213-995-8811.

American Book Company, 135 West 50th St., New York, NY 10020; phone: 212-265-8700.

Belwin-Mills Publishing Corporation, 25 Deshon Drive, Melville, NY 11747; phone: 516-293-3400.

Bowmar/Noble Publishers, Inc., 4563 Colorado Blvd., Los Angeles, CA 90039; phone: 213-247-8995.

Michael Brent Publications, Inc., 70 Winding Wood Road S., Port Chester, NY 10573; phone: 914-939-7632.

Cambiata Press, P.O. Box 1151, Conway, AR 72032; phone: 501-329-6982.

Chappell Music Company, 810 Seventh Avenue, New York City 10019; phone: 212-977-7200.

Clarus Music Ltd., 340 Bellevue Ave., Yonkers, NY 10703; phone: 914-375-0864.

Dickson-Wheeler, Inc., 208 First Street, Scotia, NY 12302; phone: 518-374-1136.

Empire Music Company, Inc., P.O. Box 279, New Westminster, B.C., Canada V3L 4J6; phone: 604-324-7732.

H. T. FitzSimons Company, Inc., 357 W. Erie St., Chicago, IL 60610; phone: 312-WH4-1841/2.

Holt, Rinehart, and Winston, Publishers, 383 Madison Avenue, New York City 10017; phone: 212-688-9100.

Kendor Music, Inc., Main and Grove Streets, Delevan, NY 14042; phone: 716-492-1254.

Hal Leonard Publishing Corporation, 8112 W. Bluemound Rd., Milwaukee, WI 53213; phone: 414-774-3630.

MCA Music, 445 Park Avenue, New York City 10022; phone: 212-759-7500.

Mel Bay Publications, Inc., 107 W. Jefferson, Kirkwood, MO 63122; phone: 314-965-4818.

Novello Publications, Inc., 145 Palisade St., Dobbs Ferry, NY 10522; phone: 914-693-5445.

Oxford University Press, 1600 Pollitt Drive, Fair Lawn, NJ 07410; phone: 201-796-8000 and 200 Madison Avenue, New York City 10016; phone: 212-679-7300.

Theodore Presser Company, Presser Place, Bryn Mawr, PA 19010; phone: 215-525-3636.

E. C. Schirmer Music Company, 112 South Street, Boston, MA 02111; phone: 617-426-3137.

Silver Burdett Company, 250 James Street, Morristown, NJ 07960; phone: 201-538-0400.

Trophy Music Company, 1278 West 9th Street, Cleveland, OH 44113; phone: 216-696-1234.

Wadsworth Publishing Co., 10 Davis Dr., Belmont, CA 94002; phone: 415-595-2350.

MUSICAL EQUIPMENT MANUFACTURERS

ARP Instruments, Inc., 45 Hartwell Ave., Lexington, MA 02173; phone: 617-861-6000.

Artley, Inc., 2520 Industrial Parkway, Elkhart, IN 46516; phone: 219-522-8696.

Barcus-Berry, 5381 Production Dr., Huntington Beach, CA 92649; phone: 714-898-9211.

CBS Musical Instruments, 100 Wimot Rd., Deerfield, IL 60015; phone: 312-948-5800.

Computone, Inc., P.O. Box 488, Norwell, MA 02061; phone: 617-871-2660.

C. G. Conn, Ltd., 2520 Industrial Parkway, Elkhart, IN 46516; phone: 219-522-3392.

Fox Products Corporation, South Whitley, IN 46787; phone: 219-723-4888.

M. Hohner, Inc., Andrew Road, Hicksville, NY 11802; phone: 516-935-8500.

Frank Holton Company, 320 North Church Street, Elkhorn, WI 53121; phone: 414-723-2220.

Krauth & Benninghofen, Inc., 3001 Symmes Road, Hamilton, OH 45012; phone: 513-874-4400.

G. Leblanc Corporation, 7019 30th Avenue, Kenosha, WI 53140; phone: 414-658-1644.

Ludwig Industries, 1728 North Damen Avenue, Chicago, IL 60647; phone: 312-276-3360.

The Monroe Company, 353 Church Street, Colfax, IA 50054; phone: 515-674-3511.

Multivox/Sopkin Music Co. Inc., 370 Motor Parkway, Hauppauge, NY 11787; phone: 516-231-7700.

Muramatsu Flutes–USA, 1414 S. Main St., Royal Oak, MI 48067; phone: 313-546-4136 or tollfree: 800-521-6380.

Music Education Group, 1415 Waukegan Rd., Northbrook, IL 60062; phone: 312-498-3510.

Musitronic Company, 555 Park Drive, Owatonna, MN 55060; phone: 507-451-7871.

Pennino Music Company, Inc., 6421 Industry Way, Westminster, CA 92638; phone: 714-897-2515.

The World of Peripole, P.O. Box 146, Lewiston Rd., Browns Mills, NJ 08015; phone: 609-893-9111.

B. Portnoy Clarinet Accessories, 1115 Brooks Drive, Bloomington, IN 47401; phone: 812-339-5820.

Rabco, Inc., P.O. Box 610782, North Miami, FL 33161; phone: 305-947-4540.

Radio-Matic of America, Inc., 760 Ramsey Avenue, Hillside, NJ 07205; phone: 201-687-0929.

Rhythm Band, Inc., P.O. Box 126, Forth Worth, TX 76101; phone: 817-335-2561.

Rico Corporation, P.O. Box 3266, North Hollywood, CA 91609; phone: 213-767-7030.

Scherl & Roth, Inc., c/o C. G. Conn, Ltd., 2520 Industrial Parkway, Elkhart, IN 46516; phone: 219-522-3392.

School Specialities, P.O. Box 2394-R, 166 Ridgedale Ave., Morristown, NJ 07960; phone: 201-538-3004.

Scientific Music Industries, Inc., 525 N. Noble, Chicago, IL 60622; phone: 312-421-0836.

The Selmer Company, Box 310, Elkhart, IN 46514; phone: 219-264-4141.

Slingerland-J.C. Deagan, 6633 North Milwaukee Avenue, Niles, IL 60648; phone: 312-647-0377.

Super Sensitive Musical String Co., R.R. 4, Box 30-V, Porter Rd., Sarasota, FL 33583; phone: 813-371-0016

Temporal Acuity Products, Inc., 1535 121st Ave., S.E., Bellevue, WA 98005; phone: 206-746-2790.

Trophy Music Company, 1278 West 9th Street, Cleveland OH 44113; phone: 216-696-1234.

Unicord, 89 Frost St., Westbury, NY 11590; phone: 516-333-9100.

Wenger Corporation, 555 Park Drive, Owatonna, MN 55060; phone: 507-451-3010.

The Wurlitzer Company, 403 East Gurler Road, DeKalb, IL 60115; phone: 815-756-2771.

PIANO AND ORGAN MANUFACTURERS

Baldwin Piano and Organ Company, 1801 Gilbert Avenue, Cincinnati, OH 45202; phone: 513-852-7000.

M. Hohner, Inc., Andrew Road, Hicksville, NY 11802; phone: 516-935-8500. ⸱

Mozart Music Corporation, 436 Granby St., P.O. Box 3, Norfolk, VA 23501; phone: 804-625-1673.

Multivox/Sopkin Music Co. Inc., 370 Motor Parkway, Hauppauge, NY 11787; phone: 516-231-7700.

Rhythm Band, Inc., P.O. Box 126, Fort Worth, TX 76101; phone: 817-335-2561.

Steinway & Sons, Steinway Place, Long Island City, NY 11105; phone: 212-721-2600.

The Wurlitzer Company, 403 East Gurler Road, DeKalb, IL 60115; phone: 815-756-2771.

Yamaha Musical Products, P.O. Box 7271, 3050 Breton Rd. SE, Grand Rapids, MI 49510; phone: 616-942-9223.

SCHOOLS AND COLLEGES

Berklee College of Music, 1140 Boylston Street, Boston, MA 02215; phone: 617-266-1400.

Blossom Festival School of Kent State University and the Cleveland Orchestra, Kent State University, Kent, OH 44242; phone: 216-672-2613.

Blue Lake Fine Arts Camp, RR 2, Twin Lake, MI 49457; phone: 616-894-8325.

College Conservatory of Music, University of Cincinnati, Cincinnati, OH 45221; phone: 513-475-2883.

The College Music Society, Inc., Regent Box 44, The University of Colorado, Boulder, CO 80309; phone: 303-492-5049.

Duquesne University, School of Music, Locust & Magee St., Pittsburgh, PA 15219; phone: 412-434-6080.

Interlochen Arts Academy National Music Camp; Interlochen, MI 49643; phone: 616-276-9221.

New England Conservatory of Music, 290 Huntington Avenue, Boston, MA 02115; phone: 617-262-1120.

Peabody Conservatory of Music, Peabody Institute of Johns Hopkins University, 1 E. Mt. Vernon Pl., Baltimore, MD 21202; phone: 301-837-0600.

Stetson University, School of Music, Deland, Fl 32720; phone: 904-734-4121.

Temple University College of Music, 13th and Norris Streets, Philadelphia, PA 19100; phone: 215-787-8301.

Fred Waring Music Workshop, Delaware Water Gap, PA 18327; phone: 717-476-0510.

Westminster Choir College, Princeton, NJ 08540; phone for information: 609-921-7100.

SHEET MUSIC AND INSTRUMENT DEALERS AND DISTRIBUTORS

Sam Ash Music Stores, 301 Peninsula Boulevard, Hempstead, NY 11550; phone: 516-485-2122.

Augsburg Publishing House, 426 South 5th Street, Minneapolis, MN 55415; phone: 612-332-4561.

Boston Music Corporation, 116 Boylston St., Boston, MA 02116; phone: 617-426-5100.

Brodt Music Company, P.O. Box 9345, Charlotte, NC 28299; phone: 704-332-2177.

Broude Brothers Limited, 56 W. 45th St., New York, NY 10036; phone: 212-687-4735.

Alexander Broude, Inc., 225 West 57th Street, New York City 10019; phone: 212-586-1674.

Ted Brown Music Company, 1121 Broadway Plaza, Tacoma, WA 98402; phone: 206-272-3211.

Buffet Crampon International, Inc., 55 Marcus Drive, Melville, NY 11746; phone: 516-420-1400.

Capitol Music Company, Inc., 1530 – 3rd Ave., Seattle, WA 98101; phone: 206-622-4013.

CBS Musical Instruments, 100 Wimot Rd., Deerfield, IL 60015; phone: 312-948-5800.

Coast Wholesale Music Company of Los Angeles, P.O. Box 5686, Compton, CA 90220; phone: 213-537-1712.

Howard Core and Co., Inc., Route 1, The Cedars, Munford, AL 36268; phone: 205-263-1891.

Coyle Music, Inc., 2864 North High St., Columbus, OH 43202; phone: 614-263-1891.

Custom Music Company, 1414 South Main Street, Royal Oak, MI 48067; phone: 313-546-4135 or toll-free: 800-521-6380.

European American Music Distributors Corporation, 195 Allwood Rd., Clifton, NJ 07012; phone: 201-777-2680.

Carl Fischer, Inc., 56-62 Cooper Square, New York City 10003; phone: 212-777-0900.

Carl Fischer of Chicago, Inc., 312 South Wabash Avenue, Chicago, IL 60604; phone: 312-427-6652.

Mark Foster Music Co., Box 4012, Champaign, IL 61820; phone: 217-367-9932.

Gamble Music Co., 312 S. Wabash Ave., Chicago, IL 60604; phone: 312-427-6652.

Hallmark Music, Inc., 55 Marcus Drive, Melville, NY 11746; phone: 516-420-1400.

Frederick Harris Music Co., Limited, 529 Speers Rd., Oakville, Ontario, Canada L6K 2G4; phone: 416-845-3487.

Byron Hoyt Sheet Music Service, 190 10th Street, San Francisco, CA 94103; phone: 415-431-8055.

Neil A. Kjos Music Company, 4382 Jutland Drive, San Diego, CA 92117; phone: 714-270-9800.

Luyben Music, 4318 Main, Kansas City, MO 64111; phone: 816-753-7111.

Magnamusic-Baton, Inc., 10370 Page Industrial Boulevard, St. Louis, MO 63132; phone: 314-427-5660.

Markham Music Company, 1651 W. 26th, Erie, PA 16508; phone: 814-452-3340.

Mobile Music Man, Inc., 175 Rock Road, Glen Rock, NJ 07452; phone: 201-445-6060.

Molzer Music Company, 1311 M Street, P.O. Box 81724, Lincoln, NE 68501; phone: 402-432-1011.

Mozart Music Corporation, 436 Granby St., P.O. Box 3, Norfolk, VA 23501; phone: 804-625-1673.

Pecknel Music Company, Inc., 1312 North Pleasantburg Drive, Greenville, SC 29607; phone: 803-244-7881.

Pennino Music Company, Inc., 6421 Industry Way, Westminster, CA 92638; phone: 714-897-2515.

J. W. Pepper and Son, Inc., P.O. Box 850, Valley Forge, PA 19482; phone: 215-666-9600. Division offices: 5201 Harney Road, Tampa, FL 33610; 4273 Wendell Drive SW, Atlanta, GA 30336; and 373 Minnesota Street, Troy, MI 48084.

Plymouth Music Company, Inc., 170 N.E. 33rd St., Fort Lauderdale, FL 33334; phone: 305-563-1844.

Morse M. Preeman, Inc., 735 So. Spring St., Los Angeles, CA 90055; phone: 213-623-7211.

Frank Richards' Music Center, 61 E. Mt. Pleasant Ave., Livingston, NJ 07039; phone: 201-994-0021 or 994-3730.

Sampson-Ayers House of Music, West 915 First Ave., Spokane, WA 99204; phone: 509-624-3193.

Southern Music Company, 1100 Broadway, San Antonio, TX 78215; phone: 512-226-8167.

Wingert Jones Music, Inc., 2026 Broadway, P.O. Box 1878, Kansas City, MO 64141; phone: 816-221-6688.

Word Music, Incorporated, P.O. Box 1790, Waco, TX 76703; phone: 817-772-7650.

SHEET MUSIC PUBLISHERS

Alfred Publishing Co., Inc., 15335 Morrison St., Sherman Oaks, CA 91403; phone: 213-995-8811.

Alexandria House, Box 300, Alexandria, IN 46001; phone: 317-724-4439.

Associated Music Publishers, Inc., 866 Third Avenue, New York City 10022; phone: 212-935-4241.

Augsburg Publishing House, 426 South 5th Street, Minneapolis, MN 55415; phone: 612-332-4561.

Belwin-Mills Publishing Corporation, 25 Deshon Drive, Melville, NY 11747; phone: 516-293-3400.

The Big 3 Music Corporation, 729 Seventh Avenue, New York City 10019; phone: 212-575-4978.

Boosey and Hawkes, Inc., Sales Office: P.O. Box 130, Oceanside, NY 11572; phone: 516-OR8-2500; Executive Office: 30 West 57th Street, New York City 10019; phone: 212-757-3332.

Boston Music Corporation, 116 Boylston St., Boston, MA 02116; phone: 617-426-5100.

Bourne Company, 1212 Avenue of the Americas, New York City 10036; phone: 212-575-1800.

Michael Brent Publications, Inc., 70 Winding Wood Road S., Port Chester, NY 10573; phone: 914-939-7632.

Brodt Music Company, P.O. Box 9345, Charlotte, NC 28299; phone: 704-332-2177.

Broude Brothers Limited, 56 W. 45th St., New York, NY 10036; phone: 212-687-4735.

Alexander Broude, Inc., 225 West 57th Street, New York City 10019; phone: 212-586-1674.

Cambiata Press, P.O. Box 1151, Conway, AR 72032; phone: 501-329-6982.

Chappell Music Company, 810 Seventh Avenue, New York City 10019; phone: 212-977-7200.

Creative Jazz Composers, Inc., P.O. Box T, Bowie, MD 20715; phone: 301-262-9099.

Walt Disney Music Co., 350 So. Buena Vista St., Burbank, CA 91521; phone: 213-845-3141.

Edition Musicus, P.O. Box 1341, Stamford, CT 06904; phone: 203-323-1401.

Editions Salabert, Inc., c/o G. Schirmer, Inc., 866 3rd Ave., New York City 10022; phone: 212-935-5100.

Elkan-Vogel, Inc., Presser Place, Bryn Mawr, PA 19010; phone: 215-525-3636.

Forest R. Etling, Publisher, 1790 Joseph Court, Elgin, IL 61020; phone: 312-695-4884.

European American Music Distributors Corporation, 195 Allwood Rd., Clifton, NJ 07012; phone: 201-777-2680.

Carl Fischer, Inc., 56-62 Cooper Square, New York City 10003 phone: 212-777-0900.

H. T. FitzSimons Company, Inc., 357 W. Erie St., Chicago, IL 60610; phone: 312-WH4-1841/2.

Harold Flammer, Inc., Delaware Water Gap, PA 18327; phone: 717-476-0550.

Mark Foster Music Co., Box 4012, Champaign, IL 61820; phone: 217-367-9932.

Gamble Music Co., 312 S. Wabash Ave., Chicago, IL 60604; phone: 312-427-6652.

Gates Music Inc., 1 Marina Midland Plaza, Suite 1635, Rochester, NY 14604; phone: 716-232-2490.

Hansen House, 1860 West Ave., Miami Beach, FL 33139; phone: 305-532-5461.

Frederick Harris Music Co., Limited, 529 Speers Rd., Oakville, Ontario, Canada L6K 2G4; phone: 416-845-3487.

Hope Publishing Company, Division of Somerset Press, 380 S. Main Place, Carol Stream, IL 60187; phone: 312-665-3200.

Jensen Publications, Inc., 2880 S. 171st St., New Berlin, WI 53151; phone: 414-784-4620.

Kendor Music, Inc., Main and Grove Streets, Delevan, NY 14042; phone: 716-492-1254.

Neil A. Kjos Music Company, 4382 Jutland Drive, San Diego, CA 92117; phone: 714-270-9800.

Lawson-Gould Music Publishers, Inc., 866 Third Avenue, New York City 10022; phone: 212-752-3920.

Editions Musicales Alphonse Leduc & Cie, 175, Rue St-Honore, 75040 PARIS CEDEX 01, France.

Hal Leonard Publishing Corporation, 8112 W. Bluemound Rd., Milwaukee, WI 53212; phone: 414-774-3630.

Lorenz Industries, 501 East Third Street., Dayton, OH 45401; phone: 513-228-6118.

Ludwig Music Publishing Company, 557-67 E. 140th St., Cleveland, OH 44110; phone: 216-851-1150.

Macie Publishing Company, Box 1207 Brookdale Station, Bloomfield, NJ 07003; phone: 201-748-0222.

Edward B. Marks Music Corporation, 1790 Broadway, New York City 10019; phone: 212-247-7277.

MCA Music, 445 Park Avenue, New York City 10022; phone: 212-759-7500.

Mel Bay Publications, 107 W. Jefferson, Kirkwood, MO 63122; phone: 314-965-4818.

Mele Loke Publishing Co., Box 7142, Honolulu, HI 96812; phone: 808-734-861.

Music Sales Corporation, 33 West 60th Street, New York City 10023; phone: 212-246-0325.

Novello Publications, Inc., 145 Palisade St., Dobbs Ferry, NY 10522; phone: 914-693-5445.

Oxford University Press, 1600 Pollitt Drive, Fair Lawn, NJ 07410; phone: 201-796-8000 and 200 Madison Avenue, New York City 10016; phone: 212-679-7300.

Peer-Southern Organization, 1740 Broadway, New York City 10019; phone: 212-265-3910.

C. F. Peters Corporation, 373 Park Avenue South, New York City 10016; phone: 212-686-4147.

Plymouth Music Company, Inc., 170 N. 33rd St., Ft. Lauderdale, FL 33334; phone: 305-563-1844.

Theodore Presser Company, Presser Place, Bryn Mawr, PA 19010; phone: 215-525-3636.

Rubank, Inc., 16215 NW 15th Avenue, Miami, FL 33169; phone: 305-625-5323.

E. C. Schirmer Music Company, 112 South Street, Boston, MA 02111; phone: 617-426-3137.

G. Schirmer, Inc., 866 Third Avenue, New York City 10022; phone: 212-935-5100.

Shawnee Press, Delaware Water Gap, PA 18327; phone: 717-476-0550.

Southern Music Company, 1100 Broadway, San Antonio, TX 78215; phone: 512-226-8167.

S.P.E.B.S.Q.S.A., Inc., P.O. Box 575, Kenosha, WI 53141; phone: 414-654-9111.

Summy Birchard Music, Box CN 27, Princeton, NJ 08540; phone: 609-896-1411.

Walton Music Corporation, 501 E. 3rd St., Dayton, OH 45410.

Warner Bros. Publications, Inc., 75 Rockefeller Plaza, New York City 10020; phone: 212-484-6215.

Willis Music Company, 7380 Industrial Road, Florence, KY 40142; phone: 606-283-2050.

Wingert Jones Music, Inc., 2026 Broadway, P.O. Box 1878, Kansas City, MO 64141; phone: 816-221-6688.

Word Music, Incorporated, P.O. Box 1790, Waco, TX 76703; phone: 817-772-7650.

MISCELLANEOUS

AGEI Publishing, Inc., 923 Illinois St., Racine, WI 53405; phone: 414-632-9983.

Alexandria House, Box 300, Alexandria, IN 46001; phone: 317-724-4439.

American Federation of Musicians, 1500 Broadway, New York, NY 10036; phone: 212-869-1330.

American Society of Composers, Authors and Publishers (ASCAP), 1 Lincoln Plaza, New York City 10023; phone: 212-595-3050.

ARP Instruments, Inc., 45 Hartwell Ave., Lexington, MA 02173; phone: 617-861-6000.

Audio House on Location Recorders, P.O. Box 219, 307 East 9th, Lawrence, KS 66044; phone: 913-843-4916.

Bandribbons, P.O. Box 145, Monmouth, OR 97361; phone: 503-838-1752.

Barker-Lins, Inc., Sheet Music Service of Portland, 34 NW 8th Avenue, Portland, OR 97209; phone: 503-222-9607.

Beatrice Foods Co., Two North LaSalle St., Chicago, IL 60602; phone: 312-782-3820.

Broadcast Music Inc., 40 W. 57th St., New York, NY 10019; phone: 212-586-2000.

Clef House, Inc., P.O. Box 13248, Portland, OR 97213.

Coast Wholesale Music Company of Los Angeles, P.O. Box 5686, Compton, CA 90224; phone: 213-537-1712.

The College Music Society, Inc., Regent Box 44, The University of Colorado, Boulder, CO 80309; phone: 303-492-5049.

Coyle Music, Inc., 2864 North High St., Columbus, OH 43202; phone: 614-263-1891.

Creative Audio Visuals, 12000 Edgewater Drive, Cleveland, OH 44107.

Creative Jazz Composers, Inc., P.O. Box T, Bowie, MD 20715; phone: 301-262-9099.

Crest Records, Inc., 220 Broadway, Huntington Station, New York, NY 11746; phone: 516-423-7090.

Dampp-Chaser Electronics, Inc., P.O. Box 1610, Hendersonville, NC 28739; phone: 704-692-8271.

Gates Music Inc., 1 Marine Midland Plaza, Suite 1635, Rochester, NY 14604; phone: 716-232-2490.

Henco, Inc., P.O. Box 547, Selmer, TN 38375; phone: 901-645- 3255.

High Fidelity Magazine, Warren B. Syer, The Publishing House, Great Barrington, MA 01230; phone: 413-528-1300.

Hope Publishing Company, Division of Somerset Press, 380 S. Main Place, Carol Stream, IL 60187; phone: 312-665-3200.

Indian River Quality Citrus, Inc., P.O. Box 3955, Fort Pierce, FL 33450; phone: 305-464-6622.

Intermedia, Inc., 85 Carver Ave., Westwood, NJ 07675; phone: 800-631-1611.

Kimbo Educational, P.O. Box 477, Long Branch, NJ 07740; phone: 201-229-4949.

KLM Royal Dutch Airlines, 2455 East Sunrise Boulevard, Suite 711, Fort Lauderdale, FL 33304; phone: 305-563-8306.

Lutton Music Personnel Service, Inc., State National Bank Plaza, Suite 405, 1603 Orrington Ave., Evanston, IL 60201; phone: 312-864-1005.

Lyons Band, 530 Riverview Avenue, Elkhart, IN 46514; phone: 219-294-6602.

Majestic Color Studios, Inc., P.O. Box 845, Cleveland, TN 37311; phone: 615-476-7531.

Malmark, Inc., Bellcraftsmen, 21 Bell Lane, New Britain, PA 18901; phone: 215-345-9343.

Mele Loke Publishing Co., Box 7142, Honolulu, HI 96812; phone: 808-734-861.

Melody Cradle, Inc., 1502 S. 12th St., Goshen, IN 46526; phone: 219-533-1085.

E. R. Moore Co., 7230 Caldwell Ave., Niles IL 60648; phone: 312-647-7950.

Music Education Group, 1415 Waukegan Rd., Northbrook, IL 60062; phone: 312-498-3510.

Music Theatre International, 119 West 57th Street, New York City 10019; phone: 212-265-3600.

National Educational Music Company, Ltd., 33-35 Union Place, Summit, NJ 07901; phone: 201-277-3324.

National Music Publishers' Association, 110 East 59th Street, New York City 10022; phone: 212-PL1-1930.

Percussive Arts Society, Room 205, 110 South Race Street, Urbana, IL 61801; phone: 217-367-4098.

Performing Arts Abroad, Inc., 8013 Church Street, Richland, MI 49083; phone: 616-629-4979.

Rico Corporation, P.O. Box 3266, North Hollywood, CA 91609; phone: 213-767-7030.

The School Musician, Director and Teacher, 4049 W. Peterson Avenue, Chicago, IL 60646.

Andrew Schroetter & Company, Inc., 55 Marcus Drive, Melville, NY 11746; phone: 516-420-1400.

Schulmerich Carillons, Inc., Carillon Hill, Sellersville, PA 18960; phone: 215-257-2771.

SESAC, Inc., 10 Columbus Cr., New York, NY 10019; phone: 212-586-3450.

Smithsonian Institution, Collection of Recordings, 955 L'Enfant Plaza, Room 2100, Washington, D.C. 20560; phone: 202-287-3350.

Sound Preservers, Co., 1915 N. Quince, Olympia, WA 98506; phone: 206-352-9097.

Tams-Witmark Music Library, Inc., 757 Third Avenue, New York City 10017; phone: 212-688-2525.

Uniforms by Ostward, P. O. Box 70, Staten Island, NY 10314.

Vogt Quality Recordings, P.O. Box 302, Needham, MA 02192; phone: 617-444-8687.

Wenger Corporation, 555 Park Drive, Owatonna, MN 55060; phone: 507-451-3010.

Western Music Sales Service, 6381 Hollywood Boulevard, Hollywood, CA 90028; phone: 213-465-2353.

MUSIC INDUSTRY COUNCIL

AN AUXILIARY OF THE MUSIC EDUCATORS NATIONAL CONFERENCE
HEADQUARTERS OFFICE:
1902 Association Drive, Reston, VA 22091 Telephone (703) 860-4000

OFFICERS

President
Norman A. Goldberg
Magnamusic-Baton, Inc.
10370 Page Industrial Blvd
St. Louis, MO 63132

President-elect
Richard J. Richardson
Musser Division
Ludwig Industries
505 Shawmut Ave.
LaGrange, IL 60525

Vice President
Arthur Gurwitz
Southern Music Company
1100 Broadway
San Antonio, TX 78215

Secretary-Treasurer
George D. Hotton
Theodore Presser Company
Presser Place
Bryn Mawr, PA 19010

EXECUTIVE BOARD

Sandy Feldstein
Alfred Publishing Co., Inc.
15335 Morrison St.
Sherman Oaks, CA 91403

Robert D. Kane
The Selmer Company
P.O. Box 310
Elkhart, IN 46515

Daniel Kobida
Baldwin Piano and Organ Co.
1801 Gilbert Ave.
Cincinnati, OH 45202

Ed Murphy
G. Schirmer, Inc.
866 Third Ave.
New York, NY 10022